MAMA BEAR *Apologetics*®

GUIDE *to* SEXUALITY & GENDER IDENTITY

HILLARY MORGAN FERRER
with AMY DAVISON

HARVEST HOUSE PUBLISHERS
EUGENE, OREGON

This book is dedicated to all those who have been willing to take up their sexual crosses and still follow Christ, even when it's really, really difficult.

Published in association with the literary agency of Mark Sweeney & Associates.

Cover design by Faceout Studio

Cover illustrations by Joe Hox

The image of the taproot on page 100 is © Annas_Kurniawan, Shutterstock # 1736201042.
The Gender-bread Person image on page 126 is in the public domain.

Italics in quoted Scripture indicates emphasis added by the author.

For bulk, special sales, or ministry purchases, please call 1-800-547-8979.
Email: CustomerService@hhpbooks.com

Mama Bear Apologetics® Guide to Sexuality and Gender Identity

Published by Harvest House Publishers
Eugene, Oregon 97408
www.harvesthousepublishers.com

ISBN 978-0-7369-9081-3 (pbk)
ISBN 978-0-7369-9082-0 (eBook)

Library of Congress Control Number: 2021935208

Printed in the United States of America

26 27 28 29 30 31 32 33 / LB / 10 9 8 7 6 5 4 3 2 1

"In *Mama Bear Apologetics Guide to Sexuality and Gender Identity*, Hillary Ferrer and Amy Davison boldly confront the sexually misguided narrative being foisted upon today's children. They do so with a deep sense of compassion, offering understanding and hope. With profound attention to biblical truth, this book provides a solid foundation for understanding sexuality and an acute observation of cultural realities. It informs, confronts, convicts, and offers practical help. It is a must-read for parents and Christian leaders and required reading for those seeking a certification in biblical sexuality ministry."

—**Ricky Chelette**, president of The Institute of Biblical Sexuality

"Every day, our kids are bombarded by messages that glamorize a broken, corrupt, and ultimately empty view of gender and sexuality. In response, Hillary and Amy have written a book that every Christian parent needs—one filled with practical insight, humor, wisdom, and biblical truth. Buy it, read it, and equip your children."

—**Neil Shenvi**, speaker and author of *Why Believe?*, *Critical Dilemma*, and *Post Woke*

"God's beautiful design for sex has been targeted for destruction. Our culture denies it, abuses it, twists it, and demeans it. That's why this updated volume by Mama Bear Apologetics is such a gift. It deals with the 'ick' of our culture's distorted perspective on sex by highlighting God's goodness. It's honest yet gracious. Logical yet compassionate. Straight-shooting yet laugh-out-loud funny. By the end of each fast-paced chapter, you'll know Scripture, the facts, and how to talk about each tough subject in a God-honoring, natural way."

—**Jeff Myers**, PhD, president of Summit Ministries and co-author (with Kathy Koch) of *Raising Gender-Confident Kids*

"With compassion, empathy, and an unwavering commitment to Scripture, Ferrer and Davison equip parents and children to defend the biblical sexual worldview. And they do not mince words when it comes to the political agenda that is pushing sexuality on kids. Through Christlike love, this book is a call to arms to defend those held captive to sex-education curricula and its damaging ideas."

—**Josh D. McDowell**, bestselling author and speaker

"Sex is never just about sex. Teens and young adults often cite biblical sexuality for the reason behind their rejection of Christianity. That is why *Mama Bear Apologetics Guide to Sexuality and Gender Identity* is a crucial resource for every parent. Hillary and Amy address the most relevant and confusing aspects of parenting in the shifting sands of sexual morality in our culture, giving examples from research, media, and education. They present foundational and complicated truths in a format that is easy to understand and apply. This book will equip you to navigate the discipleship journey with your kids with grace and truth."

—**Dr. Juli Slattery**, author of *Rethinking Sexuality*
and founder of SexualDiscipleship.com

"As mothers and avid readers, we can't recommend this book enough. The culture is poisoning the hearts and minds of our children with a twisted vision of human sexuality and identity. Ferrer and Davison not only expose these lies, but they also replace them with a wonderful vision of the beautiful and breathtaking design God intends for human sexuality. This book will help you become the wise and trusted guide your kids need, leading them to the life-giving truths about love, sex, and identity that God has for His image bearers."

—**Erin Kunkle and Sarah Stonestreet**, cohosts of the
Strong Women podcast by the Colson Center

"Hillary's book is an important parent resource to identify, deconstruct, and offer clarity to today's distorted views of sexuality. God has already created an ideal for humanity and sexual integrity, and this book reminds us to stay faithful to His truth."

—**Monica Leal Cline**, founder of It Takes a Family

"As is typical for the Mama Bear team, the *Mama Bear Apologetics Guide to Sexuality and Gender Identity* transforms confusion into clarity, anxiety into action steps, and polarization into Christ-centered partnership. This book is a must-read for anyone seeking to equip kids to biblically navigate gender, sexuality, and the cost of discipleship."

—**Elizabeth Urbanowicz**, founder of Foundation Worldview

"The *Mama Bear Apologetics Guide to Sexuality and Gender Identity* is a timely and helpful book. Hillary tackles some of the thorniest issues of sex and identity today, yet she does so with compassion, insight, and biblical clarity. She also offers some practical steps for communicating these ideas to kids. I hope you will get a copy and start implementing these ideas today."

—**Sean McDowell**, PhD, associate professor of apologetics
at Biola University and the author of *Chasing Love*

Contents

Part 3: Things That Are Tripping Everyone Up

INTRODUCTION

My Kid's Cartoon Showed *What*?

Why I Needed This Book Yesterday

HILLARY AND AMY

Once upon a time, the sex talk was simple. It was still mortifying for both parties, but it was simple. For the little ones, you talked about the anatomical differences between boys and girls. Where do babies come from? I'm so ~~horrified~~ glad you asked! You discussed how those anatomical differences allowed the mommy and the daddy to make a baby, praying that the kids didn't ask for more details. As they got older, you discussed God's design for marriage and God's purpose for sex within a marriage. You read some verses from Ephesians, gave a very (very) light study from Song of Solomon about the goodness of sex (but only within marriage—DON'T DO IT OUTSIDE OF MARRIAGE!). And then you turned these fully prepared (*cough*) youngsters over to the youth pastor, who taught them who-knows-what out of a study guide on purity. Phew! Glad that's over.

One question though: How's that been working out for us? How'd that work out for *you*? Does it feel like we're winning the culture war on this one? Because it doesn't to us. We are losing so badly that many people have just given up and opted for the "safe sex" talk because any discussion of abstinence is just laughed at. Like, *How cute! As if you can convince teenagers not to have sex...you're funny!*

To paraphrase legendary fighter Mike Tyson, everyone has a plan until they've been hit. The church, unfortunately, is no different. Between hyper-fundamentalism, the fallout of purity culture, and the at-times graceless response to LGBTQ+ issues, the church has taken more than its share of hits. As Dr. Juli Slattery points out, the problem isn't that the spiritual battle defending biblical sexuality isn't worth having. The problem is that the church *doesn't know how to fight.*[1] And the results aren't pretty.

Pew Research Center conducted a survey on views regarding sexuality and found that 57 percent of Christians believed premarital sex in a committed relationship was fine, while 50 percent said that hookups (sleeping with someone you aren't committed to) were no biggie![2] According to one study, upward of 80 percent of unmarried evangelicals between the ages of 18 and 29 have had sex.[3]

We parents aren't doing much better. Many of us grew up in a "don't ask, don't tell" household when it came to discussing sex, and we've happily carried on the tradition with our kids. For some of us, the silence is rooted in fear. We're afraid that if we talk about sex, then our kids will want sex. Or perhaps you are only now shaking off the weight of toxic sexual messages that were piled upon your teenage shoulders. The last thing you want is to make your children feel the same guilt and shame you did. And others just don't know what to say. Heck, we don't understand how the biblical sexual worldview is a critical aspect in our own walk with Jesus, let alone know how to explain it to our kids.[4] Instead, we rely on middle school health class, our kids' friends, and social apps to do the legwork for us.

Church, can we come together for a moment and acknowledge a hard truth? This isn't working. Our kids *want* us to talk to them about sex. No really, they do. When the Power to Decide campaign surveyed thousands of students, do you know who teens ages 12 to 15 overwhelmingly said had the most influence on their sexual decisions? *Parents.* Do you know who also won the influence race with teens ages 16 to 19? *Parents.*[5] Don't let their perpetual eye rolls fool you: Our kids are listening. Let's start talking.

That is why you have this book, Mama Bears. You (and your husband) are your child's primary teachers. You are the youth pastors of your home. And God has given you everything you need to shepherd your family in the truth while holding fast to loving like Christ. The enemy has come in and tried to confuse these categories, but that's where we at Mama Bear Apologetics come in. The area of sexuality is like one giant knot; its knots even have knots. Our hopes are that, through this book, we can slowly unravel the threads of confusion surrounding the area of sexuality and gender identity.

Naturally, there is a lot to unpack here. As much as our nerdy selves would love to do an in-depth study of each topic, we realize we are competing with nap time, busy schedules, and an acceptable word count for popular-level books. (You mean not everyone wants 800-page, multivolume books? Pshaw.)

What we aim to present here is a biblical perspective—to backtrack how the enemy has broken God's good design, to emphasize a loving attitude toward real, hurting people behind each of these issues, and to tackle the topics in a way that helps you reinforce biblical sexuality for your children. Are you up for it?

Amy's Story

I was recently hiding from the Texas heat and watching TV with my kids. With three prepubescent boys, my vote for *Call the Midwife* was (unsurprisingly) outvoted, so we cuddled up to catch the latest episode of *The Loud House.* This show follows a preteen boy, Lincoln Loud, as he navigates life with ten sisters.

That day, the Loud family was trying to figure out which sibling had been the recipient of a love letter. It had been addressed only to *L*, which presented a challenge since everyone in the family had a name beginning with *L*! As the show progressed, each sister confronted her valentine crush with a love note, hoping her beloved was the secret admirer. Each sister, that is, except budding rock star, Luna.

Luna was too nervous to talk to her crush, but she spent a majority of the show casting dreamy looks toward a group of kids whose ringleader was a guitar-toting heartthrob. (Boys and guitars—am I right?) With some last-minute encouragement from the Loud tribe, Luna slipped a love note into her crush's locker and ducked around the corner just as the group came down the hall. It looked like dream-boy was about to discover Luna's note...but he walked right past the locker. In the last few moments, however, my boys and I watched as guitar-boy's bandmate, *a girl*, opened the locker instead. The credits rolled as the two girls shared a googly-eyed stare.[6]

The whole scene lasted only a few seconds, and had I been scrolling through Pinterest, I would have missed it. I glanced at my kids, and thankfully the younger two had been distracted by Legos. My ten-year-old, however, had not. He turned to me with a confused look and said, "Wait, what just happened? Does she like girls?"

And just like that, my son was introduced to the LGBTQ+ world. Through a cartoon.

Proactive and Not Reactive

We realize this is a very tame example according to current standards, but Amy's story still applies: We don't know when or where this uncomfortable conversation will be forced on us. Not only do we need to be prepared, but we should probably have a game plan *in advance.* But why? Why can't we just figure it out as we go along? The answer is no, for two reasons. The first is a psychological phenomenon that I (Hillary) have not found a name for, so I'm going to call it the *founder's effect.* The founder's effect is the phenomenon that whoever is the first to introduce a concept to someone automatically becomes the expert in that person's eyes. Now we can discover other experts, but we have an implicit bias toward the person who was the first to explain something to us. Our question, Mama Bears, is: Who do you want your kids to see as the expert? You or Dr. Google? You or television shows? You or your kids' friends? The obvious answer is you!

Second—and this goes along with the first point—the worldview of the founder becomes ground zero for future understanding. We will talk about worldviews in chapter 2. Worldviews are the foundation upon which we incorporate all new information. Kids are sponges, and a child will interpret reality in light of whatever worldview is most often modeled to them. If they are exposed to alternate worldviews in these formative years, the one they hear or see the most will ultimately become their ground zero—despite that full hour of felt-board Bible stories every Sunday. This is why parents need to decide for themselves whether to use public education. The average kid can't simultaneously be a sponge *and* a missionary, holding down the fort "for God."

This is especially true with regard to sex. If the first piece of information our kids receive on sexuality is that gender is changeable, sexuality is fluid, and heterosexual relationships have no practical benefit, it will be very hard for parents to change that foundation. Every piece of information, whether the child realizes it or not, will be woven into their original understanding of sex. At that point, you cannot just tell them that boys cannot become girls and vice versa; you will have to explain, defend, and prove this statement before they'll accept it as true. In summary, the first person becomes the expert, and that person's worldview becomes the lens through which the learner evaluates all other evidence. *That* is why we need to address these concepts first with our kids!

> FOUNDER'S EFFECT: The first person to introduce a topic to a learner becomes the expert in that person's eyes; the expert's worldview will also be the lens through which the learner evaluates all future evidence.

We're Not in Kansas Anymore

I (Hillary) sometimes joke about how the Lord teaches twice—in the lecture and the lab. The lecture is the actual biblical teaching—right theology, wisdom gleaned from the Word. Amy's story reflects what I jokingly refer to as the lab portion of learning. During the lab portion, the Lord brings opportunities for you to put into practice what you've learned. Anyone who's ever prayed for patience knows what I mean. The lecture portion is fine; the lab portion knocks you to your knees. Upon embarking on this book, Amy immediately realized how real and imminent the sexual agenda was—all the way down to cartoons.

We wish we could say this was an isolated incident, but it was not. When we crowdsourced the question on social media, asking Mama Bears to share stories of LGBTQ+ characters in kids' shows, we had more than 150 comments *within the first hour*. With increasing frequency, television characters are showcasing unbiblical sexuality. Children frequently have two mommies or two daddies, and characters are every shade of trans: nonbinary, agender, genderfluid—anything but simply boys and girls. Why this sudden influx? Simple: Our culture has shifted.

Back in our day (and yes, we realize how old that makes us sound), kids' programming typically matched the biblical model, with a mommy and a daddy in the home. Girls had crushes on boys and vice versa. But now that our culture has redefined the family, we've seen cartoons, music, and programming shifting to follow suit. This makes sense when we remember that art mimics life...but that doesn't mean it'll always reflect truth.

Amy's not the only parent who's been thrown for a loop here. You could tell your own stories about the corruption of sexuality in our culture. Many parents have no idea what a worldview is, let alone that their children's cartoons are projecting one that isn't biblical. (We'll address that in chapter 2.) It snuck up on us while we were busy trying to figure out how this new math worked. (Why can't we just carry the tens anymore?!) It invaded our homes while our radar systems were focused on decoys. We missed the warning signs, and now we're in damage-control mode. Then, alas, it snowballed faster than we ever could have imagined, leaving us parents to wonder how we got here in the first place or where we went wrong.

And that's why we're glad you're here. This is a safe place where we totally understand that worries often stem from uncertainty, and uncertainty comes from not understanding. In this book, we want to help you understand what is going on in our culture and how we got here. We want to help you to define what's happening and empower your kids to live counterculturally, to stand up for truth without becoming the playground's morality police.

Our kids need to be equipped so they can refuse to call evil good, good evil, and lies truth. And make no mistake—that is being demanded of them. While some people like to compare this situation to Shadrach, Meshach, and Abednego being forced to bow before a statue or be thrown into the fiery furnace, I find that our kids have difficulty drawing the comparison. There's no physical statue and no actual furnace. But we do have evidence of Christians being required to pay lip service to another god or else face the consequences.

Say It or Else!

The Roman Empire was considered a bastion of tolerance according to ancient standards. All religions were generally accepted, and their adherents could worship whoever, whatever, and however they wanted—provided their worship didn't disturb the peace or create loyalty conflicts between them and Caesar. To weed out the troublemakers, there was basically one rule: Once a year, everyone—no matter their religion—was required to offer a pinch of incense and say the phrase "Caesar is Lord." The temple dudes didn't care if the person believed it or not. As long as they *said it*, then they were given a certificate that allowed them to buy, sell, and trade in the marketplace. No certificate, no business. Most people were willing to do this because they were already pluralistic. Why not? What's one more god? Sure, Caesar is Lord. Whatevs.

The Christians and the Jews, on the other hand, had difficulties with this. According to both the Old Testament and the New Testament, words matter. They could not speak this lie while maintaining a clear conscience before God.

Some within the faith tried to cut corners, thinking they could just obey Caesar in body and worship God privately in their hearts. These people (the ones who were willing to compromise on this technicality) were the first to crumble once real persecution came. Pliny the Younger noted these "Christians" in a letter he wrote to Trajan. Once arrested, not only would they worship the statue of Trajan, but they could be persuaded to "utter imprecations against the name of Christ." (An imprecation is basically a curse.) On the flip side, he noted that "there is no forcing, it is said, those who are *really Christians* into any of these compliances...I judged it necessary to try to get at the real truth by putting to the torture two female slaves, who were said to officiate in their religious rites; but all I could discover was evidence of an absurd and extravagant superstition."[7] (This superstition was that Jesus was resurrected.)

Summary: Once you start compromising in the little things, it's easy to compromise in the big things. The ones who refused to compromise at the temple when things were easy were the ones to stand firm in the jail once things got hard.

While nobody is getting tortured yet, people are being cancelled, bullied, fired, and fined left and right.[8] We are facing a looming crisis where Christians will be required to pay lip service to the god of our age—sex-positivity and gender ideology. Our kids are being desensitized, song by song, cartoon by cartoon, numbed to the point where immorality feels like no big deal. We want them to be able to dispense with the false ideas about sexuality that our culture sends their way, which means we need to start discipling them yesterday.

Instead of pointing us to God, sexual pleasure has become a god itself. Sexuality and gender ideology is the ruler of our age, one our kids are being required to obey and pay homage to in word (pronouns) and in deed (activism). Our children are being fed lies cloaked in the language of morality that could lead them to kneel at the altar of pleasure and deception. The call to open their eyes to false teachings is a godly conviction.

All of that starts with calling out cultural lies for what they are. After reading the first Mama Bear Apologetics book, a reader told me, "These lies were all around me in culture, and I just didn't see them. But now I do. And now that I see them, I can't not see them." That's our goal for this book as well—to shed some light on the lies so you'll know them when you see them. As we discuss each one of these messages, we'll hold it up to the Word and let godly wisdom inform our thinking.

Here's What to Expect

Part 1 focuses on the biblical view of sexuality. We look at how the way we view sexuality is actually a make-it-or-break-it issue for being a disciple of Jesus (chapter 1). Sexuality isn't just some side aspect of Christianity; what we believe about what's done in the bedroom reveals what we *really* believe about

God, others, reality, and ourselves (chapter 2). While people might think the core of the sexual revolution is pleasure (and that is a big part of it), an even bigger issue is the idea of *authority*, meaning who has the right to determine what we do with our bodies (chapter 3). And we'll frame how all of these topics should be approached—with love for people who are held captive to bad ideas (chapter 4).

In part 2, we dig into the actual standards and curricula that are being taught to your kids (chapter 5) and the tactics (like moralization and repetition) that are being used to advance the agenda (chapter 6). Then we'll look at actual curricula that is being used all over the country (chapter 7). Chapters 8 and 9 focus on the two most important movements—sex-positivity and queer theory—that undergird everything you are witnessing within our culture's understanding of gender and sex. Once you understand it, Mama Bears, you'll see it everywhere!

In part 3, we go over the specific things that are tripping everyone up. We start by taking a long, hard look in the mirror with what happened within purity culture (chapter 10), and then we'll address all the things that are coming at your kids—pornography (chapter 11), same-sex attraction (chapter 12), gender confusion (chapter 13), and the cult that is gender theory (chapter 14). For these chapters, you'll recognize the popular ROAR format (*recognize* the message, *offer* objective discernment, *argue* for a healthier approach, and *reinforce* through discussion, discipleship, and prayer).

Finally, chapter 15 reminds us that Christians with LGBTQ+ proclivities aren't the only ones who have a rough deal when it comes to obeying God's sexual commandments. Realizing that we *all* have issues gives us the courage to take up whatever cross we have been given and have compassion for others when their sexual cross is different from ours.

As an added bonus in the afterword, we go over things you'll want to repeat to your kids until they want to gag because, as we note in chapter 6, the human brain has difficulty distinguishing between truth and familiarity. There's power in good maxims to reinforce a biblical worldview, and we're not ashamed of using them! Our kids need good, bite-sized pieces of wisdom to combat the colorfully glittered bad philosophy that parades across their Instagram feeds.

Three Types of Readers

One of the things I (Hillary) have been convicted of from the moment I started speaking in public was recognizing the variety of personalities within my audience. What feels like a refreshing new idea to one parent feels like overload to another. So before we start on this book, I want to acknowledge three very different mom-types who might be reading this book.

Group 1: It's All My Responsibility

Some of you feel everything is your responsibility—from organic meals and Baby Beethoven to homeschooling and driving your kids to Awana. If it will benefit your child, you'll give it a try. You understand the gravity of raising kids in this secular world. You are doing your absolute best, but if anyone puts one more straw on your back, you fear you will finally collapse under the weight. If this is you, please sit for a moment and acknowledge that. Praise God for your zeal in shepherding your children! However, there is also a time to rest. Consider saying the following prayer before embarking on this book:

> *Father God, I know Your yoke is easy and Your burden is light. I desire to please You by being faithful with my children. Lord, please teach me how to release that which is out of my control. As I read this book, I pray that the enemy's voice of condemnation would be silenced. Lord, convict me of things where I need to improve, but please protect me from feelings of guilt or inadequacy as I learn this new information. Show me the things You would have me do to raise faithful, godly children, and help me to release them back to You, knowing that You are a good, good Father.*

Group 2: It's All God's Responsibility

Another group reading this book has mastered the art of resting in Christ's sovereignty, which is a good thing. However, it can sometimes lead to assumptions that a good Christian school, a flourishing youth group, and a few dinnertime conversations will suffice for raising children in the faith. This group may be less aware of the pervasiveness of culture's lies and might need a swift kick in the pants to realize that we're in a whole new world; we can't raise our children the way we were raised because the world in which we were raised is gone. If this is you, then be prepared for a wake-up call! It will be tempting to feel like there is too much to be done, and you might want to stick your fingers in your ears and sing, "La la la la! I can't hear you!"

Please don't. It's not too late, and it's not too hard. There is grace for being an imperfect parent. Don't give up! My prayer is that the Holy Spirit would be with you in this book, convicting and motivating you to be a warrior for your kids, raising them up into a robust Christian faith with a biblical understanding of sex and gender. Here's a prayer you can offer:

> *Lord God, I thank You for the rest I have in You. I praise You because You are sovereign. Not a single bird falls from the sky without Your knowledge. Lord, I confess the times when I have used my faith in Your providence as an excuse to not engage the culture. Lord, I pray You would open my eyes to ways I can be actively training my kids. I pray You would reveal my blind spots. I pray for wisdom, and I pray for discernment against the enemy's lying tongue, bringing condemnation where You are trying to bring conviction. Give me the strength, Lord, to face these issues head-on, so I might be a parent who purposely shepherds my kids to resist cultural lies. I do all things knowing You are with me.*

Group 3: *I've Already Blown It*

It is naive to think that all the readers of this book have squeaky-clean pasts. We have a God who came to remove our shame and bring beauty from ashes. That being said, I believe many of us are still walking in sexual shame and don't even know it.

Dealing with shame is not a process we can rush any more than we can rush the process of grief. Grieving is not fun, but it is *healthy.* It is *necessary.* It is practically a *requirement* for emotional healing. We cannot repress grief; it will come out in some other way. Similarly, there is no fast-tracking the repentance and healing process.

And here's where I want to make a bold thesis. Not until we have come to terms with our own sin—fully acknowledging, fully confessing, fully grieving, and fully receiving God's forgiveness—can we finally walk in freedom. And freedom is what I want for you and your children, friends! Experiencing God's freedom from our sexual past is key to being able to talk to our kids about sex in a healthy way.

Some of you have experienced sexual abuse or trauma and are still walking in bondage to a burden placed on you by another. For these Mama Bears, let me speak from experience that the Lord is faithful. Some healing comes quickly and some slowly. Never give up! Praise Jesus for the amazing counselors who are out there. He has given us His Word, and He has also given us His medical and counseling ambassadors who can walk us through the damage that comes from sexual trauma. For you, I pray the Lord would bring healing to the parts that have been broken so that you can walk in freedom from a burden you should never have had to carry.

For other Mama Bears, freedom means receiving the forgiveness God offers and then forgiving *yourself.* I have known amazing women, godly wives and mothers, who live in fear that someone will discover their past. For you, I want to pray peace and hope. The Lord has removed your sins as far as the east is from the west. You are *free,* Mama Bear. Don't let the enemy tether you to what the Lord has freed you from.

Now, we might have some Mama Bears who are currently in sexual sin. To you, I implore: Please realize your worth. My prayer is that you would see yourself the way the Lord sees you. He wants freedom for you. Sexual sin is the only sin Scripture calls sinning against your own body (1 Corinthians 6:18). Romans 1:24 refers to sexual sin as people "degrading" themselves with one another. Do not believe the lie that degrading yourself is empowering or fulfilling.

Each one of these types of bondage can lead to difficulties in talking with our children about sex. Slavery to shame can result in fear-based teaching, confusing kids as to the innate goodness of sex within marriage. Slavery to sin results in a "do as I say, not as I do" type of teaching, or even a tacit permission to sin because deep down you don't believe young people are capable of controlling their urges. Whatever your bondage, it will likely be passed on to your kids when you talk about sex. It's not an insurmountable issue. But it's something to keep in mind and something to pray about as we go through this journey together.

A Final Word

We are going to address a lot of topics in this book—both from a biblical perspective and from the secular perspective that is trying to rewrite God's commands regarding sexuality and gender. My prayer for you is that you don't let the pervasiveness of the secular worldview overwhelm you. We need to be aware of the adversary's schemes so we can properly defend against them. We can't defend against that which we don't understand. There is power in understanding the enemy's playbook. There is power in preparing to meet these schemes head-on, and we can empower our children to do the same—with grace, love, and truth.

You'll find problems here of which you might have been blissfully unaware, but ignorance isn't safety. Think of this book as a takedown of the enemy's manual, and now, for the first time, you can actually prepare your kids for what is coming.

Get ready, Mama Bears. It's time to ROAR.

PART 1

Things I Probably Already Knew...But Kinda Forgot

PRAYER OF LAMENT[1]

Turn to God

LAMENTATIONS 2:19; 5:1

Our young children have gone into captivity before the enemy. We pour out our hearts like water before You, Lord, for the lives of our children. O Lord, earnestly remember what has come upon us! Look down and see our reproach, our national disgrace!

Lord, hear our prayers. We are desperate. Who else can we turn to? Where else can we go? You are our only help and refuge from the onslaught of the sexualization of everything, from the normalization of all things contrary to Your will. Our kids are in a world of trouble.

Sexually Set Apart

How Sexual Holiness Is a Nonnegotiable for Disciples of Jesus

HILLARY

In the year 2000, Hollywood graced us with the poignant and moving cinematic masterpiece *Dude, Where's My Car?* The film follows two dimwitted deadbeats who, after a night of binge drinking, cannot find their car and have unexpectedly acquired an otherworldly device about which they know nothing. Well, not nothing. They know exactly two things: It's a mysterious and powerful device, and its mystery is only exceeded by its power.

A mysterious and powerful device, you say? Of which its mystery is only exceeded by its power?! *That,* my friends, is sexuality. *Selah.* (That's Christianese for "meditate on that for a hot second.")

While I am joking about the movie being a masterpiece, the mystery and power of sex are no laughing matter. You might even call sex the first command. God was like, "Here's your garden; be fruitful and multiply (wink!)." As Clay

Jones explains, "All Adam and Eve had to do all day long was to garden and play with creation's *only* physically perfect and completely naked member of the opposite sex."[1]

The idea that sexuality should be guarded is not very popular. Our society sees it as just a prudish phase we went through back in the Victorian era. Thanks to Freud, we are now supposedly enlightened, understanding that sexual repression is basically the gateway to all mental illnesses. *Be free, little birdies! It's for your own good! Don't listen to those religious nutjobs. They all craaaaaazy.*

Christians are often accused of being obsessed with sex or afraid of sex because we uphold the biblical teaching that sex is intended for husband and wife...and because we speak up when abstinence is excluded from the options laid before today's teens. We believe that far from portraying sex as a dirty act, Scripture teaches that sex is good! God created it! There's even a whole book of the Bible celebrating it. As my old pastor used to say—from the pulpit, no less—"God is not a killjoy. We serve the God who *created* the orgasm." Shock! Gasp! He actually said that? Yes, he did! And I think all our pastors should too. If we blush at declaring good what God said is good, we've already let our culture redefine the gift and steal something that doesn't belong to them.

Unfortunately, Christians notoriously blush at such statements, but the world has no such squeamishness. In fact, our live-and-let-live world can't understand why such an awesome gift shouldn't be shared with as many partners as possible. But let's take things back a bit...or a lot. If we are to understand sexuality, we must go back to the very beginning. As we will show later in the chapter, sex is intended to be a *sign* of the covenant between husband and wife.[2] Every time a married couple makes love, they are—in bodily form—*repeating their marital vows*. God doesn't place limits on sex because He wants to downplay the goodness of sex. He places limits on it because sex has *meaning*, meaning that our culture has lost.

To be fair, our culture hasn't just lost the meaning of sex; we've actually lost the meaning of *meaning*! Postmodernism teaches that there is no such thing as inherent meaning; it's a social construct *imposed* upon things by us humans.

We ascribe meaning. We determine truth. We're fashioned into little gods who can speak truth into existence...or change it on a whim.

If you read the first Mama Bear Apologetics book, you know how prevalent postmodern ideology is. Which brings me to a sad truth: If our kids can't understand the concept of unchangeable, inherent meaning, then they will never understand that *sex* has unchangeable, inherent meaning. They will not understand that sex carries a message, and that we do not have the authority to tamper with that message. When we tamper with God's plan for sex, we miscommunicate the truths that God intended to be seen through the marital union. (We'll discuss this more in chapter 3.)

The message the world is telling our kids is that sex is no longer just a behavior; *it is a person's very identity*—a foundational aspect that can be neither questioned by others nor restricted.

Our world treats sex as the inviolable truth on which everything rests. It's the big kahuna of human experience to which everyone has a right. Secular culture sees itself as the champion of the most powerful and important aspect in the world, and we Christians as the great buzzkill, trying to downplay the awesomeness of sex.

Okay, fine. We'll play that game for a second. Let's just grant briefly (for the sake of argument) that sex *is* the most important thing in the world. Shouldn't we then ask, "Doesn't *every* important and powerful thing involve boundaries and protection from misuse?" Seriously. Name one other thing that is super important and super powerful that isn't carefully guarded or meticulously controlled (nuclear warheads, controlled substance prescriptions, etc.). In fact, the more important and powerful something is, the more it is usually safeguarded. Why wouldn't we expect the same to be true about sex?

Since God created sex, He is the only one who truly knows what it means, what it communicates, and how powerful it really is—and how destructive it is when misused.

Set Apart from the Beginning

God's commands regarding sex are not just a side issue. They are a prominent theme spanning the Old and New Testaments, especially in terms of holiness. The word *holy* literally means "set apart for a special purpose." As Christians, our sexual ethic is a major way in which we are called to be set apart from the world because sexual holiness is, in essence, a sign of our knowledge of and commitment to God. It has always been this way.

Throughout Scripture, we see how God's people have been called to sexual holiness—how they are to be sexually set apart. Let's take a cursory overview through the Old and New Testaments to see exactly how serious the Lord is regarding this topic.

The Old Testament: Whoring After Other Gods...Oddly Not a Metaphor

I recommend reading through Deuteronomy 22:13-25 and Leviticus 18 and 20 to get a thorough overview of what God defines as sexual immorality and how seriously He takes it. One might notice that He's *really* specific in these passages. His commands regarding sex aren't just revealing sexual boundaries; God is actually describing the culture the Israelites were coming out of and the culture they were told to conquer.

Yahweh prefaces the Levitical sex laws by saying, "*I am* the Lord your God. You must not do as they do in Egypt, where you used to live, and you must not do as they do in the land of Canaan, where I am bringing you" (Leviticus 18:2-3). God then proceeds to list everyone (family members) and everything (animals) with whom to *not* have sex. After this extensive list, He restates His original purpose for sexual holiness: "Do not defile yourselves in any of these ways, because this is how the nations that I am going to drive out before you became defiled" (Leviticus 18:24). In other words, *This is how I am calling you to be set apart from the rest of the world! Don't mess it up, or I'll remove you just like I did them.* (And if you keep reading through Judges and Chronicles, you'll see how that's exactly what happened.)

Israel struggled with sexual idolatry from the start—and kept returning to it throughout the course of its history. For a few pockets of time here and there, they were faithful to God. But more often than not, they fell right back into the practices of the nations whom they were told to drive out of the land.

The Canaanites were not—as some people might think—just a poor, unsuspecting people who were just trying to live their lives in peace. (Admit it...you've thought this before, haven't you? It's okay. I did too, once upon a time.) But if you really dive into Canaanite history and culture, at some point—after you've recovered from your nausea—you start to think that maybe, just maybe, this was a culture that needed to be wiped out.[3]

I cannot even begin to describe the kind of sexual debauchery that went on in Canaan before the Israelites got there. I remember a pastor reading through Ezekiel 16–20 and thinking, *Holy schnikes, I've never heard someone say* whore *this many times in a row*. I'm serious. Grab an ESV translation, a two-liter of Mountain Dew, and take a swig every time you see the word. You'll be so hopped up you won't be able to sleep for two days. It's also prevalent in the book of Hosea. When I was younger, I assumed the "whoring after other gods" language was merely metaphorical, symbolic of Israel's spiritual adultery. (And yes, it's true that the Lord uses the word this way.) But after studying ancient Near East practices, I came to the horrifying realization that whoring after other gods was not—I repeat, *not*—purely a metaphor. People were literally worshipping other gods by having temple orgies.

The Asherah poles and the "high places" described in Scripture were giant phallic symbols. According to pagan worship, the gods needed to be stimulated into giving up the goodies—fertility, rain, and crops. So how did they stimulate the gods? By basically providing a veritable smorgasbord of live religious porn—complete with incest, child abuse, homosexuality, and...things that should never be done with a goat.[4] In this culture, sex with the temple prostitutes was the height of religious piety. I suspect there were lots of "very religious men" in this culture. "Honey, I'm going to the temple...again."

And what would they do with all the babies that were born from these sexcapades? They'd burn them on the altar to Molech.[5] Child sacrifice was just one more of the detestable practices of Canaan from which God called His people to separate. And before you ask (like a woman did during a lecture on Caanan), "How could anyone allow such a thing to happen in their community?" remember this: *It's still happening.* Our culture serves its own Molech. It's called Planned Parenthood. Children always have been and always will be the victims of our sexual immorality. We have not changed. We have not progressed. We've just gotten better at hiding (and renaming) our child sacrifices.

And just in case you are *still* wondering how seriously God takes sexual sin, hop over for a moment to Numbers 25. This is one of those Bible stories that will *never* be reenacted on a felt board in Sunday school, but it's an important read. Moses is giving a verbal smackdown to the entire nation of Israelite men for sleeping around with the Midianite women. In the middle of his rant, some moron traipses through the crowd with a Midianite woman on his arm and disappears with her into his tent. Aaron's grandson Phinehas sees this, follows them in, and skewers them with a spear...in the middle of the deed. How does God respond? He gives Phinehas and his descendants an eternal priesthood for being so zealous for the Lord. No, this is *not* a model for Christians to currently imitate! But it does illustrate the eternal principle that our sexual faithfulness *really* matters to God. Like, a lot.

The New Testament: Pointing Back to God's Design

The New Testament also has quite a bit to say on the topic, though not necessarily by Jesus Himself. And some people find that to be a problem. Since Jesus didn't explicitly condemn all the same sexual practices prohibited in the Old Testament (like homosexuality), some feel that His silence is tacit approval for all sexual unions. But this is just a logical fallacy called "the argument from silence." When Jesus came, He didn't spend much time reexplaining God's sexual law because He was speaking to Jews, and the Jews *already knew how God defined sexual immorality*. They had studied the Jewish law for centuries. If you were to take Christ's silence on topics as permission, then you could justify almost anything—sex with animals (Leviticus 18:23), sleeping with your mom (Leviticus 18:8; 1 Corinthians 5:1), or anyone else in your family (Leviticus 18:9-17), you name it. Don't get sucked into this bad argument from silence.

When Jesus *did* speak on sexual morality and marriage, He stuck with (as my high school biology teacher used to call it) the K.I.S.S. method ("Keep It Simple, Stupid") and simply pointed His Jewish audience back to *their own scriptures*, back to God's original design—"A man will leave his father and mother and be united to his wife, and the two will become one flesh" (Matthew 19:5, quoting Genesis 2:24).

Later, in Romans 1, the apostle Paul describes the descent of a culture into oblivion. The passage begins with people who know God but don't really care about worshipping Him (verse 21). Then their minds and their hearts go stupid (verse 22). They start worshipping something else (verse 23), and God gives them over to what they think they want: lots and lots of sex (verse 24). A few orgies later, their sexuality goes from depraved to unnatural (verse 26). At the end of the whole process they have become a group that doesn't even know what good looks like anymore. Take a peek at verses 29-32, friends. This is our society's future if things continue as they are.

> They have become filled with every kind of wickedness, evil, greed and depravity. They are full of envy, murder, strife, deceit and malice. They are gossips, slanderers, God-haters, insolent, arrogant and boastful; they invent ways of doing evil; they disobey their parents; they have no understanding, no fidelity, no love, no mercy. Although they know God's righteous decree that those who do such things deserve death, they not only continue to do these very things but also approve of those who practice them.

Sexual morality is emphasized in almost every New Testament epistle, especially the ones aimed at Gentiles, who didn't have the benefit of centuries of Jewish law. Sexual immorality is not only mentioned, but it's usually mentioned first in the long lists of sins that a Christ-follower *must* forsake—no ifs, ands, or buts.

- Acts 15:23-29: When asking which of the Old Testament laws should apply to Gentiles, there were only *four,* one of which was sexual morality.[6]
- 1 Corinthians 5:9-13: Paul is so emphatic on sexual holiness that he commands church members not to associate with those who call themselves Christians but engage in sexual immorality.
- Ephesians 5:3: Paul says there shouldn't even be a hint of sexual immorality among them.
- Colossians 3:5: Believers are told to put sexual immorality to death.

- Galatians 5:16-19: Sexual immorality is contrasted with the fruit of the Spirit.
- 1 Thessalonians 4:3-8: This might be the most convicting passage of all! It is God's will that we avoid sexual immorality, and "anyone who rejects this instruction does not reject a human being but God" (verse 8).

Praise God that we are able to repent and be forgiven! First Corinthians 6:11 says that the whole list of evil things describes what some of us *were*. None of them are an unforgivable sin from which we can't repent. Who you *were* is not the same as who you *are*. (This becomes especially important when we start talking about same-sex attraction and transgenderism!) Yes, we will probably still sin, but how we respond afterward is most important. The heart that is saved does not make sinning a deliberate, continual practice, nor does it delight in things contrary to God's commands. The transformed heart does not interpret Christ's kindness as permission to live-as-you-like now and ask forgiveness later. No. A person with a saved, renewed heart is inspired (even compelled!) to repent (Romans 2:4).

There is forgiveness seventy times seven times (and then some!) (Matthew 18:22). A broken and contrite heart the Lord will not despise (Psalm 51:17). Be encouraged by this...because I say this next scary part in all seriousness: Persistent, unrepentant sin is not the kind of sin that Christ paid for. We are warned about this in several passages:

- Hebrews 10:26: "If we deliberately keep on sinning after we have received the knowledge of the truth, no sacrifice for sins is left." Why? Because: "No one born of God *makes a practice* of sinning" (1 John 3:9 ESV).
- Revelation 2:13-16, 18-25: A lax attitude regarding sexual immorality is a deal-breaker, even in churches that are faithful, loving, and serving others in every other way. (In other words, no amount of "love" or "social justice" can make up for ignoring God's commands about sex.)

- Revelation 22:14-15: Practicing sexual immorality and loving falsehood puts us outside of God's eternal kingdom.

Do these verses sound harsh and scary? Maybe it's because God wants to be clear on how big of an issue sexuality is! I'm not sure how much more explicit we need the Bible to be. It is mind-boggling how many professing Christians are getting this wrong—redefining sexuality based on their terms and not on the Bible's.

Fine, but Where Exactly Does It Say That Sex Outside of Marriage Is Wrong?

Maybe your teenager is asking, "Where does the Bible *specifically* say sex outside of marriage is wrong?" If you're having this conversation with your teen, use this illustration. Look at the picture to the right.

Ask them what shape it is (a heart). Ask them which one of the dots "proves" that it's a heart or defines it as a heart. (Clearly, none of them.) You have to look at all the dots *together* to say definitively, "That's a heart."

This is the way the Bible communicates on some topics (which is why we always advocate Greg Koukl's advice to "never just read a Bible verse"[7]). Case in point, not every teaching in the Bible has a single, ironclad verse. Rather, *many* verses, when taken together, illustrate a particular teaching. There is no "thou shalt not have sex outside of marriage," but God gives us the picture of what marriage is in Genesis 1. We have a ton of examples of how badly things go when people have more than one spouse (alllll of the OT). We have Leviticus talking about sexuality. We find a lot of verses about sexual immorality. We've got references to things like keeping the marriage bed "undefiled" (Hebrews 13:4 ESV).

The closest to a one-and-done example of not having sex outside of marriage is probably 1 Corinthians 7:9: "If they cannot control themselves, they should marry, for it is better to marry than to burn with passion." Paul is not offering marriage as the only and ultimate remedy for dealing with sexual desire; he sings big praises for staying chastely single as well. Nor is he saying the only reason to get married is so you can have sex. What he is saying is that marriage is the proper alternative for the sinning already going on (sexual immorality). Ask your teen this: If Paul's solution to sexual immorality was to get married, then what do you think the Corinthians' original problem was? (Hint: People having sex outside of marriage!)

To which your child then tries to justify, "But they didn't have a category for long-term, monogamous, committed relationships." Stop it. Yes, they did. It was called betrothal, and it was like our engagements but more binding. (Note how Joseph was betrothed to Mary, and he couldn't just take the ring back. To break it off, he had to divorce her—even before they got married and consummated the relationship. Jewish committed relationships were even more committed than ours!) Paul closes this loophole when he addresses those who are betrothed. If their passions are too strong—meaning they're going to go crazy if they don't have sex—then by all means, they should get married! A person looking for loopholes (while hoping the text doesn't say what it clearly says) will always make things sound more complicated than they are.

It should be clear by now what God says about sexuality. But the word on every teen's mind is *why*. *Why* does God define sexual morality in such a narrow way? It seems like an arbitrary rule. If sex is so wonderful and a gift from God, why would He try to limit it so much? The answer is simple, but it won't make sense if you don't understand the power and purpose of sex.

Sex as a Sign of the Marital Covenant

All conversations about sex with our kids need to include a very important concept: Sex is a married couple repeating their marital vows in bodily form. Or in Tim Keller's words, sex is a covenant renewal ceremony.[8]

A covenant is a promise ratified and remembered by something external. God gave Noah (and us) the rainbow in Genesis 9:16-17, saying, "Whenever the rainbow appears in the clouds, I will see it and remember the *everlasting covenant* between God and all living creatures of every kind on the earth...This is the sign of the covenant I have established between me and all life on the earth." Likewise, God gave Abraham and his descendants circumcision. In Genesis 17, God says, "As for me, this is my covenant with you: You will be the father of many nations...You [and your descendants] are to undergo circumcision, and it will be the *sign of the covenant* between me and you" (verses 4 and 11).

In short, covenants include 1) a promise and 2) a physical sign reminding them of the promise. The vows we make on our wedding day are our mutual covenant promise; sex is the physical reminder of those vows. Every time a married couple makes love, they are repeating those vows in bodily form. God warns the men in Malachi 2:14-15 to not forsake the covenant by being faithless to their wives. And it's not just a covenant between husband and wife; it's between the husband and wife and God Himself. God refers to the adulteress woman in Proverbs 2:17 as one who "forgets the covenant of her God" in her infidelity (ESV).

Even if people pretend that they don't believe this about the act of sex, their instinctual reactions reveal otherwise. I don't normally point to Hollywood for transcendent truths about sex, but there is a line from one movie that has always stuck out to me. In the movie *Vanilla Sky*—not one I'd recommend for casual (or any kind of) viewing—two characters, Julie and David, have a lot (and I mean a *lot*) of what we would consider "friends with benefits" sex. Later in the movie, when David meets another woman and actually falls in love, Julie goes absolutely psychotic. At one point she screams at him, "Don't you know that when you sleep with someone, your body makes a promise whether you do or not?"[9] It's a surprisingly accurate (though incomplete) statement for a Hollywood movie. The caveat is that the act of sex is not itself a promise; the act is supposed to *point back* to a promise that was already made.

So what are you doing when you engage in the act of sex before committing to the covenant of marriage? Lying. You are lying. Your body is pointing back to a promise you never made. Our minds, unfortunately, cannot always tell the difference though. We were created to equate sexual activity with promises of forever-love. The only way to wreck that innate knowledge is to systematically deprogram it out of existence—which is basically what the sex-positive culture is doing (as we'll talk about in chapter 8).

Ask anyone and they'll tell you that having a spouse (or even a significant other) cheat on them is an unparalleled betrayal—even for people who engaged in lots of casual sex prior to commitment. Why? Because it's really hard to reprogram a built-in instinct. Beavers will try to build dams whether they are in the wild or not.[10] Cats will still chase birds whether you yell at them or not. And we can't deprogram a human to ignore the power of the bond created through sex, even if they engage in meaningless sex a million times. Return a person to even a marriage-like environment, and they instinctively return to the knowledge that when you are committed to someone, you don't have sex with other people.[11] Sex is a powerful physical statement that should not be uttered lightly.

Things That Are Powerful Enough to Be Guarded

So how do we get these concepts across to our little ones? Let's go back to something that is easy to instill if we do our jobs well: creating categories. When I was a kid, I loved playing Scattergories—a game where you have a general category, and then you think of things that belong in that category. For example, if the category was "things that are red," a participant could list apples, blood, or stop signs. When we talk to our kids about sex, we need to make sure they are already familiar with the proper categories in which sex should be placed. One category might be "things that are so powerful they need to be guarded with boundaries." Another might be "things that are good or bad depending on how they are used." Fire gives a useful analogy for both categories.

Ask your kids, "Is fire good or bad?" Some might say good because they are thinking about roasting marshmallows or soaking in a bathtub surrounded by scented candles (yes, please!). Some might say bad because they are picturing forest fires or explosions. The truth is, fire is neutral; it can be good *or* bad depending on how it's used.

Here's another question for your kids: "How powerful is fire?" If they were already picturing a forest fire, then they're on the right track. Not only is fire powerful, but it also can be used to accomplish great feats of strength that we'd never be able to do on our own.

Using fire, we can blow holes through solid rock on a mountainside, cook food, provide light, purify metal...you name it! Or we can burn down half of California. Fire is most beneficial when contained within proper boundaries and most dangerous when removed from its proper place. A fire within a fireplace can create a warm and inviting home. Take it outside the fireplace, and it can destroy everyone and everything you love in the blink of an eye. Long story short, fire can create and fire can destroy. That it can do both is our first clue that it should be handled with caution.

Enough About Fire, You Pyro...

The same line of thinking can be applied to sex. Is sex good or bad? Well, it depends on how it's used. Sexual intimacy can be used to forge bonds of intimacy between man and woman that not even Hades can separate. It can literally create a human being—from scratch, I might add! Sexual energy is *really* powerful. Sexual desire—when channeled toward one's spouse—reemphasizes the vows they made to love, honor, cherish, and protect till death do they part. When a couple takes their marriage vows seriously, they fortify their marriage, stabilize their home, and create strong families in which children can thrive. Strong families create strong communities, which lead to a strong society.

But just like fire, sex can be used to destroy as well. The sexual impulse, without restraint, can devastate an individual and destroy a marriage. If sex is—as we've stated—a recommitment to the marital vows, then even sex within a marriage can be misused. As Christopher West says in his book *Our Bodies Tell God's Story*,

> Treating a spouse merely as an object for one's selfish indulgence is never an act of love. Few Christian men understand this critical point. The books and programs that have flooded the Christian market to help us in our "pornified" culture rarely get this either. The main goal of these programs is to help husbands direct their sexual desires toward their wives—a good first step, of course. But rarely, if ever, do these programs invite men to examine *what kind of desires* they're directing toward their wives.[12]

I have known far too many women who have been at the receiving end of this misuse of sex. Just because he put a ring on it, he feels he can come to his wife and demand sexual gratification as much as he wants or in any way he chooses. Such demands in no way reflect a Christlike agape love, which honors and cherishes his wife as a person. These demands, even if made within the confines of marriage, can undo what sex was intended to do. Rather than reinforce, these selfish acts of lust can nullify in bodily form the promises he made on their wedding day. And this is not just for men. Ladies, we are not off the hook. The way we initiate or respond to our husbands sexually should also reflect the vows we made to him.

So as you have probably noticed by looking around at our culture, sex misused outside of marriage—without reaffirming a lifetime commitment—often produces broken hearts, broken families, unwanted or aborted babies, and way more venereal diseases than should ever exist. Sex misused within a marriage—without the self-giving agape love promised on the wedding day—can devastate a marriage. Like fire, sex can create and sex can destroy. That it can do both is our first clue that it, too, should be handled with caution.

Who Are Really the Ones Obsessed with Sex—Christians or Secularists?

We have established that sex can be good or bad depending on whether it is properly channeled or contained. We have established that sex is extremely powerful. Let's go one step further in our analogy and discuss the ways one can interact with something that is extremely powerful and potentially dangerous. Back to our fire analogy!

There are two extreme ways one might interact with fire: as an arsonist or as a fireman. Question: Who of these two do you think is more obsessed with fires? I'd say they are equally obsessed, just in different ways. One is obsessed with creating as much fire as possible, and one is obsessed with containing fire to prevent destruction. The arsonist doesn't care about the consequence; he only cares about the flame. The fireman doesn't hate fire—I'm sure he loves a good campfire just as much as the next person. But he takes great pains to make sure a flame doesn't turn into a raging inferno. Firefighters put their lives on the line to help curtail the negative impact of fires gone wild. Arsonists just stand back and enjoy the show.

Our world treats sex like an arsonist treats fire. Who cares about consequences? Sex, sex, and more sex! As the arsonist hates anyone who tries to put out his fires, so our world hates anyone who rains on their sex parades. They look at the church and assume we are a bunch of dumpy, frigid, sexually repressed schoolmarms sitting atop our moral high horses, wagging our fingers and chastising people for having too much fun. No. We are trying to protect what is powerful!

Like it or not, we as Christians are called by God to be set apart, and one of the defining characteristics of His followers is sexual holiness. And now we can understand why! He didn't make boundaries because He wanted to control us or stomp on our fun, but because He wanted sex to retain its original meaning. God desires for us to experience real, lasting, flourishing fellowship with Him and with others. As we'll see in chapter 3, we flourish best when we stick to the beautiful design He created.

DISCUSSION QUESTIONS

1. **Icebreaker:** Has there ever been a time when you underestimated the power or danger of something and got hurt? What happened?

2. **Main theme:** *Sex is a very powerful covenant renewal ceremony and a bodily recitation of our marital vows; anything powerful enough to create or destroy can and should be carefully guarded.* What's the most powerful thing you can think of? Are there any kind of controls or regulations that govern it? What do you think would happen if there were no guidelines for it?

3. **Self-evaluation:** What were you taught about sex growing up? Was it treated as something good? Something dirty? Did your family even talk about sex? Have you ever been tempted to think that sex was "no big deal"? What are your thoughts on it after reading this chapter? How seriously does God take sex? Why do you think that is?

4. **Brainstorm:** As a group, compile a list of powerful and dangerous things in the world that should be treated with caution. Nuclear bombs? A rabid raccoon? You name it. Make sure you have a clear category in your

head of "things that are so powerful they need boundaries" (because you're going to do this with your kids next!).

5. **Release the bear:** Here's a fun discipleship idea! Create a secret handshake with your child and give it a meaning that involves a promise. It could be something like, "I'll love you forever and ever," or, "You will always be my child." (This one is especially useful if they start falling into some of the lies we talk about in section 3. Use it often in place of the words, establishing a category in your child's mind of "things we do with our bodies that reinforce or restate a promise that was already made with their words." Ask them frequently if they remember what it means, and have them recite it to you. Later, when they are old enough for "the talk," you can put sex into this well-established category, telling them that sex is a way married couples use their bodies to restate their wedding vows to their spouse.

6. **Pray:** Have you treated sex with the gravity that God describes in Scripture? Does your sex life reflect the kinds of messages you would have said in front of friends and family on your wedding day? Is it self-sacrificial? Honoring? Focused on self or focused on the other person? Are you using marital sex as a "rubber stamp" for fantasizing or acting out sinful situations? If so, ask the Lord why that is attractive to you. (For example, who on their wedding day would ever ask their bride or groom: "Can I pretend that you're someone else?") Our society has burdened sex with so much extra baggage that even God-fearing, married Christians often don't understand the messages the act is meant to reinforce. Pray and ask the Lord to work in your heart to understand sex the way He does. Pray that He would show you when to start having these conversations with your kids so that they can understand the goodness and power of sex.

CHAPTER 2

Sex Is Spelled W-O-R-L-D-V-I-E-W

How Our Sexual Beliefs Reveal Our Beliefs About God

HILLARY AND AMY

I (Hillary) remember the exact moment when I understood the *why* behind the Bible's teaching about saving sex for marriage. My husband and I started dating in 2006, and for my birthday he got me a book titled *Sex and the Supremacy of Christ* (because that's what nerds in love give each other as gifts). I underlined a portion of the book that made two life-changing points that transformed my outlook on sex forever.

The first is that *sexuality is designed by God as a way to know God in Christ more fully.* And the second is that *knowing God in Christ more fully is designed as a way of guarding and guiding our sexuality.*

Now to state the two points again, this time negatively, in the first place *all misuses of our sexuality distort the true knowledge of Christ.* And, in the second place, *all misuses of our sexuality derive from not having the true knowledge of Christ.*[1]

Boom. Mic drop. Mind blown.

My world changed in that moment. A misuse of my sexuality could distort my perception of God? Whoa! I don't want that to happen. Or wait…when someone has a distorted view of God, His mandates regarding sex won't even make sense to them? That kinda makes sense now that I think about it.

I've had few worldview shifts of this magnitude in my life. All of them can be summarized by a quote from C.S. Lewis: "I believe in Christianity as I believe that the Sun has risen, not only because I see it but because by it, I see everything else."[2] Those two little statements made so many other things in my life make sense—especially God's biblical commands.

All of God's super detailed laws about sex? I think I get it now. *Of course! You put boundaries around anything that is powerful enough to change the way a person sees God!* The New Testament epistles telling us to flee sexual immorality used to sound all preachy. Now they sounded super practical. *Of course! These new Christians were just getting to know God, and they were supposed to be representing God to the pagans around them. If having a distorted sexual life resulted in them representing a distorted view of God, then they needed to get that nonsense out of the church. God was trying to warn them that they were misrepresenting Him to the people He was trying to save! Duh! How had I missed this?*

I have witnessed firsthand the distorting impact that sexual immorality can have on one's view of God. I've had friends who, once their commitment to sexual holiness went out the window, so did their theology. One friend with whom I had been in youth leadership just walked away from the church altogether after becoming sexually involved with a non-Christian man whom she eventually married. Another friend—a girl whom I had been in leadership with at Cru—eventually turned not only away from God but *toward goddess worship*. She now teaches classes on how sex is at the "core of our vitality," whatever that means. It was a slow process, so it didn't happen all at once. But when she changed her views (and her actions) to match a worldly view of sex, her heart didn't just reject God; it went full pagan, just as God warned the Israelites in the wilderness.

An Inconvenient Truth

Sadly, Hillary's experience is the exception, not the norm. For the past several years I (Amy) have been traveling the US sharing God's design for sex. I start out asking the crowd what they as kids were taught about sex. It's fun to watch a roomful of adults squirm and turn bright pink. The answers are usually the same:

> Nothing!
>
> Don't do it! (Ah yes, the reverse Nike campaign, a Christian sex ed classic.)
>
> It'll fall off! (Cuz that's science.)
>
> When a mommy and a daddy love each other very much...

You get the idea. After the giggles die down, I ask for a show of hands from those who were taught that sex isn't just an act between bodies, but an expression of what we believe about God, ourselves, morality, truth, sin, and what happens after we die. To date, only 32 people have raised their hands.

It's no mystery why our culture—nay, why our *churches*—are so mixed up about sex. According to studies done by Dr. George Barna, only 4 percent of Christians have a fully biblical worldview—which means 96 percent of self-proclaimed Christians only partially know the tenets of a biblical worldview.[3] Or, if they do know them, they have no idea how to *incorporate* them into their everyday lives (particularly their sex lives). If someone has only a superficial understanding of the Bible's teachings on sex, gender, and marriage—knowing *what* it says but not *why*—the message may sound good in theory, but it won't actually change the way they live.

Sure, most Christian kids know that God designed sex for marriage, but once the teen years hit, they suddenly get all Genesis 3 ("Did God really say...?"). We at Mama Bear want to help break this cycle. Given that most of us haven't gotten worldview training, we're going to start with the fundamentals: What is a worldview?

What Is a Worldview (and Why Does It Matter)?

When we think of "worldviews," we often think of religions like Buddhism, Wicca, Islam, and Christianity. But let us assure you, Mamas, *sexuality is a religion.* And just like every other religion, each worldview answers the same core questions:

> What is reality?
>
> What is truth?
>
> What are human beings?
>
> What went wrong with the world?
>
> What is morality (i.e., right versus wrong)?
>
> Finally, how can this all be fixed?

While many Christians think of sexuality as only a moral issue, the implications are much more complex. A person's core view of sexuality isn't just tied to their view of God, but to their entire worldview. The word *worldview* may be an ambiguous concept for some. A person's worldview can be like…

- **A Lens:** A lens determines how accurately we perceive reality. (How do we know truth?)
- **Rules to a Game:** Rules tell you the purpose of a game and what kinds of actions you can or can't do to accomplish the purpose. (Think of the *what* and *why* of morality.)
- **A Filter:** A filter separates things, allowing certain materials to pass through and other materials to remain. A good worldview should allow truth in while keeping lies out. If the holes are too big (in our analogy, being too tolerant of bad ideas and sin), then lies slip in, and we start looking like the rest of the world. Make the holes too small (that is, "majoring in the minors"), and we create unnecessary division where there should be unity.
- **A Puzzle Box Top:** The box top shows reality as it was created. All the puzzle pieces—if put together correctly—should mirror the

box top. Think of each of your beliefs as pieces to your worldview puzzle and your actions as putting this worldview puzzle together. Each decision you make either reflects biblical truth (the box top) or some other puzzle (whatever the worldview-du-jour is teaching). If our beliefs (puzzle pieces) do not match reality (the box top), then our actions (putting together the puzzle) will show a very different picture.

- **A Cartographer's Map:** A good worldview allows us to look around and understand where we are, how we got there, how to navigate where we want to be, and which obstacles to expect on our journey. An accurate map doesn't save me from difficult terrain; it just helps me navigate it without too many surprises.

One thing Christians need to remember is that our worldview affects more than our perception of the world. It makes identity claims that influence our desires.

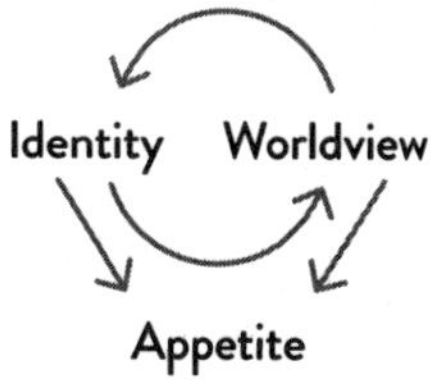

A properly understood biblical identity and worldview reinforce and protect each other... *if* they stay united around truth. For example, when a false identity claim is made ("I *am* LGBTQ+."), a robust biblical worldview recognizes the lie ("My identity is determined by my sexual attractions!") and kicks that sucker to the curb ("Nope! Not today, Satan. My attractions can be affected by sin, and they are not who I am."). When a person recognizes the identity statement as a lie, the solid worldview further protects them from rooting their identity in anything other than God (Colossians 2:8).

Reinforcing each other, a correctly grounded identity and biblical worldview then *inform* and *steward* my appetites, determining which desires I should allow myself to indulge in. The more we feed an appetite, the greater it becomes. The more we starve it, the weaker it gets. Praise be to God that we do not have to be controlled by our sinful desires (Romans 7:24). So what happens when we prioritize appetite over biblical identity and worldview? This model gets flipped on its head. Why? Because the object of worship changes. Notice the shift below.

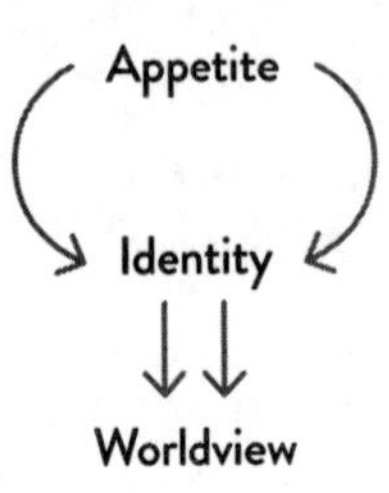

Instead of our worldview and identity shaping our appetites, the appetite *determines our identity* and then becomes the *filter* for the person's entire worldview. With this model, if something doesn't affirm what I believe about myself (whether it's straight, gay, trans, or minotaur—yes, that's a thing[4]), it's canceled as bigoted bias even if it's biological fact.

How does this affect our worldview? To be truly free from the shackles of doctrine, we have to apply this same approach to the Word of God. If you want to see what this looks like in the real world, read what the editors of *The Deconstructionist's Playbook* say about how to deconstruct your faith through the liberating process of "deciding which [elements of your faith] to keep, which to reimagine, and which to completely throw away."[5] Here's Hillary to tell you a little more about the Christian worldview.

An Overview of the Christian Worldview

The Christian worldview is a beautifully coherent story centered around the relationship between God and humans. It starts at creation; explains sin, separation, and morality; and ends with redemption. Our kids need a firm understanding of these tenets (and their implications) if they are to confidently commit to the Christian worldview, even when the culture calls them hateful, hurtful, intolerant, abusive monsters for doing so. (And, by the way, that's what they are being called now. Not Jesus freaks or goody-goodies. Nope. Our kids are facing much harsher names—names that are meant to shame them out of their Christian beliefs.)

If we think of the Christian worldview like an accurate map of reality, here are some of the landmarks we would expect to encounter along the way and how each of these aspects affects our views of gender and sex.

1. God Himself Is the Foundation of Reality and Truth

God created the world, so it's safe to say that His "map" of reality is the most accurate. While there are many differing views within Christendom on exactly how this creation took place, we should all stand united around the knowledge that God alone created, through Christ, out of nothing (John 1:1-3). If out of God all things came to be, then God *Himself* is the foundation of reality and truth. All things are derived from His attributes. God is good, so everything He created was good. And then sin entered the world, and Satan had a field day. But we must remember that all Satan can do is pervert something that was originally good. There is no independent entity that is evil. Any evil you try to conceive of is really just one of God's good gifts that has been twisted, used in the wrong way or in the wrong amount. (Except maybe scorpions. I have a hard time picturing those *ever* being good.)

What does this tell us about sex and gender? First off, since both sex and gender existed before the fall, then they are inherently good! Sex doesn't just feel good; it is *morally good* when used according to God's design! And gender differences were part of God's original design. When we reject the concept of male and female, we tell the world that God's created order isn't good.

2. Ultimate Truth Is Discovered, Not Created

Since God *is* truth and God *is* eternal, then there exist eternal truths that we can discover. And since humans were created in the image of God, our minds reflect a hunger and ability to discern these truths—truths that lie *outside* of ourselves. Since truth is ultimately traced back to God, it isn't subject to our desires or opinions.

There are truths present in creation (Psalm 19:1-2; Romans 1:20), in God's revealed Word (2 Timothy 3:16), in relationship with God Himself through the Holy Spirit (John 14:26), and even embedded within our hearts (Romans 2:15). According to Romans 1, we can *suppress* and *exchange* these truths, but we'll find it very hard to erase them completely.

What does this tell us about sex and gender? Culture is telling us that we create truth. But legit truth isn't created; it is discovered. When you find an idea that pops up among every. single. people. group. in. history, you're likely dealing with an eternal truth that was written by God onto our hearts. And guess what has been universally acknowledged in every single culture throughout time? Male and female as separate sexes, and some form of marriage for the purpose of bearing and raising children. Furthermore, the truth of male/female sexual relations is embedded in our bodily design.[6]

3. Humans Are Uniquely Created in the Image of God

God created all things, but humans are unique in that we are created in the image of God. Theologians and philosophers have debated for millennia what exactly this statement means.[7] Regardless of how *imago dei* is defined, it is an elevated status (Psalm 8:4-6) granting humanity greater worth than anything else in creation. When I say greater worth, I mean that if God has to choose between saving a thousand pigs or one human, he picks the human (Mark 5:1-20). Pigs are great. We love pigs. But they can never match the worth of a human.

What does this tell us about sex and gender? Being created in the image of God means we are valuable! We have incalculable worth! We share similarities with God that nothing else in creation shares. Amy has a story from one of her talks where a teenage girl came up in tears and said that nobody had ever told her she had value—and especially that God's design for sex helped reflect and reinforce it. She left with a lot more joy than when she arrived.

4. God Created with Purpose

Embedded within God's creative act is the concept of *teleology*—a fancy word for saying that something was designed with an end goal, a purpose in mind. Telos tells us *why* something was created, what it needs to function, and how it functions best. The telos of inanimate objects is easy. (For example, use printers for printing, not for doorstops.) Telos in animals is evident too. Try as you might to keep your sheepdog from rounding up all the grandkids, you won't succeed. If he sees little creatures that can be corralled, he *has* to corral them; he just can't help himself. It's in his telos.

Design implies a designer—an author, if you will. And what do authors have? An author has *autho*rity over that which they designed! A video game designer is the only one who knows the secret cheat code—because he or she put it there! And only God can tell us how we humans were created to function best and what will royally mess us up.

What does this tell us about sex and gender? Since God created sex in the garden, then we, as Christians, can absolutely proclaim that it is goooo-ooood! Furthermore, our bodies, our genders, sex, marriage, and family were designed for a purpose. And guess what, friends? These things are not up for redefinition. We have not been appointed to that committee. Rejecting God's design for sex, gender, marriage, or family is basically rejecting God as the authority.

5. *God's Moral Law Is Part of Our Telos*

There's a reason Adam and Eve didn't have any other rule except which tree to avoid. Their natural inclinations were already in lockstep with God's design. Imagine a world where God didn't *have* to give us any commandments because we only wanted to do that which pleased Him.[8] What delighted God delighted us! It would be like the whole array of vegetables all tasting like candy and pizza. "Eat your veggies, kids" would be accompanied by "Yaaaaaaay!" We were—by nature—everything described in 1 Corinthians 13 and Galatians 5:22-23.

What does this tell us about sex and gender? If we want to find wisdom and flourishing, we need to look at how things functioned *before sin came into the world.* "Male and female he created them" (Genesis 1:27). They were created as husband and wife to be joined together sexually (Genesis 2:24). The purpose of that sexual union was 1) to unify husband and wife (Genesis 2:24) and 2) to procreate more humans who would join them in ruling over the earth (Genesis 1:28). Being made in God's likeness (Genesis 1:27) means we rule over the earth by manifesting God's character and goodness. That was our original telos.

6. *Sin Got Us All Confused*

God wanted Adam and Eve to live with Him *voluntarily*, as Creator and creature. But you can't choose to be with someone if there's literally no other choice; similarly, someone can't choose to obey if there are literally no rules! So God even provided one arbitrary rule by which Adam and Eve could express that they were with Him by choice. (If this is confusing, see the blog on our website titled: "Why Did God Create the Tree in the First Place?"[9]) God didn't mince words; He told them that the day they ate from the tree in the middle of the garden, they would die. The choice wasn't about the eating; it was about *believing* that what God said was true.

Churchy people know this is called "sin," and it's responsible for the havoc we see in the world. But the word *sin* is easy to wave away because it's so Christianese-y, so let's talk about sin from a teleological perspective. As stated in point 5, all our inclinations before sin were good. The only real choice we had was whether to acknowledge God as our authority. We humans are made as physical and spiritual beings. When God said Adam and Eve would die if they ate from the tree, that was both a physical and spiritual death. Physically, it meant we wouldn't live forever. Spiritually, it meant our inborn telos—behaving according to God's design, reflecting His good goodness, and reflecting His character—would no longer come naturally. Why? Because sin severed our connection to God—the *source* of our goodness, design, and character. The part of us that was drawn to godliness died a spiritual death, and our subsequent behaviors got so janky that by Moses's time, God literally had to specify: "Hey! Don't verbally taunt the deaf dude or trip a blind person!" (Leviticus 19:14, my paraphrase). Why?! I'm serious! *Why* did that have to be said? It did, y'all. It really did.

When left to our own devices (disconnected from the source of our original telos—God's goodness), our inborn desires became more and more warped. That which delighted God seemed "meh," and that which God abhorred was all "Ooooooh! Yes, please!" Add a few generations of babymaking with people passing down these broken designs, and you'll land yourself smack-dab in the middle of pre-flood earth where "every inclination of the thoughts of the human heart was only evil all the time" (Genesis 6:5). Where are we now? Well, I'd say we are quickly heading toward the "fabulous" society described in Romans 1:28-32 where people are literally inventing ways of doing evil. We are so disconnected from our telos that people don't even know how to be human anymore.

What does this tell us about sex and gender? Interestingly, all worldviews seem to agree on one major truth: Things done got broke. The only way to unbreak the broken is to return to that which is good for us. The world and God's Word have two diametrically opposing game plans for restoring sexual health. God says His design is how we were created, how we will ultimately flourish, and how we are to behave if we are to accept Him as the authority on the matter. The world says God's design is what has messed us up so badly! His restricting sex between husband and wife, between male and female (and even the concept of male and female to begin with), is supposedly what prevents us from being our authentic selves. The only way for humans to be fulfilled is to decide *for themselves* what their sexual telos is. Ask yourself which worldview your sexual actions have communicated?

7. We Cannot Be Reconciled to Our Telos Until We Are Reconciled to God Through Jesus

Just as every worldview has its own version of original sin (what's ultimately wrong with the world), so every worldview has its own version of redemption (how to fix what's wrong in the world). The Christian worldview teaches that our main problem is that sin severed our connection to God, the source of our telos. Every person from the beginning of time until now has been born with a severed connection to God; humans can't reproduce what they don't have. So God Himself had to step into flesh. Only God is sinless, which means only He can afford to pay our penalty. (The best a guilty person can do is pay their own debt.) Jesus, the fleshly incarnation of God, came to earth, lived a sinless life, and paid the penalty of sin, which is death (Romans 6:23). Only Jesus could have accomplished this. Why? Only a *human* could pay on behalf of humankind, which is why God became man (John 1:1, 14), and only an innocent party (God) can take an undeserved punishment. If Jesus wasn't God, then He was only a sinful man who paid His own penalty. If Jesus was not human, then He could not have been our representative.

Unless you can find another God-man to do this for us, Jesus is it. There's no other option. No philosophy, no self-help program, no morality boot camp can restore the connection between us and God and thereby change our natural inclinations from evil to goodness. We can pretend for a while (and plenty of people in religion do pretend!). We may look all sparkly for a season, but eventually our grit and self-control gives way, and all the yuck we've been hiding in our hearts eventually oozes out because we can't get rid of our sin nature on our own. Only a true salvation experience (followed by true submission to God) can rehab our sinful hearts. And just like in rehab, it often takes a while for our natural inclinations to change.

What does this tell us about sex and gender? This one is simple: You cannot change your inclinations on your own. This was the great (failed) experiment of "conversion therapy" (as in the "shock the gay away" stupidity that occurred in the mid-1900s).[10]

8. Not Everything Is Redeemed...Yet

You'd think that all we need is to restore the connection between us and God so everything could go back to the way it was. Not quite. Anyone who has ever completely lost their health knows that regaining it is a long, arduous process. Our redemption starts on this earth but is never completed here. Instead, as Paul puts it, we "groan inwardly as we wait eagerly for our adoption to sonship, the redemption of our bodies" (Romans 8:23).

Salvation is the beginning of righting the wrong that was done in the garden. It reconnects us to our source of goodness—God. But as all rehab patients know, it takes time and a lot of work to change our bodies from doing what comes naturally to operating at peak condition.

What does this tell us about sex and gender? God's sacrifice on the cross doesn't make our transformation immediate: *It makes it possible.* Expect that your sexual desires will not immediately change. Expect to be fighting the battle against yourself for a long time. But also expect that as you submit to Christ, His commands, and His telos day after day, it will get easier. Our goal isn't mere behavioral change; those don't usually last. Rather, when we allow God to change our hearts, life gets much easier. We participate in this healing process; we can choose behaviors that increase or decrease our connection to God. The more we obey, the more His goodness changes us from the inside out. The more we disobey, the more we go straight back to the bondage we were freed from.

You *Was*, Not You *Is*

According to the Christian worldview, we can expect that things are not the way God designed them to be. We expect that many of our natural inclinations lead us away from godliness. We humbly accept Christ as the only One who can restore us to what humans were intended to be, and we have faith that living according to His design will bring us the ultimate freedom, even if our desires disagree for a time. These are our expectations based upon a biblical worldview of what went wrong and what the solution is. No surprises there. *Aaaand yet*...for some reason, even our churches are getting confused about this. I attended a conference of a well-known theologian who speaks on LGBTQ+ stuff, and he could not answer the simple question: "Are same-sex desires a result of the fall?"[11] Churches are literally changing their stance on God's sexual commandments because people have desires they feel unable to overcome. A truly biblical worldview expects this though! It expects that overcoming our inclinations will be hard! Instead, we have turned our sexualities into immutable, unchangeable "I am" statements.

"I am gay."

"I am trans."

"I am bi."

"I am nonbinary."

Friends, you am nuthin' but a sinner, loved by God and saved by His marvelous grace.

If you are in Christ, everything you are should be stated in the past tense—"I *was*"—because that is what the Bible says: "That is what some of you *were*. But you were washed, you were sanctified, you were justified in the name of the Lord Jesus Christ and by the Spirit of our God" (1 Corinthians 6:11). Only faith in God alone can change our "I am" and return our natural inclination back to how we were created. And one day, when we get our new bodies, we won't have to fight against the sin nature. Praise God! That battle will be done. I may not understand how my obedience in the present affects eternity, but I will stake my life on the fact that it does. Staking my life on that fact means I obey when I don't want to; I believe God when I don't want to; and I (or, as many in AA or therapists say) "trust the process." The process of what? Of therapy? No!

Of God's redemption through my continually choosing obedience, shameless repentance when I fail, and unending pursuance of Him as my good God, even when things are hard. Why? Because I have faith that He has told me the *truth* in His Word, and that the truth will set me free! Are you ready to prepare your children for freedom, Mama Bears? Let's teach them what to expect based on a biblical worldview.

 DISCUSSION QUESTIONS 

1. **Icebreaker:** Who wears glasses? What was it like the first time you put them on? See if someone in the group can procure a pair of wacky glasses that distorts everything. Pass them around and try to read a paragraph of this book. How much harder is it with the distortion glasses?

2. **Main theme:** *The Christian worldview is complete and coherent. It describes a good original design, what happened to mess it up, how God provided Jesus to redeem what was broken, and how He plans to continue to redeem us amid a broken world. Our sexual behaviors reflect our agreement or disagreement with this worldview.* How does the Christian worldview affect our view of gender and sexuality? How do you think it is different from how the world views sex and gender?

3. **Self-evaluation:** What aspects of the Christian worldview do you find hardest to apply to your everyday life?

4. **Brainstorm:** How does the Christian worldview change the way we view sex, gender, and our bodies? How might a person's worldview be different if they believe they weren't created, that what they do with their bodies doesn't matter, or that physical pleasure is the main goal of life?

5. **Release the bear:** Our kids need to understand that the Christian worldview explains both the good *and* the bad things in life. Make a game out of identifying original design, brokenness, and redemption in everyday life. A day with family enjoying food and fellowship? Original

design. Getting a stomach flu? Brokenness. Forgiving each other when we say mean things? Redemption.

6. **Pray:** Pray that the Lord would begin showing you areas where your worldview might be askew, and thank Him for how beautiful and cohesive the Christian worldview is. If you can't see it, ask Him to reveal to you the beauty of His ordered design.

A Pretty Great Design, When Followed

How Gender, Marriage, Sex, and Family Show Us the God We Can't See

HILLARY

Coherent and *beautiful*: Those are my two favorite adjectives for the Christian worldview. And I say that because I've studied the other worldviews. I know this is a book on sexuality and gender identity. Those are the dumpster fires du jour. If we start with sexuality, however, it's like opening a book right in the middle of the story. We cannot understand what is going on in the middle until we know what came before. And we cannot fully appreciate the significance of the middle unless we know how it weaves into a glorious ending—the telos, the purpose, the end goal of the rest of the story.

In order to address how gender, marriage, sex, and family show us the God we can't see, we must first address the giant elephant in the room: *authority*. I truly believe that much of the distortion surrounding gender, sex, and marriage can be traced back to people's fundamental misunderstanding of this one little word. Who has the authority to say what we do with our bodies? Who has the authority to define sexual morality and immorality? Who has the authority to define marriage? What does authority even mean? What does good authority look like? Can it even exist? Doesn't absolute power corrupt absolutely? How do we prevent people from abusing their authority?

Right off the bat, I want to acknowledge those of you who have experienced unhealthy authority, especially those who have been sexually abused at the hands of someone you trusted—or even worse, at the hands of a self-proclaimed Christian church leader. Sexual abuse messes with a person's ability to trust or interact with authority in a way that most people will never understand. I hear you. I grieve with you. (I am one of you.) At the same time, I want to encourage you to never let a bad representative define what God has called good. Our God is the great Restorer, the Healer, the One who makes all things new.

In reading the biographies of people who have gone from sexual brokenness to freedom in Christ, I have noticed a theme. They were never convinced of God's sexual *telos* (His purpose for sex) for intellectual reasons. Their submission to God's design was only possible when they finally understood the *goodness* of God Himself, submitting to Him out of love and not out of fear.[1] I do not expect that I can talk anyone into what the Bible describes as a good design if they've never seen it in person. So let me try to draw you a picture from my own life.

But first a disclaimer: Though my circumstances may appear picture-perfect in comparison to others, let me assure you that I have had my fair share of struggles. In and out of the hospital for most of my life, I felt ostracized by my peers and frequently jealous of all the things they could do with their healthy bodies that I could not. Most people would not want to take on the number of medications I have to take on a regular basis, deal with cancer that keeps peeking its ugly head into my life, or live through the surgeries I've had. Alas, the Lord gives us each our own burdens; we all suffer in our own ways. So don't take this section as me bragging about how awesome my life is. No. My purpose in this section is to present *one* area of my life that has not been a burden—namely my experience with authority. I'd like to paint a beautiful picture in your mind of how awesome God's plan is for marriage and family...when it is followed.

My Story

I never had a hard time submitting to my father's authority because my father is the pinnacle of provider and protector. He didn't use his authority to "get his way." He used his authority to serve us. He served our family by providing for us materially. He served our family by leading us spiritually. He served (and still serves) our family by loving my mom fiercely and faithfully. In turn, I saw her respect my father by joyfully submitting to his leadership. And as she submitted to him, he laid down his life (metaphorically speaking) for her. He didn't disrespect or martyr himself, because our first area of authority is over our own bodies and needs. However, my mother's, my sister's, and my needs and wants were always at the forefront of his mind.

I rarely ever saw my parents fight; they discussed—sometimes at length—but rarely with raised voices. They seldom made a decision without doing so together, and they made sure my sister and I couldn't play them off each other. When my dad put his foot down (which happened occasionally), none of us questioned it because my dad is such a gentle man and we trusted him. His *yes* was predicated on two things: Was it beneficial for us, and was it possible for him to provide it? He never put it in these words, but he provided us with anything we needed to succeed in our respective spheres of influence. If I made a comment about worrying about the SATs, a book of practice tests would magically appear the next day. We never had name-brand anything because (even if he could theoretically provide it) showing off name brands was *not for our benefit*; thus, he didn't provide them. But if something within his power and means would benefit us or bless us, he made it happen. Authority—to me—has always meant provision and protection.

My father also gave me (and still gives me) the most important things a father can give: time and attention. What was important to me, my mom, and my sister was important to him. I don't think I ever had a hobby in which he didn't participate in some way. When my sister became a teacher, he found ways to involve himself by taking her out to buy decorations for her classroom.

When I was an athletic trainer at Texas Christian University, he got himself and my mom season tickets to the football games, just to watch me do my thang. When I was a photographer, he went to photo conferences with me. And now that I'm a writer, he and my mom read most everything I write before it goes to press. If it is important for my work, it is important to him.

The legacy my parents left for me is one in which authority means cultivating those under your care the way God made them, not the way you wish they were. I never mistook my parents for my "best friends" growing up, but they weren't my enemies either. If I spoke to either of them with a disrespectful tone, it was addressed immediately. They made sure my sister and I knew that we were not top dogs; God was the first priority, then each other, and then us. Mom always gave Dad the best of every cut of meat, not my sister or me. Mom always got shotgun (the seat of honor) in the car no matter what. Through healthy boundaries, we developed such mutual respect that now, as an adult, I *can* say they are my best friends. It is still a joy to honor my parents because of the way they honored God's authority structure in our home. My foundation is ultimately in Christ. But a pretty big part of my emotional stability still derives from having grown up in a home with parents who modeled servant-leadership and healthy submission toward one another.

I looked forward to marriage because of how my father and mother modeled it for me. Anyone who knows me knows I can have a strong personality. I have a will of my own and plenty of thoughts on most every matter. And now, wonder of wonders, I get to write about them for a living. (Holla!) A shrinking violet I am not. So how could I not bristle at the idea of a man, my peer, being my "head" as Christ is head of the church (Ephesians 5:23)? Simply put, I don't bristle at it because authority always meant security to me, not subjugation.

When it came time to form my own family, I found a man who treated me the way my father did. I can say with no hesitation that it is a joy to submit to Dr. John D. Ferrer. A major part of that is because the submission issue very rarely comes into play. John imitates Christ through his love and provision, and I understand Christ better by the way John treats me. And that's how it was meant to be!

My husband literally calls me "his garden" and muses about how his role as my husband is to cultivate me in the Lord.[2] At the same time, he knows that the active *pruning* role belongs to the Holy Spirit—not him! Every now and then, when we are at an impasse, he'll come straight out and ask me to submit. It is always couched with, "Will you please submit to me on this one? I answer to God for our family. I think this is the right course of action, and you have full 'I told you so' privileges if I'm wrong." He pulls this card so rarely that I know he's not just saying stuff to get his way. And he doesn't demand my submission. He requests, and I have yet to refuse—because he has earned my trust in a million ways.

When it comes to providing for me, my husband passed up many jobs that would have helped him in his career in order to make sure I had health insurance—since my cancer and other health issues put me in the high-risk population. While writing the first edition of this book, my beloved Dr. John was waking up at four a.m. to work ten-hour days at a window factory. He was probably the only guy there with a PhD.

In years prior, John missed out on many academic opportunities because the organizations didn't provide health insurance—a nonnegotiable for us at the time. My current career as an apologetics writer and speaker is actually the job my husband labored *for 12 years of grad school* to do. But when he saw God blessing Mama Bear Apologetics, he put his credentials aside and said, "I see the Lord blessing this more than anything I've ever touched, so I will do whatever I need to do to make sure you are able to flourish in this role. Far be it from me to get in the way when the Lord is moving."

John knows that marriage is not 50-50 but 100-100. That 100 percent, though, is relative to the person who is giving. Unfortunately, my 100 percent is about 10–20 percent of what other people are capable of. Most people don't realize this, but in our home, John does the dishes. John does the laundry. John does the grocery shopping. And John does a lot of the tidying. Why? Because I've got, on average, about four good working hours a day, if that. John has every reason to be bitter that I'm not "giving more," but he isn't. Why? Because he knows that I give all of what I've got. It's just not much in comparison to other people.

I hope that gives you a picture of the kind of man I married and why I will never begrudge him the honor and submission that Scripture says I should pay him (Ephesians 5:22-24). I rarely think about it, it's such a nonissue.

And why should it be? What woman in her right mind wouldn't jump at the opportunity to be under a man who provides such love and emotional security? Where is the downside? I can't see it. When my husband leads with such gentle and sacrificial love, I gladly allow him to be the tiebreaker when we can't quite reach an agreement, which isn't that often. I gladly defer to him as the head of our family. And as a ministry leader, I understand the gravity of leadership. It's not a position for the faint of heart. I answer to God for the decisions I make as head of Mama Bear Apologetics, and John answers to God for the decisions he makes as head of our home. I will gladly be number two to not have that level of responsibility. Honestly, if leadership doesn't scare the pants off you, you probably don't understand it (and you're probably not ready to lead).

Putting This in Perspective

I don't share this in order to brag about what a great family I have. What have I been given that wasn't a gift? Nothing. Neither do I describe my marriage to say, "This model is true because it works for us"—rather, because it's true...*therefore* it works...when followed! God ain't no liar!

Furthermore, I tell my story because I want people who have never seen this modeled for them to know that 1) it is possible and 2) it is beautiful! God did, in fact, create a really great system! My family and I are by no means perfect. But I think we get the gist of what God was going for, and our lives have been easier for it because we purposely chose to submit to His good design.

I know there are people out there who may have never seen what healthy authority structures look like. The word *authority* may have meant that you weren't allowed to ask questions, or that trying to understand a decision was interpreted as insubordination. In some churches, a woman is held responsible for "submitting" while the leadership ignores the selfish, overbearing, or porn-addicted husband and gives him a pass. Is it any surprise that people reject God's teachings on sex when the only reason behind them is that "God says so"? If the authorities in their life never loved them or served them, then why should they trust God as an authority on any subject? And I'll say this 100 times in this book: Most issues with sexuality are rooted in the fact that people don't understand God's goodness! The sex issue is just the symptom.

Authority for many people has been reduced to blind obedience. And while authority does imply obedience, it's not obedience out of fear of punishment. Such obedience is rooted in gratitude for the provision and protection offered by the leader. Our submission to God is rooted in our knowledge of His *goodness*. If you cannot see His goodness, His laws sound like arbitrary power plays.

Leading means serving and cultivating those under your leadership. That is how God models and designed authority. But in a marriage, you can't have just one person following the design; you need two people committed to following it. When you have that, it doesn't just work. It rocks!

Authority Within the Godhead

Here's where things get dicey: Authority implies a hierarchy, and some people misunderstand hierarchy. They have rarely seen power and authority used for good, so any kind of authority structure sounds like a system of oppression. However, one of the reasons I know authority was part of God's original plan is because God chose a hierarchical authority structure within the Godhead when Christ became flesh. Before we discuss this, however, we must first understand the difference between *ontological* hierarchy and *functional* hierarchy. Otherwise, we end up as heretics! No bueno.

Ontology refers to the nature or essence of a being. We as humans are ontologically different from the rest of creation (animals, trees, etc.). We have a different essence and a different level of authority. We are, however, ontologically equal to all other humans—no matter the gender, ethnicity, or developmental level. A four-year-old child is as equally made in God's image as Einstein. We are ontologically equal.

Functional hierarchy refers to different roles between ontologically equal parties. A conductor and a violinist are ontologically equal—of equal worth and value. Functionally, they have different roles. But you know what their different roles are based on? An absolute commitment to being on the same page. Conductor and violinist must be operating on the same page—otherwise it's cacophony and chaos. We also see this within the military, when officers of equal rank preside over committees. (Sometimes, even higher-ranking officers submit to lower-ranking offices, because for the time being, they are following the leaders of that committee.) It's the same with all coequal authority structures. This is how we saw functional hierarchy working within the Godhead when Jesus took on flesh.

God the Father, God the Son, and God the Holy Spirit are not the same person, but they are all equally God. This understanding mattered to God so much that He had the Israelites repeat it every day via the Shema: "Hear, O Israel: The Lord our God, the Lord is one" (Deuteronomy 6:4). In the Gospel of John, Jesus says over and over that if we have seen Him, we've seen the Father. If we want to know the Father, we can know Him by knowing Jesus (John 8:19; 12:45; 14:7). Colossians 1:15 says that Jesus "is the image of the invisible God," and Hebrews 1:3 says that Jesus is the "exact imprint of [the Father's] nature" (esv).

The relationship within the Trinity is unlike anything a human had ever witnessed, and God basically said, "Look to me to know how you are supposed to act," but also, "Be so unified that people will recognize me." In John 17:20-23, Jesus says,

> My prayer is not for [the disciples] alone. I pray also for those who will believe in me through their message, that all of them may be one, Father, just as you are in me and I am in you. May they also be in us so that the world may believe that you have sent me. I have given them the glory that you gave me, that they may be one as we are one—I in them and you in me—so that they may be brought to complete unity. Then the world will know that you sent me and have loved them even as you have loved me.

The works of the Trinity cannot be understood apart from this kind of unity. And guess what? Same thing for husband and wife! The way we act in unity is supposed to be a way for the world to see and understand the God they cannot see or understand. And if the world cannot see it through the way we as believers treat each other, then His hope is for marriages to offer another picture. Ephesians 5:31-33 says,

> "For this reason a man will leave his father and mother and be united to his wife, and the two will become one flesh." This is a profound mystery—but I am talking about Christ and the church. However, each one of you also must love his wife as he loves himself, and the wife must respect her husband.

Take these passages together, and what is the picture God is trying to paint for the world? It is the picture of separate persons—*equal* in nature, *equal* in worth, *equal* in value—who are so united in love that even the different roles of authority in Christ's missional submission result in joy, not oppression. That is how functional submission looks—just like the Son (in His humanity) submitting to the Father.

The main message about the Godhead from Genesis to Revelation is one of love and unity, not power. Obedience is not an issue within the Godhead because there is unity—one will, just as there is supposed to be in marriage. In John 6:37-38, Jesus says, "All those the Father gives me will come to me, and whoever comes to me I will never drive away. For I have come down from heaven *not to do my will but to do the will of him who sent me.*" Likewise, the Spirit is unified with the Father and the Son in purpose as seen in John 16:13: "When he, the Spirit of truth, comes, he will guide you into all the truth. *He will not speak on his own; he will speak only what he hears.*"

Within the way the Trinity works in creation, there are different roles—some of which (and specifically during Christ's time on earth) included *obedience*. The unity and love among them make this work so flawlessly. This is what Christian marriage and family were meant to model for the world. We are raising little men and little women who may one day choose to form their own families. The way they see us *serving* in leadership and *honoring* in submission affects how they will one day view authority as well. And this isn't just authority when it comes to family, but to any authority we place ourselves under, whether that be where we choose to live (police and government officials), where we choose for school (teachers), where we choose to work (bosses), or where we go to church (elders and pastors). Is God a cosmic killjoy out to command His minions, or is He a loving Father who wants the best for His children? Their experience at home will either help or hinder the way they view God because family was intended to demonstrate the unity, love, and willful submission within the incarnational Godhead.

Can you see what an amazing civilization we would have if this model of authority and submission were followed in every sphere? It is health that breeds health, life that breeds life. Done well, it is a beautiful, harmonic order where all are elevated in value. We may not get a choice of whom we submit to as children, but we do as adults, through a thousand different choices. Let's teach our kids to choose their authorities well, and then show them how to both lead and submit in a God-glorifying way.

Why Is It So Important to Get the Concept of Authority Right?

Some might be thinking, *This is a book on sex, not on authority*. Mama Bears (and Papa Bears), understanding authority is imperative for understanding sex and marriage because, as we've discussed, sex is a bodily recitation of the marriage vows that were already spoken. But there's a really important second aspect, one that makes some people uncomfortable: Marriage itself was intended to be a picture of Christ's relationship with the church.

As Christopher West points out in his book *Our Bodies Tell God's Story*, Scripture is bookended by two marriages: the first marriage between man and woman, and the final marriage between Christ and His bride. Our very sexuality, the two different genders united in an embrace of love, is meant to be a picture of what is to come. *And if we feel awkward about that, it only serves to point out how far our understanding of sex and marriage has degraded from God's original design.* It is a beautiful picture of oneness in the midst of diversity. And without the two sexes, without the marriage, and without the coming together of two—who literally create one flesh (i.e., kids) through their union—we do not understand the purpose of our lives, the purpose of marriage, the purpose of sex, or even the purpose of our bodies.

No one explains this better than Rachel Gilson in her book *Born Again This Way*:

> When God speaks of himself and his people being "married," God is *always* the male, and his people are always the female...Why does sex difference matter for the metaphor? First, the relationship by definition can't exist without both parties. So if you lack one of the parties you destroy the picture. Lose the male from the marriage, and you lose the picture of Christ. Lose the female, and you lose the picture of the church...Second, the members are not interchangeable—Christ is not the church and the church is not Christ...Third, the male and female are different from each other yet able to be united because of shared humanity. So too, God and his people are essentially vastly different...The gospel is about an uncrossable chasm shockingly bridged.[3]

As I stated in chapter 1, we have lost the meaning of *meaning*. We have been carefully trained by culture to think that meaning is a human construct, but it is not. Within marriage is a picture of God Himself—which is why, if we get it wrong, we see God incorrectly too.

The Fashion Analogy

I want you to picture for a moment that you are a clothing designer about to present at fashion week. You have worked tirelessly for months creating a clothing line that is beautiful and functional and tells a very personal story. In fact, as the models walk down the catwalk, pieces of a poem you have written are shown on the screen behind them, and each line is only understandable by viewing the garment coming down the aisle. You have created poetry in word and in form—an artistic masterpiece!

Now picture someone coming in the night before the fashion show, cutting up all your pieces, and resewing them in some odd fashion that is neither beautiful nor coherent. The poem you carefully crafted now sounds like utter nonsense. Your name is still on the fashion show, but the work is no longer yours. And every person in the audience is judging you, your skill, and your message by this chopped-up, incoherent mess they see in front of them. Based on what they see, they don't understand you, they now reject you, your reputation is in tatters, and your message is lost.

Friends, this is what humanity has done to God.

God is the designer. Gender, marriage, and sex are the clothes, and the poetic message that united them is now incomprehensible because it has been separated from God's original design. We have separated gender from sex, and sex from marriage. Then we redefined marriage and now are in the process of redefining gender. If we are having a hard time understanding who we are, who God is, and where our ultimate destinies lie, it is not because God hasn't communicated well; it's because we have destroyed His picture.

The Message of Gender: A Picture of the Image of God (*Imago Dei*)

In Genesis 1:27, Moses writes: "God created mankind in his own image, in the image of God he created them; male and female he created them." In case we missed it the first time, he restates it in Genesis 5:1-2. And in case we *still* missed it, Jesus repeats it in Mark 10:6.

God made humankind in His image, male and female. Who is made in God's image? Not man alone. Not woman alone. Male and female together reflect the image of God.

Does this mean that a single person cannot carry the image of God? By no means! Scripture gives great dignity to those who are single—whether by choice or not (Matthew 19:12). In the words of Christopher West, "All people are called to prepare themselves for eternal union with God." Christian celibacy—keeping oneself wholly united to Christ and His work here on earth—in no way destroys the picture.[4]

The Message of Marriage: A Picture of Christ and the Church

Marriage was intended to point us to our ultimate destiny as members of the church body, and the church being joined eternally to Christ. Marriage is a tiny microcosm of that reality. But this picture has been distorted by those who twist authority and submission. Some men love to quote the Ephesians passage about wives submitting to their husbands as unto the Lord and use it as carte blanche permission to treat their wives like lesser vessels instead of *with care* as the weaker vessels (1 Peter 3:7). But if husbands are to be a picture of Christ, then their authority is not one of power, but one of service. Just look at how God defines the husband's role in Ephesians:

> Husbands, love your wives, just as Christ loved the church and gave himself up for her to make her holy, cleansing her by the washing with water through the word, and to present her to himself as a radiant church, without stain or wrinkle or any other blemish, but holy and blameless. In this same way, husbands ought to love their wives as their own bodies. He who loves his wife loves himself. After all, no one ever hated their own body, but they feed and care for their body, just as Christ does the church—for we are members of his body. "For this reason a man will leave his father and mother and be united to his wife, and the two will become one flesh" (Ephesians 5:25-31).

The command to the husband is one of *dying to his own desires* in order to serve his wife just as Christ died on the cross to serve His bride. That is what biblical authority is to look like. That is what my father modeled to me, and that is how I recognized the kind of character I wanted in a husband.

The Message of Sex: A Picture of Our Eternal Destiny

This is where I find most people get the most uncomfortable with the analogy of Christ and His bride. It sounds like a kind of cult where all the women are to have sex with the leader. But this fails to acknowledge that it is *the church* (not individuals) to whom Christ is being wed. No cell of my human body interacts with my soul apart from all the other cells. It's not some bizarre cellular orgy. Together, they form one unified body. It is a perfect example of diversity and oneness—all the cells, all the muscles, all the organs working together to form one whole person—me. Similarly, we as the bride will be made up of a diverse union of every tongue, tribe, and nation. We, together, are the bride of Christ. There is a reason why Paul calls this one-flesh union a "profound mystery." How does one understand a spiritual version of sex?

Again, we have to look at our bodies as the language of God's mystery. Our sexuality is carved into the very bodies of male and female—the man entering into the woman, and the woman willingly receiving the man. The joy, the ecstasy of oneness. There is a feeling of belonging, of being whole—almost a feeling of *worship*. There is tension, there is release, there is rest. Through this process, the man as the figure of Christ deposits part of himself into the woman, and she then unites a part of herself with the man—resulting in a bodily form of this one-flesh union. It is a *physical* representation of the Lord's *Spirit* working in us and through us—bringing us new life and multiplying that life around us. And all of this takes place within the context of two people who have pledged themselves to each other forever, forsaking all others, fully and without reservation. If sex is pointing to the greater reality of what's to come, and if it is a *lesser* version of the eternal reality to which it points, then can you imagine what awaits for us, for those who love God and have been called according to His purpose? If you can't, it's only because the picture on earth has become so perverted and distorted.

The act of sex itself is a beautiful picture of what we will one day experience for eternity: oneness, belonging, joy, euphoria, the utter giving of self, the receiving of God in holiness, in communion, forever and ever.

The Message of Family: A Picture of Servant-Leadership

The bearing of children is literally the result of *two* people becoming *one* flesh. God's original command to Adam and Eve was to "be fruitful and increase in number" (Genesis 1:28). Spiritually speaking, this is the same command Jesus gave the disciples: "Go and make disciples" (Matthew 28:19). The physical act of sex creates new physical life, just as the spiritual act of oneness with Christ creates new spiritual life.

And just as we talked about how authority was to be exercised between husband and wife, so is our authority as Mama Bears to be exercised with our children. Our children will learn to love or despise authority based on the model we have in the home. As we exercise leadership over our children, we do so by serving them. This doesn't mean we are at their beck and call. Rather, our job as parents, grandparents, aunts, and uncles is to assist them in whatever way they need for becoming mature adults.

And as we joyfully exercise our authority over them through service, we help them understand how to submit to the authority—a skill set required for any job they'll ever have. Granted, most of the time they don't understand that we really are doing things for their own good. Our "service" probably won't be recognized till later, but that's okay.

Part of this service is encouraging them to exercise authority in their own sphere of influence. Do your kids know that they, too, have a sphere of authority? They do. They have authority as stewards over their bodies. They can exercise that authority to benefit their bodies or to harm their bodies. All humans, even tiny humans, also have authority over the earth, the creatures on the earth, and whatever resources adults provide them (like crayons and toys). How are they learning to steward that authority?

If you have pets, this is a great way to teach your kids about the service aspect of authority. Feed Fido on time and in the correct amounts. Take him for a walk, even if you don't feel like it. And one of the most important aspects for cat owners is asking our kids, "Are you petting the cat the way *you* want to pet the cat, or how the *cat* likes to be petted?"

Now Back to Reality...

The sad reality is that many of us have not gotten a very clear picture of God from marriage, sex, and family. In the real world, people often use their authority for their own benefit—advancing their own agenda and lining their own pockets. They don't give a thought to the people beneath them. They demand unwavering obedience while exercising their power with an iron fist and for the purpose of glorifying themselves. I won't pretend that this kind of authority doesn't exist. Abusers abuse, people cover for them, and there's really no end to how badly authority structures can break down due to the sin nature that lies within each of our hearts.

There are even many so-called "Christian organizations" that have used the same scriptures I have used to justify turning a blind eye to men who abuse and subjugate their wives, holding the wife "accountable" to submission but not encouraging the husband to love like Christ. The fallout from this is heartbreaking—especially what I've seen it do to women's theology. As I have said repeatedly, the system of marriage, as designed by God, only works when *both* spouses are following the design. Unfortunately, when Scripture is cunningly twisted and used to validate abuse, people conclude the biblical design of marriage is flawed.

On the home front, moms and dads leave or fight. Marriages are broken. "Till death do us part" has become "till it stops working." (What is the mysterious "it," and why are our marriages contingent upon whether "it" works?) The entire system is in shambles due to human selfishness and brokenness, with only the smallest wisp every now and again of what God's original design actually looks like. And, consequently, our perception of God becomes just as ugly. What do we do?

On the one hand, if we keep emphasizing God's good design, those who have already fallen short feel like we're heaping judgment and shame on their backs. What is the husband or wife to do when they are the only ones trying to make the marriage work (while the other party sabotages their efforts)? They hear verses about this good design and feel like they are supposed to do more, more, *more*! That's not the picture of Christ and His church either. I'm so thankful that God gives us grace when we cannot attain His perfect design. There is no situation so damaged He can't redeem it, no ashes so ashy He can't create beauty. I acknowledge and celebrate this with no ifs, ands, or buts. Well...maybe one but...

Without letting go of the above truths, there can be a problem on the flip side if redemption is the *only* thing we focus on. When we stop lifting up God's original design, sometimes our kids get the message that God's ideal is unattainable or irrelevant. They subsequently don't go into marriage expecting forever. They go into marriage(s) expecting that it might take a try or two before they get it right. There's always a chance for a do-over—at least, that's what they've always heard. And, sure enough, by failing to plan for marriage, they plan a failed marriage. Like all things, we need balance. We cannot elevate God's good design to the point where people who have missed it feel like they are forever on the outs. And we cannot elevate God's redemption to the point where people feel like there's a get-out-of-jail-free card whenever things get tough. I know this is a difficult balance to convey, so I hope y'all hear my heart on this.

Living Within the Tension

I really want to emphasize this balance for us as a community of Mama Bears. We cannot stop lifting up God's design as the ideal, even if we haven't attained it. And I recognize that it hurts a lot when we realize how far we are from God's original design. You have permission to feel that pain. I don't think healing means the pain always goes away, and I'll tell you why: We will always experience the pain of living in a fallen world, but it's coupled with hope as we look ahead to the ultimate marriage to the Lamb! We are captive to evil, and we have a God who wants to slay the evil so He can pledge Himself to us—in love and faithfulness—*forever.* As my professor Clay Jones often says, it's not that the gospel is a fairy tale; rather, fairy tales reflect the gospel! But our lives don't feel like fairy tales, do they?

Are you divorced? Point your children to the goodness of marriage anyway. Are you in a blended family? It's okay to tell your kids, "This isn't the way it was supposed to be...but I'm so glad we still have a chance to be a family." Death and divorce were not in the original plan. But even in the grafting in of families, we can remind our children how we were grafted into God's family alongside Israel. Jew and Gentile—the original blended family!

Is your marriage not the greatest example for the kids? Don't be shy about directing them toward other examples of good authorities in your community. Acknowledge where your model is flawed. Whatever you have to do, let your kids see healthy, loving authority in action. How in the world will they ever mimic what they've never seen?

There is beauty in sacrificial love, and there is beauty in joyful submission. And that is precisely the point about gender, sex, marriage, and family. When done well, it helps us understand God better. We can have all the apologetics arguments in the world. We can be the smartest people in the room. But I will maintain till my dying day that the most effective apologetic (rational defense) for God is a healthy family. *We can defend the faith by defending the family.* Family is the first institution created by God. Almost everything that can be known about God was intended to be known within the context of family.

Marriage and family done well are glimpses into heaven itself, how the kingdom was intended to function. And every aspect that was intended to be a picture of God is currently being twisted by an enemy who hates the very image of God. Gender matters because within gender is the image of God Himself. Sex matters because it bodily reinforces the marital vows. Marriage matters because it points us to our eternal unity in Christ. Family matters because it teaches us all how to serve *in* authority and how to joyfully submit ourselves *to* authority. Gender, sex, marriage, and family matter because they were intended to show us the God we can't see. Even more, they point the world to the God they cannot see in hopes that what is invisible can become more understandable. Any movement seeking to destroy gender, sex, marriage, or family is destroying the message God intended, the picture He gave us in order to understand Him. And that picture is a really great design... *when followed.*

 DISCUSSION QUESTIONS 

1. **Icebreaker:** When have you experienced really good authority? When have you experienced really awful authority? How hard was it for you to obey the bad authority? Was it easier to obey the good authority?

2. **Main theme:** *Gender, sex, marriage, and family are intended to represent an invisible God in a visible way, and our understanding of authority can help or hinder this picture.* Which message and picture (gender, marriage, sex, or family) have you seen done best in your life? How have they helped you to understand God better?

3. **Self-evaluation:** How did you react to Hillary's story about her experience with authority in her life? Did it sound beautiful? Did it make you feel angry? How do you think your previous experiences (good or bad) have affected your view of authority?

4. **Brainstorm:** We cannot be responsible for how other people treat us, but we are responsible for how we respond. Ask each person to pick an area where they are under authority, and brainstorm ways they can bless their leader by their actions. Now pick an area over which you

have authority. Brainstorm all the ways you can cultivate the people under your care.

5. **Release the bear:** Our kids need to know they aren't just under authority but also have their own spheres of authority They are in authority over their bodies, the earth, and their pets. Talk to them about how good authority treats those underneath them. If you have pets, talk about the ways they can be good authorities over their pets.

6. **Pray:** Thank the Lord for the amazing way He structured authority. Pray over the ways you can exercise your authority to His glory. Has anyone in the group been under cruel, selfish, or abusive authority? Grieve together. Have the whole group pray over those hurting among you.

CHAPTER 4

Demolishing Arguments, Not People

Releasing Ideological Captives

HILLARY

I grew up on 90 acres of land. The land was heavily wooded, and I remember seeing my parents come home all scratched up and bloody from clearing away the brambles. Why the blood? They weren't just clearing away ordinary vines and bushes; they were clearing *thorny* vines and bushes. Regular bushes and vines just need a quick hack with a machete or a snip of the shears. Catch and release. Thornbushes are different beasts altogether.

Thornbushes hold you hostage. All the thorns go in different directions. The more you try to free yourself, the more the thorns dig in until the whole vine wraps around you. The only way to free yourself is for someone else to help pull out each thorn individually while holding the vine away from you—otherwise the vine will snap right back toward you. One does not simply grab hold of thornbushes; thornbushes grab hold of you. No matter which direction you move, there's pain. There's blood. Helping someone with thorny problems in their life can be a similar experience. And often in the process of helping someone, you get tangled up yourself.

The secular worldview is all over the place. It cries out: "There's no ultimate truth! Everyone has a right to their own truth. We'll fight anyone who disagrees that everything comes down to power and oppression!" (We'll get to that in chapter 6.) There's only one word for someone who adheres to such contradicting claims: *bondage*. And the more the ideas sink in, the less able a person is to separate herself from this worldview. Eventually the bad ideas are not just beliefs; they become that person's very identity.

This is the difficulty we find ourselves in today. We cannot merely tell people to let go of the lies. Like that thornbush, the lies are holding on to the person. And when it comes to sexual sin, we're often not dealing with rebels; we're dealing with *captives*. And captives need to be freed.

A captive will rarely be able to hear your rejection of his or her ideas without feeling like you are rejecting him or her as a person. It's a bit of a tricky process. But we will do our best to explain how it can be accomplished. To do so, we will break down our approach into a few important categories.

First, we will explain the difference between *people* and *ideologies* and why distinguishing between the two is imperative. If you confuse the two, you'll end up either compromising truth or coming off as a clanging cymbal (1 Corinthians 13:1).

Second, we will grapple with what it means to love God and love others.

Third, we are going to learn the anatomy of an argument. Every single idea has a flow of logic, whether it be good logic or bad logic. To break down the lies in our culture, we need to understand what reasoning is being used to justify the beliefs. (And trust me when I say that when your kids learn how to do this, to call them "empowered" will be an understatement.) We will compare and contrast emotional reasoning and deductive reasoning. Much of what passes for sound argumentation these days is really just emotional reasoning. It is important to understand how emotional reasoning works so we can best love the person. But it's also important to be able to translate that faulty reasoning into a logical form. This is how we break down the strongholds of bad ideas.

Finally, we will end our discussion by looking at how Jesus loved. He treated ideas (agendas) and people very differently.

Is This a Person or an Idea?

In 2 Corinthians 10:5, the apostle Paul tells us, "We demolish arguments and every pretension that sets itself up against the knowledge of God, and we take captive every thought to make it obedient to Christ." Notice that believers are to demolish *arguments*—not people. Later, in Colossians 2:8, Paul writes, "See to it that no one takes you captive through hollow and deceptive philosophy, which depends on human tradition and the elemental spiritual forces of this world rather than on Christ." Read these two verses together, and it becomes clear that we are dealing with two separate issues: an idea and a captive.

The polarization of our culture has made it difficult to see past labels. But we as Christians are called to distinguish the person from the ideology—*no matter our political persuasion*. Protestors rioting in the streets are people made in the image of God, every one of them. Those talking heads on the news, hollering about the downfall of America? Jesus died for them too. My husband reminds me every time we get in a fight: "Hill, remember who the real enemy is. You and I are on the same team."

An Enemy with No Scruples

No war is pleasant, but the Vietnam War was particularly heinous. Very few who went to Vietnam came back unchanged. No side was innocent in that war; each committed its own atrocities. Americans spent a decade dropping Agent Orange on the Vietnamese, exposing millions of noncombatants to toxic chemicals. Over a million people today remain disabled as a result of their exposure. At the same time, the Viet Cong were developing their own deadly tactics. They used the most vulnerable population as human shields and suicide bombers. They hid in hospitals so the Americans wouldn't bomb them. Little kids were given live grenades and told to walk into groups of US soldiers. Kids who were barely ten would suddenly pop up with machine guns. Perhaps worst of all, toddlers had their diapers or teddy bears stuffed with explosives and were then abandoned, left for the US troops to find out in the field. You only make that mistake *once*. Every piece of humanity our poor military boys had was stripped from them. They could either keep their sense of humanity by comforting the crying children (but risk killing their entire platoon), or—as usually happened—they had to silence their most basic human instinct and treat the kids for what they were: weapons of the enemy. Nobody can gun down a bunch of children and return home unchanged—even if they knew the children would have killed them first.

I find us in a very similar situation when it comes to the sexual agenda. We, too, have an enemy with no scruples. Satan is the father of lies, and he has no problem targeting the hurting, the vulnerable, and the broken—the ones who are most in need of love—and then strapping an ideological bomb to their backs. What do we do? We cannot accept the ideologies into our fellowship; upon detonation, churches are rewriting God's commands thinking they are "loving others." *Kablooey* goes the gospel. But neither can we turn a blind eye to these broken and hurting people. That profanes the *purpose* of the gospel. *Kablooey* goes our witness.

Many of us in the church have recognized this catch-22. We have been put in an impossible position; we just haven't been able to articulate it. Loving God and loving others sounds so simple...until an unbiblical agenda attaches itself to the very people we are called to love. The enemy has convinced them that the agenda is their identity, and our refusal to embrace the agenda feels like a rejection of their very selves. Like the soldiers, some of us may have even grown numb because it feels like a lose-lose situation. Why even try anymore? Our love has grown cold because to love has become deadly, from a spiritual perspective.

There was no way to disarm the children in Vietnam, but we can do our best here with the sexual agenda. Like those soldiers, we have to balance our compassion with our commitment to truth. We can encourage our sweet and compassionate kids to love the vulnerable, the broken, the marginalized, and the misfits—just like Jesus did. But unless we teach them how to diffuse the ideological bomb first, they run the risk of having their Christian worldview blown to smithereens, all because they desired to show love.

Agendas are often promoted through media and education until they become so ingrained that they define the new normal. We *must* resist agendas that rewrite the rules of truth and morality and teach our kids to do the same. Remember: "Our struggle is not against flesh and blood, but against the rulers, against the authorities, against the powers of this dark world and against the spiritual forces of evil in the heavenly realms" (Ephesians 6:12). These enemy forces have *no* scruples.

When Jesus was asked what the greatest commandment was, He replied with the Jewish Shema: Love the Lord with all your heart, soul, mind, and strength, and *secondly* love your neighbor as yourself.[1] The problem we are seeing is that people are switching the order of these two commands. Within progressive Christian circles, loving God is reinterpreted in light of a new definition of love—one which elevates feelings over truth. One popular progressive Christian author described a conversation with another Christian leader about their "different teaching styles." She told the other teacher, "In Jesus' awesome summary of life's main work—love God and love people—you lean into the 'love God' part best and I lean into the 'love people' part best." She writes, "When 'loving God' results in pain, exclusion, harm, or trauma to people...then we are absolutely doing the first part wrong."[2] (Guess the early church didn't get the memo?) This is nonsense; we can't do one without doing the other. Done right, they will never be in competition...unless a person has redefined love...which is what I suspect has happened in her situation.

Loving God means doing what pleases Him. We love people the same way—*by doing what pleases God.* Scripture famously defines love in 1 Corinthians 13. Most everyone on the #loveislove train is totally fine with all the "patient" and "kind" stuff. It's verse 6 that often gets left out of the equation: "Love does not delight in evil but rejoices *with the truth.*" Truth is included in the definition of love. And as Christians, we do not believe that truth comes from within. It is eternally grounded in God and in the person of Jesus. By scriptural definition, we cannot love people if we succumb to lies; it ceases to be biblical love. Love and truth are probably the two most primary virtues to which we as Christians must cling.

Our task then? We need to maintain our Christian worldview while loving those living in or struggling with sin. This fulfills the greatest commandment *and* the second...in the right order. We balance truth with grace, never sacrificing either. Let's dig into each in turn.

Loving God by Loving Truth

If we see an ideology pushing people away from God's precepts, we should fight that ideology on its own turf. As parents, we need to show our kids that we understand and can refute the assumptions on which the ideology is based. Refuting poor reasoning is a requirement for elders who are leading the church, so it should be a requirement for us as we help train up our kids (Titus 1:5-9). As we saw from the Romans 1 passage, when people suppress truth, their ability to reason is the first thing to go.

The Anatomy of a Logical Argument

Logical or deductive reasoning starts with assumptions and facts from which a conclusion can be drawn. If we are to teach our kids how to identify lies for what they are, we need to show them how to form a cogent argument. For the purposes of this book, I will use the following formula:

> Statement 1: **Assumption (A)** (assumed to be true)
>
> Statement 2: **Fact Claim (FC)** (data you can investigate)
>
> Statement 3: **Conclusion (C)**

Let's use the cosmological argument for God as an example:

> **Assumption (A):** Everything that begins to exist has a cause.
>
> **Fact Claim (FC):** The universe began to exist.
>
> **Conclusion (C):** Therefore, the universe had a cause.

Just who or what *caused* the universe? That can be discussed, and that's what our goal is: productive conversation.

Let's take a crack at some of the assumptions in the Christian worldview and those of the secular worldview and see how they compare:

> **A:** If human beings were created by God, then they were designed with a purpose.
>
> **FC:** Human beings were created by God.
>
> **C:** Human beings are designed with a purpose.

Let's contrast this with the secular worldview:

> **A:** If human beings evolved, then they were not designed with a purpose.
>
> **FC:** Human beings evolved.
>
> **C:** Human beings were not designed with a purpose.

The funny-not-funny thing is that many people who believe that human beings evolved also believe that human beings have purpose. But purpose implies an original intention. An intention can only come from a mind. Evolution is, by definition, *without purpose, without intention, and without a mind.* This is where we identify what it means for a worldview to be *incoherent*—meaning the desired conclusion does not follow from its foundational premises. Evolution can never tell us what *ought* to be or what *ought not* to be. At best, evolution gives us what survived over time. It can never give us purpose.

Trying to discover the purpose of a purposeless process is a waste of time. Thinking you can *get* purpose through a purposeless process is illogical. Believing one can reject the Creator God and still have purpose reflects what philosophers call "the grounding problem." A person may believe the sentiment "my life has purpose" but lack the worldview foundation on which to build that conclusion. They may decide their "purpose" is to love their neighbor, but they just as easily could have decided that their "purpose" is to *eat* their neighbor. You cannot judge these two "purposes" from an evolutionary perspective because it provides no outside standard by which to judge which purpose is better. You can't do it, friends. It's a losing battle.

I am just barely scratching the surface of logic here. As a reminder, the format I'm using here isn't the official model, but rather helps emphasize the differences between assumptions, fact claims, and conclusions. (Those of you who have studied formal logic may struggle with this format—but go with it. ☺) Many of our cultural disagreements occur at the conclusion level when the debate is actually over a person's *unstated assumptions*. Or, people think you are disputing their fact claim—then provide you with a tsunami of "evidence"—when their starting assumptions (which interpret the facts) are actually at fault. Case in point: Assumptions need to be debated, and fact claims need to be verified. If either of those is incorrect, then the conclusion is usually incorrect. But until you uncover the logic, it's just two people talking past each other.

Throughout the rest of this book, I'll be providing little vignettes of arguments so you can start learning how to recognize the difference between assumptions, fact claims, and conclusions for yourself—and then help your kids do the same! These will be phrased more for understandability than precision. In most of them, there are extra assumptions smuggled in, faulty assumptions, or debatable fact claims. Your goal, should you choose to accept it, is to *spot the faulty logic*.

As you familiarize yourself with the different types of claims, the incoherence of the secular worldview becomes more apparent. As Christians, our worldview allows for truth and morality because we have an objective standard outside of ourselves: a personal God who intentionally created us and who endowed us with purpose. A moral law requires a lawgiver, and our assumptions should stem from Scripture (not ourselves or culture). The only other option is for everyone to become laws unto themselves. The Bible is *full* of such experiments (Judges 17:6). Societies like that don't usually work very well.

When we teach our kids to recognize bad reasoning, they can stand even firmer with truth. When they stand with truth, their faith's roots go even deeper. Why? Because "faith is confidence in what we hope for and assurance about what we do not see" (Hebrews 11:1). The more confident and assured your kids can be of the truth, the more their faith grows. God does not ask us to check our brains at the door!

A well-trained mind is one of our biggest spiritual protections against the enemy's schemes. This is why Romans 12:2 commands us to renew our minds—because that renewal will prevent us from being conformed to the world, and we will be able to "test and approve what God's will is—his good, pleasing and perfect will" (Romans 12:2).

Emotional Reasoning

When dealing with people versus agendas, we need to understand a completely different type of reasoning—emotional reasoning. Emotional reasoning usually starts with the conclusion (a feeling) and then finds facts to support it. In its most basic form, the underlying assumption for emotional reasoning is, "If I feel it, it's true." Emotional reasoning works in the exact opposite direction of deductive reasoning. The feelings determine the facts in a self-fulfilling prophecy kind of way. Then the person states those facts as if they came first, and not their emotion. By confusing feelings with facts, our culture is tripping up our kids.

For example, oppression is still an issue in our world, and we need to know how to combat injustice when we encounter it. So how can we tread on this topic wisely? Here's an example of how emotional reasoning might cloud the issue:

> **A:** If I feel oppressed, it's because I am being oppressed by someone or something.
>
> **FC:** I feel oppressed.
>
> **C:** I am being oppressed by someone or something.

Based on this emotional argument, the next "logical" step is to identify the oppressor. This is what we see happening within identity politics. But notice how this reasoning does not start with facts. If we were to use *proper* deductive reasoning, it would look like this:

> **A:** If someone does [X] to me, they are oppressing me.
>
> **FC:** Someone did [X] to me.
>
> **C:** Therefore, I am being oppressed by someone.

This is a legitimate argument. This is how we identify when a real wrong has been committed. However, if someone wants to engage with this argument, they cannot start with whether someone feels oppressed. They must debate the assumption of whether [X] constitutes oppression.

Now I am not trying to make any kind of political statement as to whether certain groups are being oppressed or not. What I am trying to do is to show how confusing feelings with facts carries weighty implications for us as Christians. For example, what if culture changes the rules regarding what constitutes oppression? What happens when—*tooooootally hypothetically*—teaching about biblical sexuality, by law, becomes "oppressive hate speech"?

Those who define the terms determine who is the oppressor and who is the victim. They can paint anyone they want as an "oppressor," and according to our culture, oppressors must be silenced at all costs. In the case of gender and sexuality, things like binary language (male and female), the definition of marriage (between a man and a woman), or skepticism regarding the health benefits of sex change operations are all now considered "oppressive." But just because someone *feels* that being called female is oppressive does not make it oppressive. That is an assumption—one we should be preparing our kids to question.

Embracing Our Inner Warrior Bear and Nurturing Bear

While it's important to understand how logic and reasoning work, we cannot be content with winning an intellectual argument. Logic-ing someone to death has rarely a disciple made. Ideas are nothing outside the mind of a person—a person made in the image of God, who should be treated with kindness, compassion, worth, and value.

So we need two hats, Mama Bears. When we combat ideas, we are Warrior Bears. A Warrior Bear stands firm against ideas and agendas raised against the knowledge of God (2 Corinthians 10:5). We cannot sacrifice truth no matter how much that truth may offend.

When we address the *people* who espouse these ideas, we are Nurturing Bears. A Nurturing Bear tends to the wounded captive, loving them tenderly back to health and always pointing them toward the Healer (2 Timothy 2:24-26). We don't have to compromise conviction to show compassion (and vice versa).

One of these hats (warrior or nurturer) probably comes more naturally to you than the other. But if we want to be like Jesus, if we want to be "conformed to the image of [God's] Son" (Romans 8:29), we must embrace both roles. Let's look at how Jesus did this.

Modeling Our Speech After Jesus

When you read the Gospels, you'll notice that when Jesus speaks to crowds, He doesn't mince words. Take a few minutes to read the Sermon on the Mount, which you'll find in Matthew 5–7. In that sermon, Jesus unapologetically gives the smackdown of all smackdowns. He doesn't just condemn acts of sin. He includes the attitudes of the heart and the mind as well.

When speaking to the masses, He addresses the ideas for what they are. Look, for example, at Matthew 5:28-29. To the crowds, Jesus says, "Anyone who looks at a woman lustfully has already committed adultery with her in his heart. If your right eye causes you to stumble, gouge it out and throw it away." (Well, that escalated quickly.) Jesus's message to the public was not intended to remove shame. It was intended to convict and to convey truth. It was about destroying every single loophole people were using to excuse their sin.

Compare the force of that message with the way Jesus dealt with individuals. To the woman caught in adultery, Jesus spoke differently (John 8:2-11). He did not shame her into obedience. He first removed her shame and *then* called her to a life of obedience. She was hurting. She was embarrassed. She expected judgment. She didn't need anyone to tell her that what she was doing was wrong; she already knew. What she needed to hear was that redemption, healing, and a chance to get it right were possible for her.

For the sake of argument, does Jesus ever speak harshly with individuals? Actually, He does. But guess who it is toward? Jesus dealt very harshly with the Pharisees. The Pharisees were dead positive (pun intended) that they were doing everything right. Their own self-righteous confidence (and their scorn for the little guy who didn't compare) effectively prevented hurting and broken people from experiencing the living God. The Pharisees made people think they were disqualified from approaching God. We have these same kinds of Pharisees in the church today—hyper-critical, hyper-legalistic, super confident that they are God's chosen mouthpiece to condemn all the dirty rotten sinners. These people warrant open rebuke.

I'd like to point out a second type of Phariseeism I have noticed cropping up lately. These Christian leaders are also dead positive that they are doing everything right—except their confidence lies in their reinterpretation of

God's Word. They appeal "to the lustful desires of the flesh" and "entice people who are just escaping from those who live in error. They promise them freedom, while they themselves are slaves of depravity" (2 Peter 2:18-19). These types of modern Pharisees often rail against the traditional type of Pharisees. What they don't realize is that they, too, are preventing hurting and needy people from encountering the living God. Traditional Pharisees block people by making them feel too dirty to approach God. The modern Pharisees block people by making them believe their sin is not something that needs to be repented of.

So is there ever a time to be harsh? Yup. There sure is. But it's usually when you're dealing with a person who is puffed up with self-righteousness, not a person struggling with brokenness. It's okay to be confident as long as your confidence lies in God's Word. Everywhere else, we need to exercise humility.

Jesus dealt with ideas forcefully and without apology. He also dealt with individuals according to their need: What was keeping the person from unifying with the heart and mind of God? We should model our approach after Jesus. We don't just answer questions; we answer *people* (Colossians 4:6). There is a time to demolish arguments and a time to love a person tangled in a thornbush of bad ideas. Ultimately, we need to teach our kids how to do both.

DISCUSSION QUESTIONS 

1. **Icebreaker:** Have you ever had to help an animal who was in pain? How did it act toward you?

2. **Main theme:** *Biblical love means demolishing bad arguments while showing compassion to those held captive to the lies.* What do you think it means to demolish the argument while loving the person? What does that look like in a practical way?

3. **Self-evaluation:** Have you ever been trapped in emotional reasoning, starting with a feeling and then trying to find people or events around you that justify the feeling? How can this become a self-fulfilling prophecy?

4. **Brainstorm:** My friend Elizabeth Urbanowicz, founder of Foundation Worldview, has created a great worksheet to practice your argument mapping skills. Head over to www.MamaBearApologetics.com/logic-worksheet to download the worksheet and map out the arguments.

5. **Release the bear:** Look for an opportunity this week to discuss emotional versus logical reasoning with your children. You'd be surprised at how much they can understand at a young age. For inspiration, see Natasha Crain's article "How I'm Teaching My 6-Year-Olds to Be Critical Thinkers," located at NatashaCrain.com.

6. **Pray:** Our world is filled with so many hurting people who are held captive to bad ideas. Pray that God would begin letting the scales fall from their eyes (Acts 9:18) so they can finally come to the God who loves them so much.

Wait, My Kids Are Being Taught *What*?!

PRAYER OF LAMENT

Bring Your Complaint

LAMENTATIONS 1:9, 16; 2:14

Look at our affliction, LORD, for the enemy has magnified himself in triumph. For these things we weep; our eyes overflow with tears...our children are desolate and perishing, for the enemy has prevailed.

Lord, we are sickened by the lies our children are being raised to believe are truth. Our children are enticed to follow their hearts, do what makes them happy, and let feelings be their god. They're taught a foreign language of promiscuous activities that distort Your image and Your message. We have been blindsided by all the portals to filth, debauchery, confusion, lies, and deception. Our insecurities pile up like dirty laundry because when we try to speak the truth, others look at us like we are soiled by lack of "compassion."

Biblical marriage is mocked. What is evil is called good. What is wrong is called right. What is truth is called an opinion. The nonsense makes us nauseated. We too often go silent for fear of being misunderstood, of our disagreement being labeled hate. We feel unequipped. Overwhelmed. Uninformed. Defeated before we toe the starting line. Afraid of not finishing the course. Even family members, close friends, and fellow believers aren't necessarily running the race beside us. We feel alone and want to quit. Do You see this? Do You care?

Are You Sex-Smarter than a Fifth Grader?

Understanding the New National Sexual Education Standards

HILLARY

When I was in fifth grade, I was obsessed with *The Little Mermaid*, and my biggest ambition was to win the Jump Rope for Heart competition with the ragtag group of misfits I had managed to assemble. (And yes, we crushed the competition, thanks to my choreography.) My sister and I had just moved from a private Christian school to a public school, and I was shocked to hear what one of the guys did to a girl in the movie theater on a date. (A date? In fifth grade? Who were these kids' parents?!) Of course, it could have all been gossip. I only heard it through the grapevine, not from the health teacher.

Fast-forward to the fall of 2020. According to the National Sex Education Standards (NSES), by the end of fifth grade, your children should be able to explain the following:

- Distinguish between sex assigned at birth and gender identity and explain how they may or may not differ.
- Define and explain differences between cisgender, transgender, gender nonbinary, gender expansive, and gender identity.
- Describe the role hormones play in the physical, social, cognitive, and emotional changes during adolescence and the potential role of hormone blockers on young people who identify as transgender. (Um…most doctors don't even fully understand this, but our fifth graders are supposed to?!) (See pages 279-282.)
- Explain common human sexual development and the role of hormones (e.g., romantic and sexual feelings, masturbation, mood swings, and timing of pubertal onset).[1]

Oh, and by the way, this is how "common human sexual development" is defined earlier in the NSES document: "The developmental process for young people often involves *experimenting with many different identities*…and sexual identity is not exempt from this type of exploration" (emphasis mine). Yes, you heard that right. Experimenting with different genders and different sexual orientations is apparently a "normal" part of sexual development. To this I have to ask, "How did *we* all turn out okay? Were we all doing it wrong up until now?" In this chapter, we'll get an understanding of what the NSES is, its ramifications for your child's education, and its guiding mission and vision.

The New National Sex Education Standards?

The NSES were written by a group called SIECUS—Sexuality Information and Education Council of the United States—in conjunction with several other advocacy groups. SIECUS was founded in 1964 by Mary Calderone, former medical director at Planned Parenthood. And where did she get the seed money to form this organization? Hugh Hefner.[2]

First off, standards and curricula are different. Standards dictate what must be included in the curricula, and the curricula are the actual lesson plans created to satisfy the requirements of the standards. These NSES standards are being used to create the many comprehensive sex education programs—and those curricula are making their way to a school near you (sooner rather than later if you are in the Northeast or the West Coast). And while they sound super official, SIECUS is not an official government group. That's the first thing you need to know. If you go to the Department of Education, there are no curriculum standards for sex education (for now).

This doesn't mean schools aren't fooled by the name though. The standards have already been adopted by more than 40 percent of school districts in the United States.[3]

What Are Your Rights as a Parent?

First off, I'd like to reiterate that, as of this book's writing, there are no national sex education standards on the Department of Education's website. This might change depending on who is president and how much they emphasize sexual orientation and gender identity (SOGI) laws. Currently, sexual health education is still up to the states, and it's the responsibility of individual school boards to comply.

So what's your first step? Gather information. Contact your local school district to find out what sex education standards and curricula will be used in your children's classrooms. You can also contact the teacher to find out when the curriculum will be taught, who will teach it, and what class time will be used. Will the girls and boys be separated? How will questions be handled? (This one is important because if questions are a free-for-all, there's no telling what topics will be covered.) Find out who wrote the curriculum. Do they have ties to the abortion industry?

Ask if the curriculum teaches sexual risk *avoidance* or sexual risk *reduction*. *Avoidance* means the curriculum teaches unwanted pregnancy and STDs can be prevented by abstinence. *Reduction* means the curriculum assumes kids will be having sex and teaches them how to suffer fewer consequences. This is a critical difference. Technically—according to research partially funded by Planned Parenthood—the "risk reduction" programs correlate with the lowest number of teen pregnancies (the only real metric they care about). It's worth noting that it also correlates with higher abortion rates.[4]

Finally, pay attention to how the curriculum defines "safe sex." Is it in terms of *how to have sex safely* or *how to have more pleasurable sex*?[5] You can get a good idea of the agenda by specifically asking if the instructors plan to address lubrication. If they do, you can make a pretty accurate assumption of what they mean by "sex education." I recommend asking if they use Amaze.org[6] or Planned Parenthood videos. If they do, *run away.*

If, after researching, you want to object to your school's sex education curriculum, you must file a notice first with the instructor, then the principal, then the schoolboard, and then the state. But you need that paper trail. It is important (and helpful for your cause) to honor the chain of command and the prescribed process for making a formal complaint as dictated by the school district. Also, it's extremely helpful to document any conversation in person or on the phone with the date, the time, the name of the person you spoke with, and the most important points of the conversation. You might even email the person you spoke with, thanking them for talking with you, and then describing the important points of your conversation. If that person replies without challenging what you wrote, you now have a reliable document for future reference. But make sure your conversation or email doesn't feel adversarial.

Keep in mind that, while your primary job is to protect and educate your children, you also have the opportunity to be salt and light to teachers and administrators in the way you conduct yourself during these conversations. Don't let your objection to the curriculum be the only contact they have with you, reinforcing the stereotype of the neurotic Christian parent. The more you engage your child's teacher with a helpful attitude, and the longer your track record of service grows, the more likely they will be to give you a gracious reading if you object to the sexuality unit. And remember, sometimes the teacher is someone who shares your values but doesn't know how to implement a Christian worldview in the classroom while still protecting her job. Theirs is a tough position to be in. Our conversations need to be seasoned with grace and discernment.

What's New About These Standards?

Six main topics are covered in the NSES. These topics repeat every year, from kindergarten through twelfth grade, with more details and descriptions added at each successive grade level.

If your school district is using these standards to develop their curricula, they're likely complying with the second edition, published in 2020. This edition contains notable changes from the first edition, published in 2012. And, unfortunately, these changes reflect a worldview that doesn't even come close to reflecting the one we discussed in chapter 2. Here's a small sampling.

Consent

Previously called "Healthy Relationships," this section has been retitled "Consent and Healthy Relationships." Every single grade level now focuses on *consent* being the new moral standard for sexuality. The message our kids will be getting every year, for 13 years, is that if someone consents to a sexual activity, then it's okay—*healthy* even. And just in case they aren't sure what consent is, Planned Parenthood made a super awkward little video explaining allllll the ways your child can get consent. Check it out.[7] It's basically a voice-over on videos with (mostly same-sex) couples making out. Oh, and FYI, it has dozens of comments from kids who were *required to watch it for health class.*

Emphasizing consent isn't necessarily bad. Rape is still rampant in our society. So is childhood sexual abuse. Your kids should know they have control over their own bodies. (That's part of their sphere of authority, remember?) Nobody should have the right to touch them without their explicit permission. But the type of consent the standards are emphasizing is more about sexual autonomy—meaning that all kids at any age should have the right to decide when and with whom they want to have sex, and nobody else's input matters. What the standards are pushing for is sex-positivity, a topic upon which we will expand in chapter 8.

What Exactly Do They Mean by Healthy Relationships?

Healthy is a sneaky little word. You can only know what's healthy if you know what is good for someone. And you can only know what is good for someone when you have properly defined *good* to begin with. You don't quite see what the standards mean by "healthy" until twelfth grade, where they finally define it as consent, communication, and freedom from gender stereotypes. I gotta say, that's a pretty low bar for "healthy."

From the perspective of sex-positivity, the goal is to help kids become familiar with their own sexual wants and needs so they know what they do and don't want to consent to. (And as we saw on page 92, healthy sexual development is now defined as exploring all these options.) Under this definition, not being able to explore these options is "unhealthy." Progressive pastor Nadia Bolz-Weber totally agrees. She muses in her book *Shameless* (after talking to a girl who felt awkward during her first sexual encounter),

> *You were robbed.* The church took away over a decade of [this girl's] sexual development. All this time, she could have been gaining the kind of wisdom that comes from making her own choices, from having lovers, from making mistakes, from falling in love.[8]

That's basically the mindset behind these standards. Under the new definition, "healthy" means experimenting; consequences are just "mistakes." This definition of health has nothing to do with what is actually good for your kids. If your 12-year-old decides that being choked sounds like fun, then a "healthy relationship" is one in which he or she and their partner can weigh the pros and cons of that decision together and learn how to choke without anyone getting injured. That technically meets the standard's criteria of "healthy."

Sexual Orientation and Identity

Instead of sex education being about puberty and reproduction, it is now about exploring *who* you want to have sex with.[9] And only you can decide that for yourself. As mentioned above, experimenting with different orientations is being taught as a normal part of sexual development. Children are introduced to this concept as early as kindergarten when they start learning about the "different kinds of families"—same-sex parents being one of the categories. By eighth grade, students should be able to define the whole range of sexual orientations.

Gender Identity and Expression

According to gender identity and expression, a person's biological sex can be different from their self-perceived gender, and both can be different from the person's gender expression (that is, which societal gender norms they adopt). Chapter 7 will go through an actual sample curriculum (the Genderbread Person) that is teaching these views of gender and sexual identity in public schools to kids as young as kindergarten.[10] While I was writing this chapter, one of my Texas Mama Bears confirmed that this curriculum has made its way into the San Antonio school district, and now Houston.[11] If it's in Texas, y'all, it can be anywhere.

The Guiding Principles and Values of the NSES

We must remember that practices and procedures don't just come out of thin air. They come from an ideological background, which, in turn, stems from a worldview—how a person perceives reality and what they think needs to happen in order to improve the world. There is an end goal in mind—a worldly telos that is competing with the telos of God. If you don't understand the worldview behind the policies, you'll find yourself unable to see the pattern that is emerging, the picture that is created from putting all these little puzzle pieces together. So let's break these down, bit by bit.

I will here give an overview of each guiding principle of the NSES. For the sake of brevity, I'll treat each like a mini-ROAR, briefly describing what it is and discerning the truth from the lies. For the record, these are all *explicitly listed* in the "Guiding Principles" of the standards.

Equity and Reproductive Justice

Equity is another word like *tolerance* or *inclusion* that sounds biblical. When people hear the word *equity*, they assume it means that people should all have equal opportunities to everything. That sounds good, right? But there's a catch. Smuggled into the definition of equity is the idea that equal opportunities will necessarily produce equal outcomes, so if we don't see equal outcomes, there must not have been equal opportunity. Commitment to equity rightly acknowledges that society should not prevent people from pursuing life, liberty, and happiness. But this definition removes any causal connection between personal agency and final results. Anytime there are unequal outcomes between various demographics, it is assumed there is a *structural impediment* (that is, a "system") preventing people from achieving the same amount of success. To have true social justice, it is said, we need to root out whatever "system" is holding people back. The problem with this is that it teaches our kids that we are just helpless pawns in the hands of fate. It downplays personal responsibility.

Also, our politically correct culture dictates what factors we are allowed to look at. There are multiple studies showing that religiosity and family structure have a much larger impact on the future success (especially academic) of individuals than do school or government interventions.[12] Under equity, however, we are not allowed to discuss these out of fear of "stigmatizing" anyone for their family structure or religion (or lack thereof).[13]

Spot the Faulty Logic

A: Justice means equality.

FC: Biology allows men to walk away from a pregnancy, but not women.

C: Reproductive justice means allowing women to (equally) walk away from a pregnancy...via abortion.

Reproductive justice is a fancy way of saying "right to abortion." The argument is that since a man is never forced to carry a baby to term in his body, then a woman should never be forced to carry a baby to term in her body. Equal outcomes, therefore, necessitate allowing a woman to choose whether she wants to be pregnant, even if conception has already occurred. While facing an unwanted pregnancy is indeed very scary, we shouldn't be so quick to lump *biological differences* into "human rights." It opens a Pandora's box of bad ideas. For example, a woman can choose to have a child without the father's permission and demand child support for 18 years. Wouldn't "equity" then mean that men could theoretically demand that they, too, be allowed to terminate the pregnancy without the mother's consent? All in all, "equity" when it comes to reproduction is not necessarily the goal we should strive for.

Language Inclusivity

As mentioned above, the new standards state, "The developmental process for young people often involves experimenting with many different identities, forms of expression, and behaviors, and sexual identity is not exempt from this type of exploration."[14] Medicinenet.com identifies and defines 72 different genders.[15] Facebook used to give you 58 genders to choose from but now just has a fill-in-the-blank drop-down menu.[16] I'm hoping this section will shed some light on why there are so many options.

This emphasis on terminology and language is a hallmark of queer theory, which we will explore in much more depth in chapter 9. In short, queer theory teaches that words are not just information. They are a means of actually *creating and regulating reality*. (Let that sink in for a second.) As Michel Foucault says in his book *The History of Sexuality*,

> It is in discourse [the words we use to talk about things] that power and knowledge are joined together.[17]

In postmodern babble, words are a socially constructed power used by the oppressor class to "regulate and police sex," thereby controlling sexual minorities and women.[18] When I say "socially constructed," I mean like how the meaning of red and green lights are social constructs telling us "stop" and "go." There's nothing universal or inherent about these colors to define them this way. It's something we made up—a social construct.

According to queer theory, words—more commonly called "the discourses"—work by arbitrarily defining *normal*, marginalizing anyone who doesn't fit the mold, and then maintaining this stranglehold on society by only allowing in the words that reinforce this knowledge or truth. A person steeped in queer theory will argue, for example, that the words *male* and *female* are a human-made binary that wrongly assumes there are only two genders.[19] After establishing these two genders as the only options, this language can now marginalize (strip away the power of) those who fall outside traditional gender norms or gender stereotypes. Therefore, according to queer theory, how language makes you feel becomes the most important barometer. In order to have a fair and just society, we need to expand our language so that all feel included and nobody feels marginalized.[20] (Emphasis on the word *feel.*) So, like I said, people can create whatever reality they want with the words they use. It's almost like a secular "name it and claim it" philosophy.

Spot the Faulty Logic

A: If I *feel* marginalized, then I'm *being* marginalized.

FC: Not using my preferred language makes me feel marginalized.

C: You *must* use my preferred language.

Furthermore, since queer theorists believe that words have created an unfair power differential, then the way to correct this unequal distribution of power is by changing the language we use. Norms are redefined so all variations are considered viable. But expanding biological categories to encompass psychological categories feels backward; why should the genders expand? Have we, perhaps, been too rigid in our understanding of appropriate ways to express one's masculinity or femininity? As you'll see in chapters 7 and 9, that's exactly what happened! Queer theorists firmly believe that gender is a social construct independent of biology. And if society made the two-gender rule, they can make the 72-gender rule. No harm, no foul.

The Postmodern Marxist Taproot

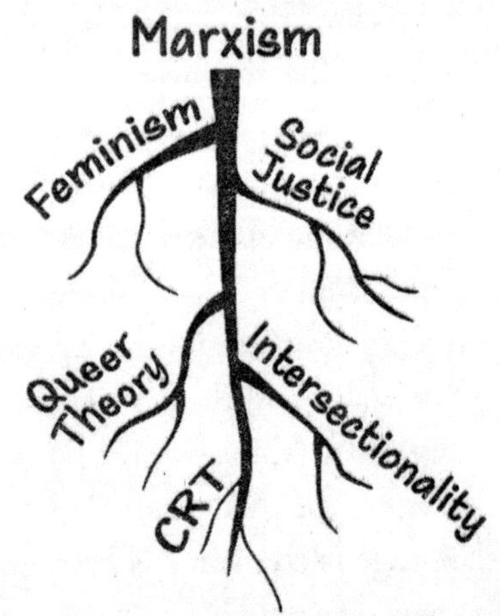

The rest of the "guiding mission and values" section cannot be understood without first understanding their parent categories: Marxism and postmodernism. (It's important to be familiar with these terms because they are fully orbed worldviews completely at odds with the Christian worldview.) The social justice movement is basically neo-Marxism in skinny jeans—virtually identical to

Marx's views, except it defines the "haves" and the "have-nots" in terms of *social* power instead of money and capitalism. If that sounded like gobbledygook, then let's take a step backward...

Picture a plant. The roots of a plant start with one large taproot from which numerous smaller roots branch out into the soil. If we want to uproot the whole root, we need to get both the taproot and the secondary roots. The taproot is postmodernism and Marxism, and from them flow all the other ideologies like intersectionality, social justice, queer theory, critical theory, and critical race theory—most of which are (again) *explicitly mentioned* in the standards. But Marxism and postmodernism are the lifelines of the whole shebang.

Postmodernism essentially erased society's belief that objective truth existed. And once we get rid of truth, all we are left with is power, which is where Marxism swoops in. Marxism rarely shows up the same way twice. Once people discover how it destroys a society, they are loath to allow the same thing to happen again. So it keeps cropping up in new and inventive ways meant to disguise and distance itself from past failures. But when push comes to shove, it's the same circus, same monkeys.

There are three main assumptions within Marxism from which all other theories derive. The first is that *all of society can be divided into the haves and have-nots.* In Marx's day, he defined these groups in terms of who owned the businesses and who worked the businesses. The owning class was unfairly reaping the benefit of the workers' toil. To have a fair and just society, resources should be distributed equally.

This same ideology is at play today, except instead of business owners and workers, everything is about power differentials—who has social power (the haves) and who does not (the have-nots). Social justice teaches that those in the privileged class have a duty to champion the cause of the oppressed. (What do you think happens to our kids when they are taught that Christians are the privileged oppressor, and people who identify as LGBTQ+ are the oppressed minority that needs protecting?) Loving the oppressed and the marginalized now means championing alternative forms of sexuality and a redefinition of gender. And *you,* my sweet Mama Bears, are the old-fashioned fuddy-duddies who are basically standing in the way of universal civil rights for your kids' friends who use they/them pronouns.

Spot the Faulty Logic

A: The Bible oppresses LGBTQ+ people.
FC: Jesus said to protect the oppressed.
C: I need to protect LGBTQ+ people...from the Bible.

The second assumption of Marxism is that *in order to have a fair and just society, the have-nots must overthrow the haves.* What might that look like when we are talking about sexuality? Have you seen what is happening in our culture?! From pride parades to sexually explicit graphic novels, the sexual have-nots (i.e., the oppressed minority) are currently overthrowing every sexual norm within western civilization—the nuclear family, the importance of moms and dads, and parental rights.[21] You are watching the cultural overthrow predicted in Marx's theory!

The final Marxist assumption? *The ends justify the means.* The end goal is to have a fair, just, peaceful, and stable society. This in itself is not a bad goal. Who doesn't want this? The Marxist, however, believes the route to achieving this utopia can only come by forcefully disrupting the current structure of society—family, government, all of it. And since the assumed final outcome is so wonderful, one must be willing to do whatever it takes to bring about this transformation. The only moral imperative is progress toward "utopia." As long as you are pushing society in that direction, then no action you take to accomplish it can be considered unethical or wrong. As C.S. Lewis said in *God in the Dock*,

> Of all tyrannies, a tyranny sincerely exercised for the good of its victims may be the most oppressive...Those who torment us for our own good will torment us without end for they do so with the approval of their own conscience.[22]

In other words, a person will go to any lengths they deem necessary when they are convinced they are acting for the greater good.

All in all, as a worldview, Marxism answers many of the same questions the Christian worldview answers, albeit very differently.

Why are we here? *To create a fair and just society where everyone is equal.*

What is morality? *Anything that brings about this fair and just society.*

What is wrong with the world? *Unequal distribution of resources and power.*

How are we redeemed from what is wrong with the world? *Through the redistribution of resources and power so they are equally shared among all.*

It must be noted that the end goals of Marxism are not bad goals. The difference between it and Christianity is that we differ greatly on how (and when) we think these goals will be accomplished. (Hint: probably not until there are incorruptible people in power—that is, in eternity, when Jesus and the saints are the ones ruling and reigning.)

Social Justice and Intersectionality

Now that we understand the unstated taproots (postmodernism and Marxism), we can examine the explicitly stated secondary roots listed in the curriculum—social justice and intersectionality. According to social justice theory, society is made up of "systems" that give certain types of people more power (namely white, male, Protestant heterosexuals). Those who belong to these groups have—whether they realize it or not—played a part in marginalizing (oppressing) those who don't belong to these categories. In order to have a fair and just society, the whole "system" needs to be dismantled. This comes by 1) recognizing that the systems of power exist and by 2) identifying where one is within the system of power.

If you are in the privileged class, you must repent of your privilege and "ally" yourself with an oppressed group. If you are not sure how privileged you are, take a handy-dandy online quiz to see where you fall on the "Matrix of Domination."[23]

Social Identity Categories	Privileged Social Groups	Borderline Social Groups	Oppressed or Targeted Social Groups	"ism"
Sex	Biological men	Intersex and transgender	Biological women	Sexism
Gender	Gender-conforming bio men and women	Gender-ambiguous bio men and women	Transgender, genderqueer, intersex	Transgender oppression
Sexual Orientation	Heterosexuals	Bisexuals	Lesbians, gay men	Heterosexism
Religion	Protestant Christians	Roman Catholics	Jews, Muslims, Hindus	Religious oppression

(There are technically a lot more categories, but these are the most relevant ones for the purposes of this book.) These categories are intended to help individuals identify who is part of the privileged "system of power" and who belongs to the oppressed minority class that has historically been robbed of social equality.

Intersectionality comes from an observation that a person may have intersecting identities—some of which are classified as privileged and some as oppressed. Pay close attention to the categories here involving gender, sexual orientation, and religion. In this new framework, a Protestant man or woman who is content in the body God gave them and who is living out God's design for sex and marriage is in the oppressor category. This would be a person who would need to acknowledge their privilege and stand in solidarity with oppressed groups. Not doing so will earn a person the label of hateful, homophobic, transphobic, Islamophobic, and hater of all underdogs. Our kids aren't just being called "goody-goodies" anymore. They are being shamed out of their Christian beliefs and brainwashed into defending actions the Lord has called sin.

Spot the Faulty Logic

A: Having social power means you are an oppressor.

FC: Heterosexual Protestant men have social power.

C: Heterosexual Protestant men are oppressors.

To be fair, do some groups in our country have less power than others? Yes. Do we need to correct *actual* injustices when and where they occur? Absolutely! That's one of the main purposes of the Offer Discernment section of the ROAR. We should always be dignifying when someone has a legit point. But again, when we take action, we should *also* make sure we are doing so on the basis of real information and specific situations, not someone else's categorical terms or claimed identity. (We'll explore the relationship and differences between categories and actual information in the next chapter.)

With instruction in social justice and intersectionality, our kids are having a category hammered into their brains from kindergarten through their senior year of high school. The category consists of "oppressed people I should defend." This is a great category when teaching our kids to defend *individuals* who are experiencing mistreatment of some kind. This is *not* a great category in teaching our kids to defend entire classes of people. Why? Because doing so teaches our kids that guilt and innocence are derived from one's demographic, not from one's actions. That is definitely not a part of the biblical worldview! Protect from legitimate oppression? Yes. Defend in all circumstances just because of particular demographic? No.

What Is the Outcome of These Ideas?

Part of being an ally to a marginalized group means stepping aside and elevating the minority group's voices, experiences, and opinions. This, too, hits our kids where they are most vulnerable. Who doesn't want to be cheered on for their identity? Who doesn't want to be celebrated as a hero just by adopting a label? Who doesn't want their words to carry more weight?

As a result, we are witnessing an alarming number (one in five) of Gen Zers self-identifying as LGBTQ+. This is almost *double* the number of Millennials, which was itself more than *double* the number of Gen Xers.[24] And these are all adults we're talking about! If this trend continues, we should expect *one-third* of our kids under 18 to soon self-identify under the LGBTQ+ banner.

For some, this is a legitimate sexual cross for which they need love and compassion. They need loving guidance to know how to deny themselves and take up that cross while remaining faithful to Christ (see chapter 15). But for others, this new identity is an experiment—the one they were encouraged to have by the curriculum. Once a person starts messing with hormones and the image of God, certain effects are difficult to undo.

Church, here we are still singing songs about Father Abraham while our kids march like proverbial lemmings over the cliff of bad ideas. For starters, we have allowed society to redefine truth and goodness under the banners of love, inclusion, and protection for the oppressed. It is very difficult to remain an orthodox Christian once truth and goodness are redefined.

Our kids are seeking what we all sought back when we were young: a way to fit in and be accepted. They used to want to grow up to be firefighters and astronauts because that is who our society lauded as heroes. Today, there is a virtual parade of new "heroes" whose only claim to fame is who they sleep with or what has changed between their legs. Declaring oneself to be a sexual minority is not just accepted but celebrated, and our kids are interpreting it as the fastest fast-track ever to celebrity. Kids who used to be bullied suddenly find themselves sitting with the cool kids once they declare themselves transgender. (One study showed that 60 percent of kids claimed that their transgender "announcement brought a popularity boost."[25])

The Remnant

I know this chapter was a bit of a downer, and I don't want to end on that note. Yes, these philosophies are wreaking havoc, but think of this section like a visit from Dickens's ghost of Christmas future. *This does not have to be the fate of your kids.* Just in reading this book, you are preparing yourself and your kids to spot the lies before they ever take root.

Take a deep breath and remember the world will do what the world is gonna do, just as it's done in every pagan society throughout the course of history. Yes, in this world we will have trouble, but our God has overcome the world (John 16:33). He has given us the power to demolish ideas raised against the knowledge of God (2 Corinthians 10:5). Remind yourself of this truth: No matter how bad things have ever gotten, *the Lord has always preserved a remnant.* There will always be a group, however small, who will not bow its knee to another god. And that remnant has a beautiful future: "They will do no wrong;

they will tell no lies. A deceitful tongue will not be found in their mouths. They will eat and lie down and no one will make them afraid" (Zephaniah 3:13). No one. Not even a Marxist sex ed teacher.

Mama Bears and Papa Bears, when we are committed to Christ, to loving our neighbor, to standing for truth, and to immersing ourselves in the Word, *we are the remnant.* The Lord reserves for Himself those who have not bowed their knees to worthless idols (1 Kings 19:18). That idol right now is sex and gender ideology and all the agendas that go with it.

You are not alone, even though the enemy is trying to make you feel that you are. We are not responsible for the entire direction of culture. We are only responsible for what happens in our families while our kids are under our roof. Daniel 12:3 says, "Those who are wise will shine like the brightness of the heavens, and those who lead many to righteousness, like the stars for ever and ever." The Lord has given us everything we need for wisdom, and the ones you are leading in righteousness are your children.

The beauty of this modern era is that we have the resources to anticipate what the world will throw at our kids. This book is just one such tool. We're not saying this book will guarantee your kids' salvation. We're responsible for doing what we can, but the results are ultimately up to God and (gasp!) our kids' free will. Neither are we saying that by "knowing the right things" your kids are guaranteed protection from the seduction of bad ideas.[26] (And if your kids have already fallen for some of these lies, that doesn't make you a bad parent.) Our kids are responsible for their choices, and we are responsible for ours. There is no magic formula.

All the apologetics in the world cannot substitute for faith, a good understanding of God's Word, and the inner work of the Holy Spirit. We can't control our kids' free will, but we can make it a little easier to rip away the deceptions of this world. (Can I get an amen?!) Mama Bears and Papa Bears, you are choosing, right now, to inform yourself so you can better shepherd your kids. Titus 1:9 says the role of a church elder is not only to teach sound doctrine, but also to refute those who oppose it. Who are the spiritual "elders" in your family? *You are.* And guess what? By investing in this book, you are one step closer to understanding the worldview that is being taught to your kids so that you can refute it like Titus tells us to! Remember, we cannot refute that which we do not understand. When you prepare your kids to recognize the unbiblical worldview, the teachers can say whatever they like. Your kid will be empowered to see right through it.

DISCUSSION QUESTIONS

1. **Icebreaker:** Which of the "by the end of fifth grade, your children should be able to explain [fill in the blank]" statements was the most shocking to you? How old were you when you had to grapple with those concepts?

2. **Main theme:** *The sexual agenda is coming from a blatantly anti-biblical worldview using Christian-sounding virtues.* What are some good points that social justice and equity make? What lies have they slipped in that conflict with the Christian worldview?

3. **Self-evaluation:** How involved have you been in what the schools are teaching your children? Does understanding these principles make you want to get more involved?

4. **Brainstorm:** Take a look at the guiding principles from the NSES document (pages 97-101). Get a whiteboard and draw a line down the middle. Label one side "NSES Worldview" and the other "Christian Worldview." Brainstorm how you think each of these worldviews would answer the following questions: 1) Where did we (humans) come from? 2) What is original evil? 3) What do we need to do to fix the evil in the world? 4) What is the definition of *good*? 5) What is the definition of *bad*? 6) How should we treat our bodies? 7) What is the purpose of sex?

5. **Release the bear:** It is going to take a movement of Mama Bears to stem this cultural tide in the schools. Contact your school this week to find out what curricula they are using for sex education. Go over it on your own or with a group. Do you see any of the principles from

this chapter at play? While we need to speak up when we see dangerous ideologies being taught to our kids, as Christians we should *first* ask ourselves: "How can we as a group first *bless* the teachers and administration?" Build some rapport…and then lovingly start to question the ideologies being presented—moving up the chain of command as necessary (as described on pages 93-94). Why is it important as Christians for us to earn trust before we try and criticize and change the system? How might doing so ensure our efforts are better received?

6. **Pray:** Discuss what it means to be "the remnant." Pray for the courage for you and your children to face hostility for not going along with the cultural tide.

CHAPTER 6

The Enemy's New Playbook

The Language and Morality of the Sexual Agenda

HILLARY

In the previous chapter, we discussed the mission and vision behind the new sex education standards as well as some of the expectations that are being required of our fifth graders. We must remember that this didn't happen overnight. As we continue this journey through sex and gender, it would behoove us to understand not only what is going on but also *how we got here* (and which of the enemy's schemes we have unknowingly fallen for). The agenda (yes, agenda!) to erase biblical sexuality is not new, nor is it an organic, grassroots movement. It is extensively funded and has been strategically planned and executed.[1] And very successfully, I might add.

We trip and fall when we can't see what's in front of us. The enemy loves for us to operate in the dark, but no more, Mama Bears! It's time to shine a big ol' spotlight on his schemes. And remember, when we say the "enemy," we mean *the* enemy—Satan and his demons who have captivated people through hollow and deceptive philosophies, and not the people he has captured (2 Timothy 2:24-26).

The first two tactics—moralization and repetition—are prevalent for everything in this book. Next, we will discuss the importance of words and how our culture has hijacked language, tricking our Christian kids into affirming unbiblical principles using biblical words, concepts, and virtues. These tactics are all being used to establish a new moral code and erode our kids' ability to understand and live out God's design for sexuality. Helping our kids anticipate the secular sexual agenda is the best protection we can give them.

The Power of Moralizing Evil

This is the number-one tactic that we Mama Bears need to understand. The new sexual agenda is being pushed on our kids under the guise of love, tolerance, and inclusion. There is no limit to what a person will do if they are convinced they are acting for the greater good. This tactic is especially effective in manipulating the kids who are particularly empathy-driven.

Moralizing evil means that a person has taken something that would normally be considered immoral and *dressed it up to look good.* No one has codified this process more than the 1960s community organizer Saul Alinsky in his book *Rules for Radicals*. Alinsky's thesis reads as follows: "My aim here is to suggest how to organize for power: how to get it and how to use it." So let's be clear: His goal is to gain power to manipulate people toward seeing and doing things his way. How does one accomplish this feat? Alinsky writes, "Do what you can with what you have and *clothe it with moral garments*," because "all effective actions require the passport of morality."[2]

Let's unpack this: Alinsky is not advocating for actual morality. He is using the concept of morality as a *tool.* He's exploiting the fact that people generally want to do the right thing. If you can't get them to adopt an agenda straight-out, you can trick them by using moral language. God's view of morality is for us to know the right thing, and then do it. Alinsky's moral rationalization means: "I do what I want to do, and then I go back afterward and explain how it was the moral thing to do." That's essentially what he's training his followers to do.

This, Mama Bears, is how the enemy is tripping up our kids—by rewriting the moral code. Our kids need to realize that the secular agenda is being clothed in moral arguments, meaning it will sound Christian. We should expect nothing less as even Satan himself "masquerades as an angel of light," and "his servants also masquerade as servants of righteousness" (2 Corinthians 11:14-15).

The Effects of Repetition

Advertisers have long understood the effects of repetition on consumer behaviors. (How else do you think our girls got convinced that "mom jeans" were a cool fashion trend? Not from objective reasoning, that's for sure.) A slurry of scientific studies documents the effects of repetition on the brain. As psychologist Daniel Kahneman states in his book *Thinking, Fast and Slow*, "A reliable way to make people believe in falsehoods is frequent repetition, because familiarity is not easily distinguished from truth."[3]

But remember, Mama Bears, repetition in and of itself is not good or bad; it's a tool like any other. Repetition serves to burrow stuff deep into your brain until the thought or action becomes second nature. *What* gets burrowed in there is up to us, based on what we choose to focus on. We can be purposeful in reinforcing biblical ideas, or we can let the unbiblical ideas dominate by default. As parents, we need to be repeating the biblical worldview so often that our kids threaten to gag if they hear it one more time. But sometimes a good eye roll is the best proof that you're doing something right. In fact, this book's afterword is dedicated to things you should be repeating until your kids want to gag.

Remember our discussion of cartoons in the introduction? The media is reinforcing their secular worldview through constant repetition. Below, we will describe many of the secular worldview components that our kids are hearing ad nauseum. It is changing what they think is true about reality, humanity, gender, and sexuality. And if you remember nothing else, Mama Bears, remember this: We can't refute what we don't understand. So let's start understanding what's going on, shall we?

Why Words Are Worth Defending

As we discussed in the section on queer theory (pages 99-100), words themselves are being used as a weapon of the enemy, who distorts reality by twisting words. Distorted reality leads to a distorted worldview. So if we want to protect our kids' ability to accurately perceive reality and piece together a biblical worldview, we cannot ignore what is currently taking place with words.

Defending words is a type of apologetics I never expected to have to do, and yet here we are. Some people view apologetics as a side issue to evangelism—a cool hobby, but not really *that* important. Evangelists and pastors do the real work, they say. There are even some who view apologetics as if it's in *competition* with evangelism, or worse—*damaging* to evangelism! Church, we need to stop this. We are all on the same team, and we are all working toward the same end—spreading of the gospel to the ends of the earth. That is what we were commissioned by Jesus to do. Apologists and evangelists are coming at it from two different angles, but it is all in service to the gospel. And here, I would like to make an argument for the purpose of this particular chapter: the apologetic importance of defending words.

The gospel is, in essence, humans and God coming back into right relationship with one another through the sacrifice of Jesus on the cross. This gospel requires that humans understand their true identities as sinful rebels in need of saving. It also requires us humans to understand the true nature and identity of God—a perfect deity whose goodness and justice demand payment for sin—a payment He was willing to accept through Christ's death. To have an effective gospel, you have to correctly identify the parties involved. Distort either of these identities, and you cannot have the true gospel.

If humans are redefined as their own little gods, without sin, under no one's authority, with no need to repent, then they will never end up in right relationship with God. A distortion of their true identity leads to an inability to understand why they need the gospel in the first place. Likewise, if we have a God who winks at sin, or who is not all-just or all-good, then we don't have the God of the Bible. Try as we might to reconcile with that god, we are reconciling ourselves to a figment of our own imaginations, a god of our own making. Such a god cannot save.

Identity requires (at minimum) truth and words. You cannot *have* a true identity without the concept of truth, and you cannot *convey* a true identity apart from the use of words. Distort truth and words, and you essentially distort identity; distorted identities rewrite the gospel, and a rewritten gospel is no gospel at all (Galatians 1:8)!

Furthermore, this tactic of twisting language should come as no surprise when we remember how Jesus Himself is referred to in the Gospel of John: "In the beginning was *the Word* [the Logos], and *the Word* was with God, and *the Word* was God" (John 1:1). Christ is the Logos of God. If the enemy is to attack Christ, it makes sense he would attack words. Words are under attack because the Logos is under attack. Words are also under attack because, by them, we understand truth about God, the truth about humans, and the saving message of the gospel. In this chapter, we're going to take a look at the ways the enemy is trying to trip our kids up—all by messing with language.

The War on Words

Just as our ideologies are shaped by underlying assumptions, our worldviews are also affected to an enormous extent by the language we speak. Words are constantly evolving—that's just how language works. Take, for example, the word *silly*. We think of it like *goofy* or *humorous*. Read *Pride and Prejudice*, and you'll realize they understood it as something like "someone who doesn't have two brain cells to rub together." Semantic shift, y'all; it's a real thing. But that's not what we are talking about in this chapter.

What we're talking about here is much more sinister and much more purposeful than an innocent evolution of language. In the first Mama Bear Apologetics book, I refer to a tactic called *linguistic theft*. Linguistic theft occurs when a person purposely takes a concept, abstract virtue, or idea and changes the definition to promote their own agenda. Without understanding that this change has taken place, many people swallow an agenda to which they would normally object. We must teach our kids to expect that sin and secular agendas will be promoted using Christian-sounding virtues like love, tolerance, justice...and healthcare.

In researching for this book, I realized that linguistic theft was just scratching the surface. There are so many weird word games going on (which we introduced in the previous chapter with queer theory). The second kind of wordplay I'm seeing is what I'll call *linguistic smuggling.*

Categories Versus Actual Information

Categories (or categorical words) are umbrella terms used when describing. There is no concrete object that is good, evil, moral, or immoral. We can use these words to *classify* thoughts, beliefs, or actions, but interpretation is involved; we are not providing *actual information.* Hang with me here. I promise I'll make this more understandable.

Information is very specific. It refers to a concrete thing or behavior. For example, a child might use the categorical word *mean* and say, "My friend was mean to me." At this point, we could challenge his category by asking for actual *information.* "What did your friend *do* that was mean?" What if your child answered, "He sat with the new kid in the class instead of with me at lunch"? This statement is informative—we know exactly what happened and what action was categorized as "mean." But was his friend being mean? I would say the child improperly categorized this action. Maybe we could challenge him to understand that his friend was not being mean to him, but rather being "nice" to a new student. Being nice to someone else isn't the same as being mean to us. Your child thought he was providing you with information, but he didn't. He provided his perspective on the situation using a *categorical term.*

The secular agenda is being packaged in the same way, smuggling unbiblical ideas into the categories of moral, immoral, harmful, beneficial, inclusive, oppressive, etc. The only way to know if we are on the same page with someone is to have them provide *actual information.*

Linguistic smuggling is when someone slips an unrelated action under a well-known categorical word and hopes nobody asks for more details (or refuses to provide any). We have seen this happen with the word *bullying.* Most schools now operate under a zero-tolerance bullying rule—which I heartily agree with! We shouldn't allow kids to bully each other. (I was mercilessly bullied in middle school by a kid in my class.) The problem our kids might face, however, is when an agenda smuggles something unrelated under the banner of bullying.

When most people think of bullying, they think of teasing, humiliating, name-calling, shoving kids into lockers, and (of course) the time-honored and infamous wedgie. But what do we do when "using the wrong pronoun" is smuggled into the umbrella category of bullying? What about refusing to tell someone that all religions are equally valid ways to God? Or that all manners of sexual expression are equally healthy?

When things like these are put under the banner of "bullying," and there's a zero-tolerance policy, do our kids have the language to understand what is happening? If your child has been raised to respect authority, he or she may do or say whatever their teacher or principal tells them to do when it comes to not bullying, even if that means affirming something that isn't true. Affirming things that aren't true in behavior is just a step away from our kids starting to believe the lies they are forced to affirm—all in the name of tolerance, love, and anti-bullying.

Spot the Faulty Logic

A1: Not using someone's pronouns is bullying.
A2: Bullying should be punished.
C: People should be punished for using the wrong pronouns.

How Does Linguistic Theft Work?

Messing with language through linguistic theft or linguistic smuggling is an effective tactic of the enemy for a variety of reasons.

1. It Divides Us

Confusing the language is how the Lord divided the people at Babel, and it's what the enemy is using to divide us now. If two people are using the same word with two different meanings, they are talking past each other and productive conversation is hopeless. As Voltaire is said to have mused, "If you wish to converse with me, you must first define your terms." Similarly, when we hear someone use a familiar word but something seems "off," we should seek information by asking, "What do you mean by that?" followed by, "How did you come to that conclusion?"[4] The goal is to figure out what actually happened without interpretation being smuggled in. Use these questions often in your home; they're key for productive communication, which should always be our goal. We may not always agree with one another, but at least we should aim for clarity.

2. It Can Redefine Morality

Linguistic theft and smuggling assume that our culture still has vestiges of the Judeo-Christian ethic. Thus, if secular culture can redefine biblical concepts like love and tolerance (or place our Christian worldview under the banner of "oppression" and "injustice"), then they can literally rewrite morality. It doesn't happen all at once. This tactic is especially effective when coupled with repetition—because the human mind confuses familiarity with truth.

3. It Pits the Underdog Against the Villain

Everybody loves a good underdog story, and villains are the people we all love to hate. But these are both category words. If secular culture can redefine or smuggle stuff into words like *harm*, *damage*, and *oppression*, then they can decide who is the victim and who is the villain. This is what our culture is doing with gender identity and sexual orientation. And guess who the villain is? You got it. It's we who hold to the Christian worldview. With a few simple changes to definitions, our kids might begin to believe their identity is as a privileged oppressor whose primary job is to sit down and be quiet, even when truth is being maligned.

4. It Allows Subjective Experiences to Define Reality

Many of the words we'll see require a person to experience them. In other words, someone's feelings are allowed to define what *category* an action falls under. If someone *feels* hurt, then they assume they have been harmed. If someone feels like something is unfair, then injustice has occurred, at least in their mind. And if we have learned anything, it's that we cannot reason with someone's emotions. We need to remind our kids that feelings don't always reflect reality.

Stolen Words

In the first Mama Bear Apologetics book, we addressed the oft-stolen words of *love*, *truth*, *tolerance*, *justice*, *equality*, *bigot*, and *authentic*. For the purposes of this book, we are going to focus on the specific words that the sexual agenda is cramming down the throat of every person in the West (and more conservative parts of the world too!). The words are *diversity*, *inclusion*, *harm*, *injustice*, *marriage*, *power*, *authority*, *oppression*, and *healthcare*.

Diversity

Don't let this word fool you. When you see the word *diversity*, it rarely means diversity of thought or ideas. Usually, it means diversity of demographics. Diversity often means people who all look differently but who basically believe the same thing. And when diversity is championed in society, and sexual orientation and gender identity are considered their own demographic, then we—by default—are required to champion non-biblical gender identities and sexual orientations.

Spot the Faulty Logic

A: Diversity makes society stronger.
FC: Sexual and gender identities can be diverse.
C: Society will be stronger by embracing diverse sexual and gender identities.

Inclusion

This word sounds *so good*. We should be including everyone! However, as we'll see in the queer theory chapter, inclusion means getting rid of the idea of normal, because if someone doesn't *feel* like they are seen as "normal," then they are (by fiat) being excluded.

Spot the Faulty Logic

A1: Inclusion means nobody feels excluded.

A2: Not feeling "normal" is exclusion.

FC: People don't treat my [fill in the blank identity] as normal.

C: [Fill-in-the-blank identity] must be normalized or I'm being excluded.

Harm

This one is big in all the LBGTQ+ and progressive Christian literature. The going narrative is that advocating for biblical sexuality is not only outdated but *harmful* to people. Progressive pastor Nadia Bolz-Weber writes in her book *Shameless* that she wishes she could "sit down with the people who wrote the Nashville Statement" and show them how "their loyalty to a doctrine or an interpretation of a few Bible verses has created *harm* in the bodies and spirits of the people" under her care.[5] (The Nashville Statement was the multidenominational effort to define biblical gender, marriage, and sex. It's a really good document. I suggest reading it.[6])

Most of the dictionary definitions of *harm* involve two more words: *injury* and *damage*. We must remind our children that something can hurt without injuring. For example, resetting a broken bone hurts, but it is actually helping, not harming. Likewise, demolishing a bad idea causes damage to the idea, but bad ideas deserve to be damaged! We should not confuse it with damaging a person.

We don't want to minimize the real harm that has been done to people who identify as LGBTQ+ by self-righteous zealots who have treated these individuals like they are less than human or like their struggles are worse than others. Furthermore, our kids can acknowledge that when someone's feelings are hurt, that person may *feel* harmed. But we must also remind our children that we do not have control over other people's feelings. We can control whether we are kind, patient, and caring. We cannot control if biblical truth will cause another person distress.

Injustice

Romans 2:15 tells us that the law of God is written on our hearts. This means that everyone (psychopaths aside[7]) has an innate sense of right and wrong. God makes Himself clear in Scripture that He is a God of justice (Psalm 50:6; Isaiah 30:18). The Greek word *dikaiosýnē* is translated as justice or righteousness. Justice, then, can be understood as righteous living—obeying the commands of God.

But let's look at how our society is using the word *justice*. Our world treats justice as synonymous with equal. If anything is unequal, then it is unjust. As we discussed on pages 97-98, abortion rights are being argued for under the umbrella term of *reproductive justice*. Similarly, *marriage justice* assumes that marriage itself is a right. Denying anyone equal access to that right is unjust. But, of course, this assumes a linguistically stolen definition of marriage. Here's a thought experiment: Whenever you see the word *justice*, replace it with the word *righteousness*. What would reproductive righteousness look like? Marital righteousness?

Marriage

The word *marriage* is currently being redefined out of existence. In most every culture, marriage has been rooted in the purpose of bearing and raising of children. However, once birth control separated sex from procreation, and abortion separated pregnancy from childbirth, then marriage for the purpose of family became nonsensical. If marriage is about who you want to live with and have sex with, then who cares how we define it?

But God is the One who created marriage, so I say He gets to define it. While different forms of marriage are *represented* in Scripture (usually multiple wives), that is not God's *definition* of marriage. (And let's face it, there's not one "multiple wives" situation in Scripture that worked well. Am I right?) Genesis 2:24 says: "A man leaves his father and mother and is united to his wife, and they become one flesh." *A* man (singular) unites with his wife, not wives. Jesus affirms this original design when people start asking Him about divorce in Matthew 19:4-5. Later in 1 Timothy 3:2, we learn how church leaders are required to be above reproach; one of these criteria is being "faithful to his wife." Marriage, according to the Bible, is a man and a woman united for life, until death do they part. And while Jesus is clear that concessions were made by Moses because of the hardness of people's hearts, concessions do not change God's original purpose or His original design.

Health and Healthcare

The last one I want to bring up is the concept of healthcare. What does it mean for someone to be *healthy*, and what role does the healthcare system play in helping people get and stay healthy? Should "healthcare" include tampering with functioning body parts, leading to a lifetime of taking medications to maintain the changes? That sounds more like bodily abuse than healthcare. But remember, we cannot define what is healthy unless we understand how we as humans were intended to function—which assumes design...which suggests a designer...which implies an *authority*. It is crazy the amount of mental gymnastics people are doing to get around the concept of an authority outside of themselves. The same applies for mental health. We keep hearing about the rapid decline in public mental health while simultaneously not wanting to explore the real causes of mental illness because it might infringe on someone "living their truth."

Power, Authority, and Oppression

Power properly defined is merely the ability to act or produce an effect, but it has been redefined as a person exerting their authority to get what they want. This bad definition of power is now being touted as synonymous with authority—both of which now have negative connotations.

As we saw in chapter 3, however, the concept of authority is biblical. God describes submission and authority occurring on most every level—within the Trinity, the family, government, and church. And biblical authority *always* goes hand in hand with greater responsibility. We see this in the parable of the talents when Jesus concludes: "From everyone who has been given much, much will be demanded" (Luke 12:48).

Spot the Faulty Logic

A: Anything that promotes abuse is bad.

FC: Authority can be used to abuse.

C: Authority is bad.

Just because bad authorities exist doesn't mean authority itself is bad. As we saw in the previous chapter, the concept of oppression is getting really watered down, being equated with the haves and have-nots of social power rather than oppressive actions. But I'd like to point out that under this definition, our children are oppressed. And while this might sound like I'm making a silly joke, I'm not. As we write this book, transgender surgery for young children is being argued for under the guise of "children's rights"—as if the kids are now an oppressed class. If they are the oppressed, guess who is the oppressor? The woman in the mirror, my friend. You and your husband.[8]

You Fired Up Yet?

I hope so! Because when you awaken your inner Mama Bear, I know there's almost nothing you won't do to protect your kids. Moms are the sleeping giants of our society. I'm reminded of the line from *Robin Hood: Prince of Thieves* where Kevin Costner says, "One free man defending his home is more powerful than ten hired soldiers." To that I'd say, one Mama Bear defending her cubs is more powerful than ten hired activists. And when you get a whole *bunch* of Mama Bears together? Sweet heavens to Betsy, stuff is 'bout to get real!

DISCUSSION QUESTIONS

1. **Icebreaker:** Did you ever come across a statistic or story that you thought was true because you'd heard it so many times, but then later found out it wasn't true after all?

2. **Main theme:** *The secular agenda is being advanced through repetition and the use of Christian-sounding words, and it's tricking our kids into adopting beliefs that are contrary to the Christian worldview.* Why do you think that co-opting words is so effective?

3. **Self-evaluation:** Have you found yourself adopting any of the linguistically thieved words on pages 119-123?

4. **Brainstorm:** What is the difference between categorical words and actual information? Pull out a newspaper or online publication and find headlines that use some of these buzzwords. Read through the article. Did they provide information for what actually happened, or does the article only use the buzzwords? To figure out if they provided actual information, ask yourself: *If I were to reenact the scene, would I know what to do?* If you're not sure, then the article has not provided actual information.

5. **Release the bear:** Make a buzzwords board to put next to the television. Add words to it whenever you or your kids encounter "category words" that seem to be pushing a narrative without giving any facts.

6. **Pray:** Jesus is the Logos, the Word of God. Praise Him for being the true Word, and pray for the ability to discern when words are being stolen or used to promote ideas raised against the knowledge of God (2 Corinthians 10:5).

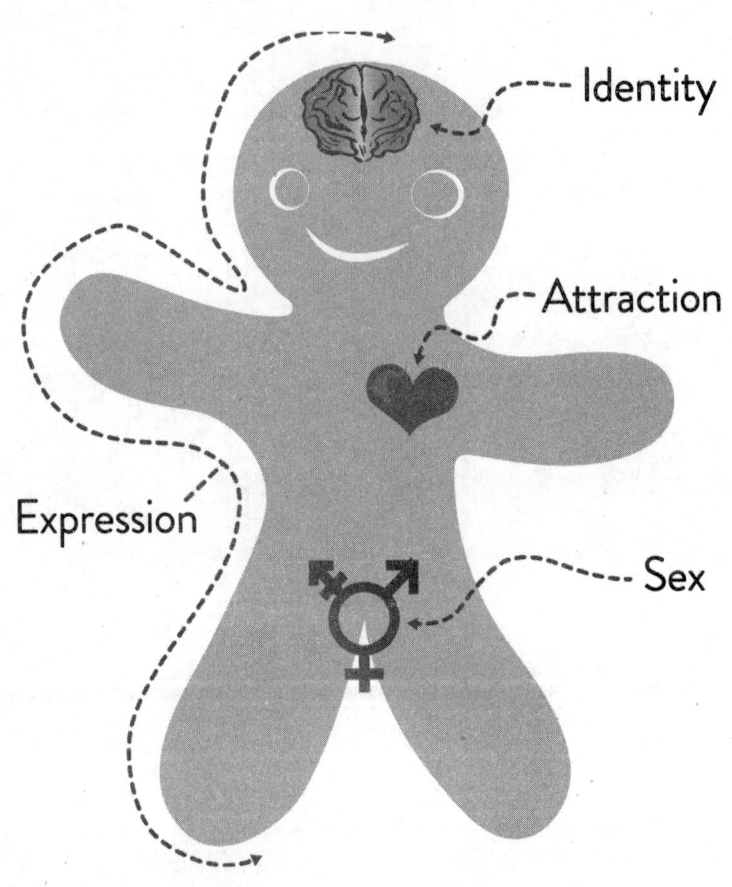
Identity
Attraction
Expression
Sex

CHAPTER 7

The Genderbread Person

The New Definitions of Identity, Expression, Sex, and Attraction

HILLARY

In the previous chapters, we've led you through the maze of what is going on in the schools. We've looked at the new sex education standards and discussed the language and morality being used to advance an agenda. Now, let's take a look at an actual curriculum being used with the littles.

Forget the muffin man. Do you know the Genderbread Person? The Genderbread Person is a commonly used tool for teaching kids about sexual orientation and identity. (The Gender Unicorn is a similar curriculum.) You need to be aware of this curriculum so you can understand and discuss the implications of it with your kids. Hold on tight, Mama Bears. First grade just got a lot more confusing.

In a lesson plan titled *Genderbread Person and LGBT+ Umbrella*, kids as young as kindergarten are taught all about sexuality.

> LGB all represent sexual identities. And the T represents a gender

> identity, as well as an umbrella term for many gender identities. Queer means different things to different people, for some it describes sexuality, for others their gender, for others both. When we say "sexual identities or sexual orientations" what we are talking about are the ways we categorize and define who we are attracted to, romantically, sexually, or otherwise. When we say "gender identities" we are talking about the ways we categorize and define our genders.
>
> Gender is best understood when broken up into three parts: gender identity (which is how you, in your head, define and understand your gender based on the options for gender you know to exist), gender expression (the ways you demonstrate gender through your dress, actions, and demeanor), and biological sex (the physical parts of your body that we think of as either male or female). Let's talk about these one-by-one.[1]

Yes. Let's. Starting with how they define gender identity.

Identity

I didn't know the slow loris existed until I saw a fabulous YouTube video of one being tickled. However, my lack of awareness had *no bearing* on the slow loris's existence. Reality is independent of my knowledge.

The Genderbread curriculum teaches the opposite, saying identity is all in the head. And make no mistake, that is where this kind of curriculum is headed—to remove gender from the realm of objective reality to subjective preference or experience.

The logical law of identity states that a thing is itself and not something else. For example, an apple is an apple and not an orange. Twelve equals twelve, not twenty-four. But according to the Genderbread Person curriculum, identity is not set. It is based on an individual's current perceptions. And if those perceptions change, a person's identity changes. Essentially, an apple can turn into an orange as soon as it becomes aware that oranges exist—if fruit were conscious.

Merriam-Webster defines *identity* as "the distinguishing character or personality of an individual" or "the relation established by psychological identification."[2]

Did you catch that second definition? A relation established by *psychological* identification. We have just defined the essence of a thing as contingent on a person's psychological state. What could possibly go wrong? If identity is defined by a person's psychological state, then we cannot tell people in the midst of depression that they are not worthless. They *feel* worthless, and according to this definition, they are worthless—that's the relation that has been established by their psychological identification.

I can't tell you how many times my emotions have been hijacked to feed me lies. (You can ask my husband though. He probably knows. He's the one who gets to hear *all* about it.) Mama Bears, if our kids think their identity is based on how they identify in the moment, then there is no security in Christ. If they don't *feel* saved, then they aren't. If they don't *feel* like God is close to them at the moment, then He's not. If they *feel* ugly, then they are. Don't try to talk them out of it: The Genderbread Person taught them all about how to determine their identity.

When it comes to identity, the Genderbread Person also relies on completely regressive gender stereotyping. The curriculum states, "Gender identity can be thought of as the aspects of man-ness and woman-ness you either do or don't align with."[3]

Hard stop right here.

Who defines this "man-ness and woman-ness"? And if there are a bunch of different definitions, how could a child possibly know which they align with? Don't worry. The Genderbread curriculum will define it for you.

> In this case, we are talking about the norms (social expectations) and roles (ways we fulfill or act out those expectations) placed upon "men" and "women" in a society. A few typical norms of man-ness might be *strong-willed, logical, athletic* and roles of *leader, builder, protector*. For woman-ness, we might think of the norms *empathic, sensitive, caring* and roles *teacher, caretaker, supporter.*[4]

Raise your hand if you have a daughter who is strong-willed, athletic, logical, and maybe a bit scant on the sensitive caretaker role. (My mom should be raising her hand right now.) Is there a tendency for guys and girls to fit into these roles? Absolutely. Does it change their gender if they don't? No! This curriculum is *literally* telling your sensitive son who wants to be a nurse that he is actually more of a woman, and it's telling your athletic, leader-oriented daughter that she is actually more of a man. (Didn't the feminists take on this gender stereotyping back in the '80s? Have we really regressed to such one-dimensional definitions of man and woman?)

Furthermore, if gender identity conforms to society norms, then according to this definition, a person's gender can theoretically change when they travel. (I'm not saying this is what the Genderbread Person curriculum is teaching. However, this is a logical conclusion that cannot be refuted by their definition.) If gender identity is based on norms, we cannot ignore that masculine and feminine norms are different in different countries. There are cultures where it is considered more acceptable for a man to cry. Does this mean an emotional and sensitive person is more feminine in America and more masculine in...I don't know, Italy? (Disclaimer: I am only speaking from my husband's comments while watching Italian soccer matches. Apparently, the players get overly dramatic when it comes to fouls.)

Again, an identity *is what something is* and not something else. Reality doesn't change, no matter what's in your head or where you are on earth. A person's psychological state might feel like reality to them, but it is just a perception. And while we should not ignore the impact that perception can have upon a person, we shouldn't give that perception the power to shape reality.

When we turn to Scripture, we see two clear genders from Genesis to Revelation. Jesus even affirms this in Matthew 19:4: "At the beginning the Creator 'made them male and female.'" Scripture doesn't include a single instance of a male or female identifying with the opposite gender. What *do* we see? We see people defying gender stereotypes all over the place. Deborah was a female judge. David played the harp and cried a lot. The Proverbs 31 woman is a complete entrepreneur. (No, seriously. Read her résumé.) And our current translation "wife of noble character" sadly misses the traditionally understood Hebrew translation "woman of *valor*." Valor was generally reserved for praising military prowess. This is the Hebrew equivalent of saying, "Here's a woman in beast mode."

God has poured out His gifts on both men and women, and He doesn't discriminate based on gender. If you have a child who conforms to gender norms, praise them for their qualities! If you have a child who doesn't conform to gender norms, *praise them for their qualities.* Reinforce that God has made them logical or empathetic, athletic or artistic, no matter if they were born a boy or a girl. Reinforce the ways God has created them *male and female* with these characteristics. (More on this in chapter 13.)

Expression

> Gender expression can be thought of as the aspects of masculinity and femininity you display in your clothing, grooming, speech, actions, demeanor, and more. As examples, masculine dress might be considered baggy, unprimed, or functional. Feminine dress is form-fitting, colorful, and frivolous.[5]

My first thought upon reading this part of the Genderbread Person curriculum: *This is a really schizophrenic view of gender. I mean, what happened to just being a good old-fashioned tomboy?* (A tomboy is, of course, a girl who has more traditionally masculine interests and energy levels and hates wearing dresses.) Why do we have to separate our genders based on fashion and grooming? When I was a teenage girl, we called that our "mood." What mood am I in? Am I in a cargo-pants-with-boots mood, or a sundress-with-sandals mood? If I had to wrestle with being told I had different *gender* expressions on different days...good grief. I would have grown up so confused.

My second thought? *Ohhh. I think I see the problem now.* Because if I'd finished my thought above, it would have sounded like, *Why can't we just have tomboys and uh...and...uhhhh...*

What about the boys? When I was growing up, what options did they have except being a Mr. T, Tyrannosaurus rex–loving, G.I. Joe–backpacking, rough-and-tumble boy? *They didn't.* Sure, there were boys who didn't fit the stereotype, but they were often relegated to the sidelines in terms of status. They didn't fit the mold, so they lost punches on their man-card, whether it was stated verbally or not. Often, it was stated physically in the form of bullying.

This was, and is, a problem. Girls could be girly girls or tomboys and were affirmed in their womanhood for both roles. We looked up to female athletes, artists, and intellectuals equally. But the boys could be rough-and-tumble boys...or sissies. Them's the options. These "tomgirls," as I've heard them called, are guys who might be a tad more on the soft-spoken, artistic, sensitive side of the spectrum. Where did they get to fit into society's gender norms while maintaining the same level of masculinity the jocks had? They didn't—unless they created their own little subculture (which high schools are full of). I suspect the seeds of our current gender schism may have started there.

The fact is, there is a spectrum of gender expression. Not all women express their femininity in the same way, but it doesn't make them any less of a woman. Not all men express their masculinity in the same way, but it doesn't make them any less of a man. As Bible teacher Sue Bohlin writes, "Narrow gender stereotypes don't honor the creativity of the God who makes varieties of girls and boys on a femininity spectrum and a masculinity spectrum."[6]

In my parents' generation, boys were boys, men were men, girls were girls, and women were women. No ifs, ands, or buts. Even the girls' softball team wore dresses to school every day. Everyone was equally shoved into a gender-conforming stereotype. You fit in—or you became a pariah. (I think of Eugene from the first *Grease* movie.) But that all started to change in the '80s.

It was pretty awesome to be a girl in the '80s as opposed to previous decades. We girls were told early on that we could be anything we wanted to be. Dream big! Play sports! Wear pants! Wear sneakers! Home ec is optional! (No complaining from me yet. Except for the '80s shoulder pads—like a weird mix of businesswoman and football player.) Girls had all the freedom of expression in the world. But the boys...nope. They were still shoehorned into their stereotype—or mocked mercilessly if they failed to conform.

Can we all just take a deep breath and recognize how incredibly unfair this was for little boys who loved to dance, or paint, or sing...or shower on a regular basis? To be treated like they were less of a boy, and later, less of a man?

I think we tried to fix this inequality by creating a new category, but it was too little, too late. The category I'm referring to is "metrosexual." The metrosexual movement was for guys who liked to groom themselves, shower, and wear nice clothes but didn't self-identify as homosexual. These guys were often artists, musicians, and philosophers who loved craft brew, specialty coffees, and beard-grooming products. They put the *man* in *manicure*. The metrosexual movement made it acceptable to be refined and artistic without sacrificing one's perceived masculinity. (Just look at all the youth pastors and worship leaders who adopted the skinny jeans.) These guys can wear tight, colorful, "frivolous" clothing without anyone questioning their manhood.

This was probably a really healthy movement. It allowed guys to express themselves in a legitimately masculine way that would have otherwise been seen as feminine. But even this movement is starting to take an unhealthy turn. Instead of teaching little boys that their God-given masculinity can be expressed in a variety of different ways, we are instead telling them that these gender expressions make them girls.

When a person backs away from some ideology—in this case, rigid gender stereotypes—they often back into something worse. In our society, people have backed into an outright denial of gender as an objective fact about a person and turned it into this messy, fluid, confusing, daily-changing spectrum of expression that will leave even the strongest of kids confused about who they really are.

Sex

Nothing summarizes our discussion more today than the famous scene from *Kindergarten Cop* where a little boy respectfully raises his hand to speak and waits to be called upon. His words of wisdom for the class that he so ardently and patiently waited to share? "Boys have a penis. Girls have a vagina."[7]

In 1990, this was considered so obvious that it was part of the joke. Fast-forward 30 years, and a statement like this could be prosecuted as hate speech in some places![8] According to the Genderbread Person curriculum, the simple definition of biological sex is "the physical traits you are born with or develop that we think of as sex characteristics, as well as the sex you are assigned at birth."[9]

Sex, then, is all a matter of perception. The physical traits are those "*that we think of* as sex characteristics"—not those that objectively correspond to biological sex. Notice this shift in language—a literal, physiological, scientifically testable statement has been reduced to a perception. The Genderbread Person's shift in language—from biological sex being absolute to being subjective—is something we need to make our kids aware of.

Along these same lines, the Genderbread curriculum defines biological sex as the "sex that you are assigned at birth," as if the doctor just flipped a coin and slapped a label on you as male or female. I don't want to oversimplify this, but this really is a simple concept. For millennia, unless a baby was born with a genetic abnormality—which does happen[10]—assigning a sex was as simple as looking at their nether regions. Unless there is some sort of abnormality, this method of announcing biological sex has, historically, been extremely reliable.

But before we accuse the curriculum of only looking at body parts, I do applaud it for being more comprehensive than the kid in *Kindergarten Cop*.

> Let's consider biological sex in the ultra-reductive way society does: being female means having a vagina, ovaries, two X chromosomes, predominant estrogen, and the ability to grow a baby in your abdominal area; being male means having testes, a penis, an XY chromosome configuration, predominant testosterone, and the ability to put a baby in a female's abdominal area; and being intersex can be any combination of what I just described...In reality, biological sex, like gender identity and expression, for most folks, is more nuanced than that.[11]

Is this as "ultra-reductive" as they claim? In some ways, yes. Being female doesn't necessarily mean you have certain body parts. Women who have had hysterectomies or cancer-related removal of the uterus and ovaries are no less female than those with these organs.

If I were to tweak this statement to be more accurate, I'd say a woman is "a human being whose body is organized around gestating another human life." Even if something goes wrong or is removed, or she chooses not to—her body was still organized around growing a baby. It pains me that we have to get this specific, but part of (successfully) engaging in the cultural battle means we have to use words that cannot be refuted. We *must* take objective arguments and create objectively true statements. Otherwise, we will be arguing over nuances, technicalities, and perceptions.

And speaking of nuance, intersex individuals are worth our consideration. Intersexuality and transgenderism are *not* the same thing. While a variety of genetic abnormalities can render the simple XX/XY distinction confusing, those situations are different from "gender dysphoria"—feeling that you were born in the wrong body. True intersex conditions occur when the chromosomes and genitals do not align, resulting in reproductive or physical abnormalities. I think about these individuals every time I mark "female" on a survey. I can't imagine how truly confusing and frustrating that one little question must be for this group *every* time they fill out a form.

This group has a real, legitimate difficulty in that they are truly intersex. And it should be noted that this particular group—the one group that has a science-based reason to question their sex—is not the group that is advocating for a redefinition of sex outside of the binary of male and female. According to the Intersex Society of North America, "We are trying to make the world a safe place for intersex kids, and we don't think labeling them with a [third] gender category that in essence doesn't exist would help them."[12] This condition is real, and confusing, and individuals who were born with it cannot be lumped into the same category as the rest of those who identify as LGBTQ+.

Remind your children that while abnormalities exist, they do not redefine normal. Science (and especially medicine) cannot progress without a concept of "normal." For example, some people are born with six fingers, but we will never see textbooks redefining human hands as having anywhere from five to six digits. Normal human hands have five digits. And abnormalities do *not* make a person "less than."

All this talk of normality aside, the word *atypical* might be better to use with your kids than *abnormal.* While *abnormal* just describes deviation from the norm, it has the connotation of being "weird" for kids. Nobody wants to be abnormal. Like me—I have an abnormal kidney, but that doesn't make me weird. (I'm weird for a whole lot of *other* reasons.)

When you talk with your children, affirm that they can use the reality of their bodies to understand the truth about their gender. In a popular TED talk, cardiologist Paula Johnson says, "Every cell has a sex—and what that means is that men and women are different down to the cellular and molecular level. It means that we're different across all of our organs, from our brains to our hearts, our lungs, our joints."[13] In other words, no matter what your gender philosophy, when you are ill and the doctors put you on the operating table, they still need to know your original biological sex in order to give you the best possible healthcare.

Our physical bodies are an objective reality. If kids can't even use their bodies to tell them who they are, how can we expect them to understand themselves in any meaningful, non-transient way? We can't. Life becomes an ever-shifting reality that can't be pinned down by anything. That, friends, is a really confusing worldview to expect our kids to live in.

Attraction

> Sexual attraction can be thought of as the want, need, or desire for physical sexual contact and relationships. Romantic attraction is an affinity and love for others and the desire for emotional relationships. Some folks have both, some folks have neither, many experience more of one than the other. Sexual orientation is all about who you are physically, spiritually, and emotionally attracted to (here we've broken it out specifically into sexual and romantic attraction), and the labels tend to describe the relationships between your gender and the gender types you're attracted to.[14]

In the Genderbread Person curriculum, sexual attraction refers to the gender with whom you want to be sexually active. Romantic attraction is the "affinity and love for others and the desire for emotional relationships." I don't mean this in a condescending way, but isn't this what *friendship* is—having an affinity toward another person with whom you would like to have an emotional relationship? We need to emphasize to our kids that desiring an emotional relationship with someone does *not* change their sexual orientation. Even loving someone does not mean we are in love with them. You would be surprised at how confused many kids are regarding this concept.

Friends, we were created by God for relationship, and healthy relationships include an emotional component. What has happened to our understanding of healthy, platonic, same-sex friendship? If our kids are buying into the propaganda that a desire for an emotional attachment with someone of the same sex means they have a same-sex sexual orientation, then be prepared for a lot of confusion. Healthy relationships begin with healthy same-sex friendships.[15] We cannot take a normal desire and make it a predictor of sexual identity. By this definition, everyone is romantically attracted to their best friends.

So let's figure out what romance looks like according to the Genderbread Person, getting a better idea of the terms the curriculum is using.

> If you are a man and you're attracted to women, you're straight. If you're a man who is attracted to men and another gender, you're bi-sexual. And if you're a man who is attracted to men, you're gay. These are the labels most of us know the most about. We hear the most about it, it's salient in our lives, and we can best understand where we stand with it.[16]

A quick pause here to point out that this statement can't make sense if we've already redefined what it means to be a man or a woman. According to this statement of attraction, we need to know what *we ourselves* are and what the *other* person is in order to even put a label on our sexual identity. However, as we've already seen, this curriculum has sawed off the branch it is sitting on. If one's gender is determined by subjective and mental associations that can be fluid throughout life, we have lost the ability to identify who is a man and who is a woman. And it is impossible for us to determine what someone else is apart from their informing us. We cannot even call someone gay or straight unless we are willing to commit to a definition of male and female! I think the authors of the Genderbread Person foresaw this issue because they say:

> It's pretty cut and dry, right? Maybe. There's much more to attraction and sexuality. Some folks define and experience attraction without gender as a factor; they might identify as "pansexual." If you experience romantic attraction but not sexual, you might

identify as asexual or "ace," or, depending on the gender(s) you're attracted to, hetero-, homo-, or panromantic.[17]

Truths to Affirm

Your eyes may be swimming with all these "identities," so let's just keep to our main question. What do we need to emphasize to our children?

1. We Were Created for Relationship

The Genderbread Person curriculum provides a range of orientations, but not one of them includes the concept of healthy, nonromantic, nonsexual friendships. Our God exists eternally in relationship within the Trinity, and He created humankind because He desired a creation with whom He could relate. Our kids need to know that as children of God, our identity is rooted in that relationship. We were created by a relational God for relationship, and our families, friendships, and communities give us a picture of the way God relates to us.

2. Not All Love Is That Kind of Love

Our society has taught children that all strong feelings of love have a sexual component (that is, eros—romantic love). This misconception can be easily fixed if we help our kids understand the different categories of love, especially platonic love (*phileo* in Greek). Let them know that sometimes their attraction for another person is really respect for traits they admire. Those traits can even be physical beauty. That doesn't make them gay. We are by nature attracted to beautiful things, but appreciation for beauty does not equal sexual attraction. The more you talk with your kids about the distinctions between the different loves, the less they'll be confused about their own feelings of love. The different categories will already be in their minds.

Spot the Faulty Logic

A: All strong attractions are erotic in nature.

FC: I'm strongly drawn to my BFF.

C: I must be in love with my BFF (and am therefore bi or a lesbian).

3. Touch Isn't Always Romantic

We were created for physical contact. In fact, babies in the neonatal ICU are able to leave more quickly when a person engages in "touch therapy" with them. And boys, in particular, face a crisis now that the category of platonic touch between men has been removed. Psychologists call it "skin hunger."

When I was a kid, we had roller-skating parties. The DJ always played a "couples only" song. It never once occurred to any of us that picking a friend to hold hands with during the couple's skate meant we were anything other than friends. It was a couple's skate. We were two people. We fulfilled the requirement. Let's hold hands and skate!

This is a luxury our kids no longer have. I'm a really touchy person. (Just ask any of my close friends or family.) I've hated how my innocent instincts for snuggles and physical touch have been perverted by society. Before my sister died, we got to the point where she wouldn't hold my hand in public because she didn't want people to think we were a "couple." As her sickness got worse, I think she got over it and unashamedly held my hand in public. I have to admit that even I felt self-conscious when I could tell people were looking at us and wondering what our hand-holding meant. I just chose not to care and held her hand anyway, and I don't regret it—especially now that she's gone and I can't hold her hand anymore.

We need to reaffirm to our kids what kinds of touch are appropriate and inappropriate. This isn't just important for helping them understand themselves, but also for helping protect them against predators when they know what kinds of touch are inappropriate. In fact, the more appropriate touch your kids receive from you, the better they will be able to tell when someone is touching them inappropriately. They can say, "Mommy and Daddy don't touch me like that." Affirm and model *phileo* love and platonic touch.

4. Male and Female He Created Them

Together, we reflect the *imago dei* in a way that man and woman cannot on their own. We need words and categories to defend this *imago dei* to our kids, and we need the care, tact, and understanding to model healthy relationships to a world that is, frankly, starving for love.

Yes, the new sexual ethic is concerning. It seeks to normalize sexuality that mars the *imago dei*. We should not support an agenda raised against the knowledge of God. But *do not confuse the ideology for people.* We are called to love *all*—no matter their understanding of sexuality and gender. We are called to love people and demolish bad ideas. May we never mistake the two. Never.

 DISCUSSION QUESTIONS 

1. **Icebreaker:** As a child, how did you understand gender expression? Did you feel that you fit the norm established by your peers, or did you have to change to fit in?

2. **Main theme:** *Kids are being taught to deny gender as an objective fact, leaving them confused about God's design, romantic attraction, and even their identity.* Describe ways you're already seeing the faulty logic of the Genderbread curriculum play out in culture.

3. **Self-evaluation:** Have you ever tried to urge your child into a gender stereotype? How about discouraging them from doing something that was gender atypical? How did that affect your son or daughter?

4. **Brainstorm:** Together, make a list of ways you can affirm your children in their sexuality. How can you nurture your kids' tendencies toward athleticism, leadership, or quiet contemplative work no matter their gender?

5. **Release the bear:** This week, talk with your kids about friendship. Discuss how admiration and attraction are not necessarily romantic, but simply appreciation for the way God designed one of His children.

6. **Pray:** Pray over your children's friendships this week. Ask the Lord to provide them with close, intimate, same-sex friendships so they can grow up knowing the difference between friendship and sexual attraction.

Sex-Positivity

Anything Goes If It's Consensual

AMY AND HILLARY

Sex-positivity. You might not have heard the term, but you've definitely heard the concept—and this new movement is actively shaping your child's view of sexuality. It shares a good amount of ideology with the sexual revolution of the '60s, but with fewer tambourines and more deodorant.

Its ideas can be traced back a century to a man named Wilhelm Reich, the man who popularized the phrase "sexual revolution."[1] His goal was to free sexuality from the social and religious structures that taught that sex should be limited to married adults. He encouraged open sexual boundaries for all (including young adolescents), was a champion for abortion, and taught that sex could cure mental disorders. This made even Sigmund Freud (his mentor) roll his eyes. (Good grief—if *Freud* thinks you've gone too far with the whole sex thing, you've *definitely* gone too far.)

So why would a chapter on current sexual issues reference someone that even Freud found excessive? Because the beliefs of Reich (and others like him) are now being promoted en masse. Today, sex-positivity websites praise Reich as the leader of sexual liberation. His views supporting promiscuity, abortion on demand, and comprehensive sex ed are being pushed as healthcare. His materialistic view of the universe asserted that the physical world was all there is, and it promised health and even salvation through sex.[2] In short, Reich's views advocate a sexual worldview that is still leading the charge on school campuses across the country.

I probably don't have to tell you that this sex-positive lifestyle is everywhere in mainstream media. Take Cardi B's song "WAP." When this moral dumpster fire of a song hit the airwaves, business partner Brooklyn Johnny defended the explicit lyrics as a way for women to level the sexual playing field: "Men can talk about whatever...they aren't getting scrutinized."[3] Women should be able to be just as confident.

Who cares that this definition of "confidence" is degrading toward women and men? Nope, let's demand the right to objectify ourselves just like the guys do because nothing says "I'm a confident female" like grinding in a pool of water around colorful fountains shaped like a woman's backside! What do you think, Mamas? Sound about right?

I can't begin to tell you how tantalizing this sounds to teen girls. Yes, even yours. From an early age they have absorbed the cultural message that being sexy gets you ahead in life. They see it in their toys, they see it in their clothes, and they see it dancing across their afternoon shows. Social media expands a teen's social peer group to global levels while fostering an addictive, perform-reward cycle for validation (which we'll talk about in chapter 11). By the time they are in high school, sexually explicit material barely makes a blip on the conviction radar. So when their hormones are kicked into overdrive and a cleverly titled sexual movement paints promiscuity as a positive way to know thyself, many girls will happily leave their convictions at home. As for the guys? Well, let's just say the guys are happy that the girls have *finally* gotten the memo.

If our kids are to stand a chance, they have to be able to recognize the lies of progressive movements like these and, in Nancy Pearcey's words, see the "Christian worldview as a viable alternative."[4]

ROAR Like a Mother!

RECOGNIZE the Message

Activists will point to Reich for the origins of the sex-positivity movement, but much of the undertaking has been shaped by the desire to soothe past hurts and prevent future harm. Even sex-positive activists struggle to define what the movement is and isn't.[5] However, there are three key points they all agree on.

1. The Only Thing That Matters Is Consent

Like all worldviews, sex-positivity has a source of morality, and it's found in the concept of consent. (Remember the new sex ed guidelines in chapter 5?) It's like the mythical philosopher's stone, but instead of turning whatever you consent to into gold, you turn it into *good.* The label *good* can apply to anything from strict abstinence to the kinkiest kink that ever kinked. As long as you and whomever you've got tied to a bedpost have consented to what's going on, then nothing is wrong with the pleasure it brings. Whatever you mutually approve of is now considered moral, valuable, and worthy of celebration and protection.

2. Thou Shalt Not Judge

Not only has "good" been redefined as "consent," but sex-positive people would never dream of judging anyone else's decisions. (On the plus side, no one can say anything against you for being "cisgender" and abstinent until marriage.) In turn, however, you're not allowed to discourage someone from, say, having an anonymous tryst with some couple they met on a partner swap website.

Sex-positivity emphasizes personal agency and pleasure while minimizing any kind of moral judgment.[6] To be truly sex-positive, says one expert, you "have to genuinely believe that other people can have sex any way they want with whoever they want, so long as consent is involved."[7] If you find yourself cringing at another person's choices, then you're being sex-negative.

This anti-judgment platform means your personal convictions and sex-positivity will be at odds. Like someone being pulled out of a cult, you'll have to work to deprogram your conscience—and silence the Holy Spirit, for that matter—from reacting negatively to any sexual choice that's consensual. Only when you have been fully desensitized and support your brothers and sisters (and children too) in navigating their sexuality can you truly be sex-positive.

3. There Are No Taboos

This open-mindedness isn't going to come on its own. Nope, it has to be fostered. Any sexual stigmas that have existed in the past—whether because they were grossly immoral or just physically unhealthy—must be erased. This is accomplished through open and comprehensive discussion about *alllll* the things. Every question is welcome. The goal of sex-positivity is transparency, affirmation, and the nurturing of sexuality at each developmental age, from childhood on up. This is one of the objectives of the comprehensive sex education movement. What better way to get people to value sexual "diversity" than by discussing every possible sex act in all its glory through the 12 most formative years of a child's life?[8] But don't worry—it's done in an "age appropriate" (cough) manner, of course. But then again, according to the NSES standards, it's "age appropriate" to ask middle schoolers to explain the difference between oral, anal, and vaginal sex.[9]

OFFER Discernment

Before we go into the lies of sex-positivity, let's look at the biblical truths we can affirm. For one, the brokenness of our fallen world is never more obvious than when we have to sit our boys and girls down and explain the importance of consent. But it's much broader than #MeToo. Sex-positivity highlights the importance of continued respect and autonomy in all relationships—something we here at Mama Bear Apologetics fully support.

Sex-positivity also makes huge leaps where some churches have traditionally fallen flat. I mean—seriously, folks. Have you read some of the descriptions of what the bride and groom are looking forward to doing in Song of Solomon? They weren't eating raisin cakes for the fiber. They were looking forward to getting *busy*! Sex-positivity points out what the church should have been shouting all along: Sex is good! Pleasure is good! Desire is good! As my

(Amy's) son once shouted as he tore through the house naked, "My body is beautiful!" Yes, it is, but put some pants on, son. You're scaring the neighbors.

We also affirm how sex-positivity encourages better communication when it comes to sex. Frankly, the church has tiptoed around this topic far too much. Christian kids have been ridiculed as being notoriously ignorant about the human body and sometimes clueless about STDs. Treating sex as such a hush-hush topic has led to young Christian married couples either suffering in silence when things don't go smoothly, or seeking out secular resources for help because the church hasn't provided many. We don't have to affirm everything to teach both medically accurate and biblical information.

So yes, sex-positivity is highlighting some important points, but not everything that glitters is gold. Beneath the shiny surface is an entirely destructive worldview masquerading as a "healthy and positive" viewpoint.

Lie #1: If It's Consensual, It's Moral

Obviously, everyone agrees that consent is vital in any healthy relationship. It shows that we are being respectful of ourselves and others. But it makes a terrible foundation for morality. Why? Because consent doesn't actually make a moral claim about an action. It only says that you're willing to let that action occur.

The concept of pleasure suffers from the exact same problem; it cannot make any moral claims. Pleasure only says that you enjoy what you're doing. News flash: *Sin is usually enjoyable.*

Lie #2: Pleasure Is the Only Purpose of Sex

There is a reason pleasure takes center stage in the sex-positivity movement. Well-meaning Christians have sometimes painted *pleasure itself* as sinful (or at least secular).

Yes, physical pleasure without any acknowledgment of the spiritual ramifications of sex treats the body and the soul as two separate things. Sex is an intensely spiritual act, and when we separate the physical act from the spiritual, it's like we are trying to separate our bodies from our souls. Do you know what an actual separation of the body and soul is called? Death. That is literally what death is—when the soul separates from the body.[10] And when people figuratively separate their body and their soul during the act of sex, is it any wonder that they might psychologically long for its completion?

I (Hillary) noticed a trend while researching all the ways we humans have strayed from God's design. Almost every deviation is accompanied by an *increased risk of suicide and suicide attempts.* As we'll see later in this chapter, there are statistically higher suicide rates and attempts among those who identify as LGBTQ+, with sexually active teens, and even within the BDSM community.[11] (BDSM is sexual activity whereby participants are aroused by inflicting [or receiving] pain during the act of sex.) When we separate physical pleasure from the *soul* purpose (pun intended) of sex, it makes people vulnerable to thoughts of suicide and death—at least, that's what the research seems to show.

Yes, sex is intended to be pleasurable. God created orgasms. But its pleasure was intended to reinforce a man's and woman's wedding vows in bodily form and prophetically point forward to the mystery of the church's eternal oneness with Christ. Even the chemicals involved (as we'll see in chapter 11) are intended to bind husband and wife together—spiritually, emotionally, and physically.

When we deviate from His plan, our bodies know it—even if our minds don't. If the Christian worldview is true—and especially what the Bible teaches about sex—then these suicide statistics make sense, sad as they are. We have separated our bodies from our souls and have an unfulfilled telos, which creates a longing that nothing in this world can satisfy.

Lie #3: All Judgments (Except This One) Are Wrong!

If you read our first book, you might remember the relativism chapter titled, "You're Wrong to Tell Me That I'm Wrong!" Moral relativism is the belief that objective truth (that is, truth that applies to everyone) doesn't exist. Only personal, subjective truth exists. (Thanks, postmodernism!) You can believe whatever you want so long as your truth doesn't say my truth is wrong. Because it's wrong to tell anyone that they're wrong—right?

While sex-positivity claims there are no objective standards (do whatever you want!), it *still* has an objective standard: Judging another person's sexuality is objectively wrong. Sex-positivity is basically just relativism applied to your sex life.

This is especially difficult for our kids when they are taught that affirming a biblical sexual morality is not only wrong but *oppressive*—which is essentially the message they are getting through their sex ed curriculum.[12] According to the new standards of worldly morality, they are required to not only affirm but *celebrate* the sexual choices of others.[13] Not doing so is a hateful form of disrespect. This is where our "I'm supposed to love like Jesus loved" kids are getting all turned around.

Lie #4: Sex-Positivity Leads to Freedom

The apostle Peter didn't know the phrase sex-positive, but he actually addresses this false teaching in his second epistle:

> They mouth empty, boastful words and, by appealing to the lustful desires of the flesh, they entice people who are just escaping from those who live in error. They promise them freedom, while they themselves are slaves of depravity (2 Peter 2:18-19).

What he means by "people who are just escaping from those who live in error" are the people turning to Christianity from their sex-positive culture. They *just escaped the error*, and then these false teachers hooked them right back in by teaching that Christianity and sexual immorality were compatible. Far from freedom, this kind of teaching leads people right back to the bondage they escaped from: bondage to their sexual desires.

The ideology also leads to some disturbing inferences about your worth as a person. But human beings have inherent value. This means your value isn't determined by anything outside of you. Not your job, your beauty, or your bank account. You are irreplaceable and immeasurably precious, with all the dignity and perks to life and liberty simply because you are a human being, made in God's image.

Remember the necessity of boundaries around something incredibly powerful and potentially destructive that we discussed in chapter 1? The same principle applies to things that have *value*. The more value something has, the more rules and boundaries we erect to protect it. This is why the *Mona Lisa* is behind glass—it is far too valuable to be exposed to a group of hacking, sneezing tourists all jockeying to snag a quick selfie for their Instagram.

Only when something doesn't have any inherent value can you do whatever you want with it, which turns out to be the skeleton lurking in the closet of sex-positivity. It encourages you to do whatever you want with whomever you want. The implicit message (that most people don't pick up on) is that you and your partner(s) have no inherent value worth protecting. Consent can't provide this value, and neither can pleasure. Sure, sex-positivity may sound like freedom, but in reality, it's saying that your body and what you do with it don't matter.

Lie #5: All Expressions of Sexuality Are Healthy

The new sex education standards place a huge emphasis on healthy sexuality. But as we saw in chapter 5, they define *healthy* as consensual and enjoyable. A big problem with this is that it outright denies that many of the sexual decisions that arise from sex-positivity (also called safer sex) are themselves dangerous.

Within the last 40 years, we've gone from two main STDs to 25.[14] Every day there are 8,000 new cases—three million a year—and that's just among teens.[15] And what is the medical community telling our girls about HPV? Do they tell them that, due to what is called the "transformational zone" on their cervixes, young women are at greater risk for contracting an infection?[16] Nope. Do they tell them that this zone gets smaller with age, so it's probably a good idea to wait for sexual activity? Oh, heck no. What about how birth control actually *enlarges* the transformational zone, increasing their risk? Of course not! That's sex-negative. So what are they told? Well, according to advice from Dr. Vanessa Cullins, the vice president for medical affairs at Planned Parenthood, "*Expect* to have HPV once you become sexually intimate."[17] You know, no biggie.

How is this the advice from a medical professional? Myriam Grossman states, "Instead of aiming for disease *prevention*, as is done in the fight against heart disease or obesity, the goal [of this ideology] is risk *reduction*—aka 'safer sex'—followed, when it fails to be safe enough, by *damage control*."[18]

That's just the tip of the physical effects. What about the emotional toll? As Grossman says, there is no condom for the heart.[19] One study that sampled 6,500 students showed that teens who were sexually active were more likely to be depressed and attempt suicide.[20] Another study with 8,000 youth showed similar results among teens who were romantically involved.[21] And in both these studies, girls were impacted far more. A low-commitment sexual encounter, Grossman reminds us, is a heart risk.

This is common sense, people. Yet common sense has suddenly become politically incorrect rocket science for the sake of sparing people's feelings. What was once considered "risky behavior" is now promoted as healthy sexual exploration. As far as we can tell, about the only behavior designated as "risky," according to sex-positivity, is not having regular checkups to find out *which* disease you just picked up. Oh, and not using condoms. They're all about condoms.

Lie #6: You Can Be a Sex-Positive Christian

Perhaps the most subtle lie our kids have swallowed is that Christianity and sex-positivity are compatible. To be both a Christian and sex-positive requires that you deny that God designed sex to be shared only between a man and woman in marriage. All those passages warning believers to flee from sexual immorality? Yeah, there's really no sin to repent of if you're sex-positive. In fact, there's even a Bible app your kids can use which will help them avoid such uncomfortable passages so they can "ditch toxic theology."[22]

The whole "God loves you and He wants you to be happy" thing suddenly means that anything that gives you pleasure gets the heavenly green light of approval. With just a few quick "positive" concessions, the believer denies God's wisdom and design, ignores the existence of sexual sin, and rejects Jesus's atonement for those sins. That isn't Christianity, folks.

Lie #7: If You're Not for Us, You're Sex-Negative!

The final lie we'll mention here really stacks the deck against our Christian kids. Sex-positivity says unless you affirm that all consensual pleasures are good and healthy, you are sex-negative! Booooo, you negative Nelly! This basically makes Christians sound like they hate sex, which is a flat-out lie and poor logic.

At the end of the day, the sex-positive movement is really just Romans 1:18-32 repackaged. Same outcome, different branding. If being the world's definition of "positive" means we have to ignore God and His teachings, enthrone our sexual urges, and encourage everyone else to do the same, then you can keep it. We'd rather be countercultural anyway…(#Romans12:2).

ARGUE for a Healthier Approach

As we can see, the whole sex-positive approach is more mud than marble. Like the seductress in Proverbs 5, this worldview tells you everything you want to hear. But each lie leads to brokenness, hurt, and more than a few rounds of penicillin. If we want our kids to be wise to the schemes of the world, they have to be able to see beyond the pretty packaging. Here are a few reminders of truth.

Truth #1: God Created Sex

This concept is best summed up by the fictional demon Wormwood in C.S. Lewis's book *The Screwtape Letters*.

> Never forget that when we are dealing with any pleasure in its healthy and normal and satisfying form, we are, in a sense, on the Enemy's ground. I know we have won many a soul through pleasure. All the same, it is His invention, not ours. He made the pleasures: all our research so far has not enabled us to produce one. All we can do is to encourage the humans to take the pleasures which our Enemy has produced, at times, or in ways, or in degrees, which He has forbidden.[23]

God created sex and God created pleasure. We would do better to allow an all-good God to determine what's positive rather than sinful man.

Truth #2: Not All Judgments Are Bad

There's a difference between making a judgment and judging like God judges. Even the most tolerant person makes hundreds of judgments every day. We are judging when we decide which parts of town are unsafe to walk in alone at night. We are judging when we take a sniff of that chicken to see if it's gone bad. We are judging when we decide to marry our spouses instead of other people. Even our kids are judging when they decide to hold our hand while they cross the street. Making judgments involves using a set of standards to make decisions. It's a requirement for wise living, and there is nothing wrong with that.

God gave us His commandments in order that we might live in right relationship with Him. It's not judging (in the McJudgy-pants way) to abide by those standards while encouraging other *Christians* to do the same. Neither is it judgy to point out the health risks and benefits of particular actions. That's just called knowledge, and we recommend er'body getting some, Christians and non-Christians alike!

Truth #3: Pleasure Is a Great Gift but a Terrible God

Sexual pleasure is a good thing. God designed us to experience it, and we are grateful for this aspect of our humanity. But all good gifts can be turned into idols, and pleasure makes a terrible one. Solomon experienced everything pleasure had to offer, and you know what he concluded (in basically all of Ecclesiastes)? It was all meaningless apart from God. Men and women who seek the comfort of pleasure are overwhelmingly left depressed and saddened to find that it fails to give them hope and purpose.

A Final Word

To paraphrase General James Mattis, the most important battlefield is the six inches between your ears.[24] Mamas, that's exactly where sex-positivity is waging war right now. And it's happening on every media platform. If we want our kiddos to stand firm against the cultural tide, then we have to help them understand God's design. They need to know which falsehoods are masquerading as truth and understand how God redeems the brokenness each lie brings. Once our kiddos can do that, they'll become beacons of hope to those around them. Let's do our part to help them shine!

REINFORCE Through Discussion, Discipleship, and Prayer

1. From infancy on up, we need to remind our kids where true pleasure comes from. Whenever our kids enjoy something, remind them that God was the One who created that enjoyment. Horseback riding? Sugar? Laughter? Puppy snuggles? Sex? All designed by God for our pleasure.

2. We don't need to go into sexual appetites with our little ones, so let's use another appetite to help them form the correct categories. In this instance, we'll use tongues and our bodies. Our tongues are part of our bodies, but they are only a *part*. There are things that our tongues enjoy, like ice cream. Ice cream is good! God created sugar so we could enjoy ice cream! But ice cream doesn't have a lot of potassium or magnesium or zinc or vitamins. There are other parts of our bodies that need these things in order to function well. How disrespectful would it be to our bodies to only eat what makes our tongues happy and not what makes the other parts of our body happy? As they get older, we can reinforce the same concept with sex. Instead of only making the tongue happy, it's...other body parts (wink!).

3. Pleasure can easily take over when we and our kids lack self-control. Discuss with your kids the importance of self-control. A few great passages you can use are Ecclesiastes 3:1-11, Proverbs 25:27-28, and Titus 2:11-12. Ask your kids (especially your teens) a few reflection questions: What does this passage say about the importance of self-control? Without self-control, how can pleasure turn out to be a bad thing? What are some practical benefits to controlling our desire for pleasure? What reasonable boundaries can we put in place to protect ourselves from walking into temptation? Which friends can we count on to help keep us accountable?

4. If you have older kids, read *The Screwtape Letters* together. Talk about different kinds of pleasures that can lead to disadvantageous outcomes because they are not being used the way God intended. How can food be misused? Alcohol? Nasal spray? I'm serious when I say that literally *anything* can be used to excess or in the wrong way and cause harm. As unfortunate frat boys have discovered, a person can even die from drinking too much water.

5. For high school or college kids, read Miriam Grossman's book *Unprotected* and Nancey Pearcey's *Love Thy Body* together. Then take an honest look at how media (movies, television shows, music) portray sex. Is it an accurate representation or not? What truths are missing? What messages have you believed that aren't actually true? Why do you think it's a struggle for young people to avoid believing the messages like the ones found in sex-positivity? When do you find yourself most tempted? What steps can you take to safeguard yourself and a (current or future) boy or girlfriend from falling into sin?

PAWS for Prayer by Julie Loos

PRAISE God for Who He Is

Father God, I praise You for You reveal what is true, good, and positive. You are the protector of Your children. Your peace guards our hearts and minds through Christ Jesus (Philippians 4:7). You and You alone are the Creator of life and therefore our sexuality. As its Creator, You have authority over it.

ADMIT Where We Have Fallen Short of His Standard

Search me and show me, God, where I have fallen prey to the lies of the world about sexuality and not upheld Your view. Forgive me and forgive our nation for untethering sexuality from Your strong cord of goodness. Forgive us for promoting promiscuity, advancing abortion laws, and selling a sex ed curriculum that leads young people to "sell" their bodies to an unholy alliance with the world. For equating morality with consent, for making pleasure our god, for silencing Your Holy Spirit and common sense. We repent of celebrating sins clothed in deception.

WORSHIP WITH THANKSGIVING for the Things He Has Done

Thank You for the gift of sex and that in Your goodness You set up appropriate boundaries within which it should be opened. You have gifted us with worth and inherent value because we are made in Your image. Your words and Your ways are the true definition of sex-positivity.

SUBMIT Yourselves and Your Requests to God

Help us, we pray, that we may live and proclaim, positively, that the only healthy sexuality is holy sexuality. That we may value faith over feelings, logic over labeling. Give us the wisdom to recognize lies and point them out to our children. Help us be sensitive to Your Spirit and not desensitized by culture. Show us how to teach our children that Your boundaries for sex and marriage are not oppressive but freeing. That when they honor their bodies, they honor You. Help us raise up a generation as fierce as lions who will roar in the face of false narratives and positively proclaim that Your ways are higher and better.

 DISCUSSION QUESTIONS 

1. **Icebreaker:** Was hookup culture a thing when you were in high school or college? Was dating still common? How have you noticed the dating scene change throughout the decades?

2. **Main theme:** *Sex-positivity teaches that sexual morality is summed up by pleasure and consent and nothing else.* Where have you seen the messages of sex-positivity in your parenting journey? Why are consent and pleasure bad litmus tests for health and morality?

3. **Self-evaluation:** Have you ever had any habits you enjoyed that really

weren't good for you? Where have you believed the lie that one part of your body deserved pleasure to the detriment of your whole self?

4. **Brainstorm:** How have you seen the sex-positive movement displayed in recent movies? List as many reasons as you can think of for why our enemy is trying to sexualize our culture. In what ways does a lax view of sex prohibit the gospel? (Hint: Think in terms of chapter 3 and Romans 1:18-23.)

5. **Release the bear:** Sometimes it's time for a media purge. Go through your movies and music with your kids. Really look at the messages there. Are there any DVDs or songs that are better left in the trash? Choose to not be a part of sex-positivity's messages, and make your home a safer place for *good* movies and music.

CHAPTER 9

Queer Theory

A Whole New World(view)

HILLARY

My friend Cassy's husband (a self-proclaimed Christian) left her several years ago to pursue a bisexual, polyamorous lifestyle with a revolving door of multiple simultaneous partners—some men, some women, and some men who identify as women. She has joint custody of the kids and can't shield them from this. A few years into this arrangement, her son began identifying as a transgender woman and (see if you can keep this all straight) is now dating a girl who identifies as a transgender boy. To summarize, he's a boy who claims he's a girl, dating a girl who claims she's a boy. He calls this transgender-male-identifying girl his "boyfriend" and she calls him (her transgender-female-identifying guy) her "girlfriend." Mama Bears: Welcome to the "modern family." This story is the epitome of what it looks like when the ideologies from sex-positivity and this chapter (queer theory) meet the real world.

By now you can see that the education your kids are getting is very different from the one we got as kids, especially as it relates to sex and gender. In chapter

2, we discussed the Christian worldview and how it interacted with our understanding of sexuality and gender. In this chapter, we're going to do two things. First, we'll present what is, as of 2025, the competing worldview to the Judeo-Christian sexual ethic. Secondly, we're going to ROAR through it!

As a refresher, the Christian worldview answers the big questions like:

- Where did we come from? (Created by God with a purpose—telos.)
- What does it mean to be human? (Male and female in the image of God.)
- What is our purpose? (Worship and relationship with God, community with each other, multiply and fill the earth, and exercise wise stewardship/dominion over it.)
- What is morality? (Living according to our original design as seen through God's moral commandments and the law of love.)
- What went wrong in the world, and how do we fix it? (Sin, salvation, and sanctification.)

For centuries, we in the West structured laws around reinforcing morality and punishing evil as understood by the Judeo-Christian worldview. School sports even left Sundays and Wednesday nights open, assuming kids were at church and youth group. But times they are a-changing. As my parents' pastor often says, "We (Christians) are no longer the home team." Christianity is being pitted against a worldview that answers the above questions very differently—especially the questions regarding morality. (It felt straight-up symbolic that Easter 2024 fell on the same day as the National Day of Trans Visibility.)[1]

Up until recently, many of Christianity's tenets were considered common sense. Truth exists and we should try to find it and live by it (John 8:32). Let kids be kids; don't introduce them to anything that might take away their innocence (Matthew 18:6; Song of Solomon 8:4). Remember that all are born as little narcissists who need to learn how to deny their own desires (1 Peter 2:11) and treat others the way they want to be treated (Matthew 7:12). We should punish bad behavior and reward good behavior (Romans 13:3-5). You know, stuff like that. Why should we defend these ideas if everyone essentially agrees?

But that's the thing, Mama Bears: Not everyone agrees anymore! Or they at least disagree on what counts as good, bad, age appropriate, family, and even responsible. And I don't think many people are aware of the *degree* to which this new worldview disagrees. Friends, we are living in a whole new world... No one to tell anyone "no" or where to go, or say they're only dreaming. Our world is getting turned upside down, and we are losing a major cultural battle because the average Christian doesn't even realize we're in one—at least not one that will affect *them.*

From Critical Theory to Queer Theory

If you remember the section from page 100, the two main roots for the sex education standards were postmodernism (everyone can determine their own truth) and Marxism (everything comes down to people trying to leverage power to oppress others). Mama Bears, truth and common sense have left the building! These are both seen as crafty tools used by the powers-that-be to manipulate the common folk. Supposedly, the elites have tricked the have-nots into thinking that marriage and family are normal, but it's really just a ruse that allows them—the haves—to consolidate their wealth. Even what we consider "knowledge" in the educational sphere (including scientific knowledge) is a ploy! It's a trick! It's just imperialists leveraging their "power," convincing those who are ignorant that there is such a thing as truth when it is *really* just the elites imposing their own social norms onto the rest of society so that they—the dominant class—can stay in power.[2]

So what does the whole truth-is-a-power-play mantra mean for things like morality, law, and Christianity? In Marx's words, "Law, morality, [and] religion are...[oppressor] prejudices behind which lurk...[the oppressor's] interests...Communism abolishes eternal truths, it abolishes all religion, and all morality."[3] Translation: Law, morality, and religion are just disguises for "rich-people privilege," and Communism don't play that game. Mama Bears, this is not me "getting political." This is a Christian issue because you cannot advocate for an ideology that reduces truth and morality to power plays and still believe in the truth of Christ and our obligation to submit ourselves to God's moral law.

Spot the Faulty Logic

A: All truth claims are power plays.
FC: Christianity claims to know truth.
C: Christian truths are power plays.

The next step in this ideological mudslide was critical theory (CT), which arose in the 1920s and 1930s. CT adopted a broader definition of power. Instead of money determining who was the oppressed and who was the oppressor, CT focused on who did and did not have *social power*—meaning the influence to determine what was considered "normal" or acceptable in a society. When CT expanded into identity politics, oppressors and oppressed became defined by race, class, sex, gender, ableness, religion, or age. Within each category, a person could be an oppressor (with social power), oppressed (without social power), or somewhere in between (basically me in high school). And each type of "oppression" was associated with its own kind of *ism* or *phobia* like racism, sexism, ableism, homophobia, transphobia, etc. (See the chart on page 104 for an abbreviated version.)

Basically, according to CT and identity politics, you have the top dogs (middle-aged, white, cisgender, heterosexual, Protestant men) on one side and everyone else (non-white, disabled, too young or too old, transgender, women, and other minorities) on the other side, all vying for whatever scraps of influence are left. And here's where we get to the crux of queer theory: norms.

As hinted at above, queer theorists believe that social power on the societal level *created* "cultural norms" (which supposedly benefit those in power and push minorities to the edge of society). These "norms" show up in things like gender stereotypes and heteronormativity (a fancy word meaning that sex between men and women should be the norm). Cultural norms determined what kinds of sexual relations were permitted (heterosexual), promoted (marriage), or penalized (homosexuality or polygamy). Norms also dictated what kinds of sexual activities were taboo (incest, pedophilia, or sadomasochism). But again, these were seen as *power plays* by those who embodied the gender binary and traditional marriage.

The confusing thing about queer theory is that it isn't (what I'd call) a *positive* theory, meaning that it aims *at* something. For example, Christianity aims *at* holiness. Sex-positivity aims *at* sexual autonomy. Queer theory is the opposite; it is defined primarily by what it stands *against*. And what does it stand against? Anything that is considered *normal*. Authors Logan Lancing and James Linsdsay unpack this in their book *The Queering of the American Child*.

> Queer theory adopts the disposition that certain people illegitimately declared themselves to be "normal" and branded everyone else "abnormal," "deviant," even "degenerate" and "perverse" in order to include themselves in mainstream society and marginalize the *Others*..."To queer" is "to destabilize the social cultural and political normalizing structure that work to solidify identities and in doing so skew power toward the "norm." Put simply, "to queer" is to challenge and eliminate *normalcy*.[4]

Queer theory takes critical theory a step further and asserts that everything (and we mean e.v.e.r.y.t.h.i.n.g.) that is considered "normal" is just a socially constructed rule meant to oppress people who don't fit in. To truly free people from oppression, we need to remove all the "normal" constraints imposed by society so everyone can discover and express his or her "authentic" self. And to play devil's advocate, who's *really* to say what is normal? "Normal" is not exactly something I've ever been accused of being.

However, queer theorists aren't just advocating for people to be their little oddball selves in terms of clothing and career choices; no, they are rebelling against the innate design of humanity (can we also be animals or fairies?), sex (does procreation even matter?), and gender (does it exist?). Queering—as a verb—means pushing against what is considered "normal." For example, queering gender means purposefully doing the opposite of what would be expected according to gender norms. (One chap who was helping me check out library books explained that his red nail polish was for a class assignment where they were *required* to do something for a whole week that went against gender norms. Yes, universities are queering homework!)

And while most queer theorists currently stick to challenging gender and sexual norms, it won't stop there; *all norms* are now up for redefinition. I recommend going to Google Scholar and just typing in the word "queering." It has research on how to queer anything—from health to history.

The body-positivity movement advocates for "queering the body" to "disrupt binaries" and "reimagine the fat body as healthy."[5] Books like *Nobody's Normal: How Culture Created the Stigma of Mental Illness* question the "norms" of mental health. Or how about the "normal" classroom where teachers teach and students learn? University educator programs now promote Paulo Freire's model where teacher and student learn "alongside each other" as co-learners. Interpreting poems in English class? Maybe I can understand a teacher learning from a student's fresh perspective...but surely they don't mean things like *math*, right? Actually, they do, as seen with curricula like *A Pathway to Equitable Math Instruction*, which questions the "norm" that there is only "one right answer." Apparently, this is a relic from "the industrial revolution where precision and accuracy were highly valued."[6] As opposed to now, where it's not?! #facepalm

So when we say someone isn't following "the norm," we do not just mean, "Oh, she's quirky and likes blue, spiky hair."[7] According to queer theory, people "not following the norm" in their dress or behavior is them *being true to their identity*. For example, a person doesn't just enjoy dressing like an animal (furry), but they identify *as* an animal (therian).[8] A person doesn't just wear a fairy or elf costume (cosplay); they now identify *as* a fairy or an elf (otherkin).[9] Forget male and female; what it means to be *human* is now up for debate.

So how is this affecting our kids? Remember, the only requirement to have a queer identity nowadays is to be outside what is considered "normal." And really, who considers themselves totally normal? Nobody I know—which is why I don't think it's a coincidence that we are seeing such a rise in our kids identifying as the *Q* in LGBTQ+. And once a kid starts identifying as queer, they start going down allllll the queer rabbit holes.

Furthermore, since "queer" is now considered a "protected" (that is, oppressed) minority identity, it is being championed and defended by all the activists. You can bully kids for having big noses or red hair, or being skinny, or just plain weird. But if that same kid claims to be *queer* and is bullied, then the entire pride brigade will hunt down the (queerphobic) perps and destroy them. What kid doesn't want to be protected from bullying? And if all I need to do (as a white, cisgender, heterosexual person) to be part of the protected group is to identify as nonbinary or queer, then *sign me up.*

A Whole New World(view)

Queer theory may sound ludicrous to anyone not steeped in its tenets. But sadly, if our kids are exposed to enough of its assumptions, then QT's conclusions sound logical and consistent. Even though queer theorists deny that it is a "worldview," it still *operates* as one. In this section, we'll discuss how it answers each of the main worldview questions, and what that means for sexuality.

Origin and Identity: Where Did We Come from and What Does It Mean to Be Human?

When it comes to origins, there really are only two options: Either we were created for a purpose, or we evolved.[10] And if we only evolved, then we can continue to evolve...however we like. This leads us to the topic of identity, where you'll hear the phrase "authentic self" tossed around a lot. Queer theory teaches that the authentic self is who (or what) the person *would* have been (or how they would have identified) had they not been constrained by society's norms. Perhaps they'd have a different gender, have multiple genders, or even belong to completely different species. In short, who I am is who I imagine myself to be, and no outward reality can constrain me. Trying to change who I am is a type of cruel conversion therapy, no matter if it's my sexuality, gender identity, or any other aspect of my authentic self.[11] Who I am is based on *my* psychology alone, and only I have access to that—so listen when I tell you who I am!

Why This Matters for Sexuality: As we saw in chapter 2, the Christian worldview teaches that God created us for a purpose, in His image, and therefore we have worth and value. But if humans simply evolved, then we have no real way to argue that humans have any of these qualities. Sure, "human rights" can be ascribed later, but what is ascribed by one human can easily be *un*ascribed by another—as we've seen happen with things like slavery, abortion, antisemitism, and other genocides. Furthermore, if we were *not* created for a purpose, then neither were our bodies; therefore, what we *do* with our bodies doesn't matter. Any sexual identity we adopt or sexual behavior we choose is no better or worse than monogamous sex within marriage.

Truth and Reality: What Is True (And Says Who?)

If humans evolved through a mindless, unguided process, then there's no author (i.e., *author*ity) outside oneself; the concepts of healthy and normal merely represent people vying for power—shoehorning everyone else into an arbitrary box so that their own version of "normal" rules the roost. And how do they accomplish this? Through language. Language is how we pass down knowledge from the past. (And if you remember the Foucault quote from page 99, words are where "power and knowledge are joined together.")

And here is where QT gets really subversive. If truth and reality are just social constructs *conveyed* by the language we use, then we can *create* truth and reality by inventing (or redefining) words however we like. Essentially, truth and reality can be fashioned, refashioned, and refashioned again for each new generation. We can be liberated from the antiquated norms of bygones past—and our children should feel free to do the same! (So use their pronouns and accept their sexual nomenclature.) Mama Bears, have you noticed all these language games? And are they starting to make sense now?

Why This Matters for Sexuality: As stated on pages 25 and 47, our sexual behaviors—and the language we use to describe it—tell the world who (or what) our authority is. And make no mistake, all worldviews ultimately come down to the big *A* (authority). For Christians, our authority is God, but for queer theory, the authority is self—and not just any self, but the *authentic self*, which a person has to first discover. Our words, Mama Bears, tell others who our authority is; calling oneself a "gay Christian" (even if celibate) claims an identity (and thus authority) apart from Christ.

Brokenness: What Went Wrong in the World?

According to queer theory, the "sin" that entered the world was cultural norms—and more specifically, gender and sexual norms. The norms are supposedly the enemy of the authentic self because they stop us from expressing who we really are. Sexual norms are merely boundaries to be shattered and destroyed. Any barrier to doing exactly what I want is oppression. Who says I can't strap on size-Z prosthetic breasts and teach high school shop class?[12] You're *privileging* all the people who *don't* want to wear prosthetic breasts and teach shop class and *marginalizing* those who do!

Why This Matters for Sexuality: God created sex and gender. Male and female were created to come together in marriage, make babies, and raise boys and girls to become men and women. Sexual norms were intended to reinforce His design! We cannot jump on the cultural bandwagon and concede that it is "unloving" to reinforce God's sexual design if we still want to call ourselves Christians.

Remember that slippery slope we were told didn't exist when the Obergefell decision redefined marriage? Well, friends, that was a Slip 'N Slide we can't ungrease. We now have people identifying as fictosexual (only attracted to fictious characters) and marrying avatars.[13] We have a growing movement called *infantilism* where adults identify as toddlers; they even have their own conferences and conventions.[14] The prohibitions against incest were always predicated on not causing harm to children born from that union. But now, having children is considered a "choice" rather than a natural byproduct of sexual activity. So should we start ignoring that taboo as well? And Mama Bears, you need to be aware of what is going on within the MAP (Minor Attracted Person) community. Apparently they have been persecuted and stigmatized for far too long, according to a bunch of recent TED talks and academic papers.[15]

When we argue for one kind of "sexual minority," then no other sexual minorities are off limits—and yes, this will apply to someone identifying as a MAP who wants to teach your kindergartner.[16] Denying them the equal right to teach kids will be considered bigoted, unjust, and a byproduct of unfair stigmatization.

How steep can this slippery slope get?! Consider the 2024 Australian headline where ninth graders were taught about how to have "respectful conversations" around *bestiality*...in a presentation that began with the phrase: "I can see queerly now."[17]

Morality: What Constitutes Good and Evil? And How Do We Know?

If the original problem is oppressive powers that force people into strict roles, then evil is any system that maintains these norms (*cough* *Christianity* *cough*). The "highest good" is discovering and living as one's true self. Morality, according to QT, means allowing people to 1) accurately identify their true selves and 2) live freely as those selves without feeling stigmatized or having societal constraints. In a society that embraces those two tenets, evil ceases being something people do; rather, evil becomes anyone preventing anyone from doing what they want.

Why This Matters for Sexuality: As Catholic priest Dwight Longenecker tweeted,

> First we overlook evil. Then we permit evil. Then we legalize evil. Then we promote evil. Then we celebrate evil. Then we persecute those who still call it evil.[18]

Friends, there is a difference between culture not agreeing on things like biblical sexuality, and a culture actively promoting sin. FYI: Sin is never content living "peacefully" alongside righteousness. It usually becomes an all-or-nothing totalitarian takeover. We will get to the point (as if we're not there already) when *judging* sexual perversion is considered more evil than the perversion itself. You might even find society trying to break down your door and kill you for promoting such hate. And no, I'm not exaggerating; this has already happened at least once in recorded history. Go take a look at Genesis 19:9.

Spot the Faulty Logic

A: It is evil to stigmatize people who are living as their authentic selves.
FC: My authentic self is sexually attracted to children.
C: It is evil to stigmatize sexual attraction to children.

Redemption: How Do We Fix What Is Broken?

Just as Christianity has two stages of salvation and sanctification, queer theory has two stages: fixing what is wrong and then living what is right. If queer-salvation is attained through *discovering* one's authentic self, then queer-sanctification is achieved through *living out* one's authentic self. Queer evangelism, then, means advocating for others to do the same by actively and publicly tearing down all the norms—especially in front of impressionable kids. This is the entire crux of drag queen story hour. It teaches kids that bravery means bucking against the norms imposed upon them—just like the nice lady with the deep voice and lots of makeup.

Activism is essential for queer sanctification. It is not enough to quietly believe what you want to believe or even to be tolerant of everyone else's identities and behaviors; to truly fix what went wrong in the world, you must also be an agent of social and political change. This is why *advocacy* is one of the 12 pillars in the NSES curriculum.

Why This Matters for Sexuality: What does this look like in practice? You've already seen it; it looks like pronoun pins,[19] rainbows in the classroom, LGBTQ+ clubs,[20] and pride parades at schools.[21] Justice means representing LGBTQ+ characters in cartoons,[22] books,[23] and even *The GayBCs* for your toddler. Mama Bears, this especially looks like protocols (and punishments) for misgendering (using the wrong pronoun) or deadnaming (using the person's birth name, and not their new chosen name). These are now classified as harmful[24] at best, and full-on criminal at worst.[25] If nothing else, it's at least considered a human rights violation.

ROAR Like a Mother!

I am hoping by now your heads are exploding in the best way possible and that you are feeling empowered to tackle these topics with your kids! Are all the things you've noticed going on (but couldn't quite explain) finally making sense? Queer theory is a worldview issue, Mama Bears. A whole new worldview. Let's review with a good ol' fashioned ROAR!

RECOGNIZE the Message

1. Biological Sex and Gender Identity Are Totally Different

The separation of biological sex and "gender identity" is still pretty new. It was first introduced to the public in the November 1966 press release for the Johns Hopkins Gender Identity Clinic and soon after entered the common vernacular. And just like that (ba bada baaaaa!), sex and gender identity became totally different, with sex referring to anatomy and gender referring to how closely a person psychologically identified with masculinity or femininity—a problematic concept we'll discuss in the gender identity chapter.

2. Gender Is a Social Construct

According to QT, any perceived differences between men and women are baseless relics of older generations, telling people what boys and girls were (or should be) like. Society-past decided how boys and girls were supposed to act, and we perpetuated the myth by conforming to these made-up stereotypes. In the words of Judith Butler, "Gender is culturally constructed…gender cannot be said to follow from a sex in any one way."[26]

3. The Gender Binary Is Oppressive

According to QT, the terms *male* and *female* say nothing about who a person is inside. Forcing individuals to "pick" a gender limits how they can express their "authentic self." And as we saw in the worldview section, limiting people from expressing their authentic self is oppression, and oppression is injustice. And injustice anywhere is a threat to justice everywhere! Thus your little bears will be told that loving like Jesus means freeing people from the oppression of any and every gender norm. Gender justice now requires helping to disrupt and dismantle any norms associated with male and female. Just watch how quickly proponents trip over themselves praising your son for donning a princess dress.[27]

3. Stop Telling Me I Don't Exist! (Or: You Are Erasing My Identity!)

Language is super important to queer theorists because they believe language and reality interact in a reciprocal manner. As we said before, QT teaches that words don't just *describe* what is real; rather, reality can actually be *created* through words. To refuse to use the words for someone's reality (that is, their preferred terminology for their pronouns, gender, or sexual identity) is to "erase" their existence by denying the language that they feel identifies them. No language = no existence. If a person claims to be a non-binary lesbian and you say, "That doesn't make sense," you have essentially erased their existence if that is how they identify.

OFFER Discernment

As in all things Mama Bear, we need to acknowledge the *truths* queer theory is based on. Were it not based on any kind of truth, nobody would follow it. And the original proponents of queer theory had some very legitimate beefs which we—especially the church—need to grapple with if we are going to teach our little bears how to live as boys and girls and later godly men and women.

Can we agree that some norms are wrong and oppressive? Absolutely. (When did it become "normal" to force kids to sit for eight hours a day with no recess?) Are some *gender* norms oppressive? Also yes! (Why are wives who work full-time often still expected to do the lion's share of cooking and cleaning on top of their 9–5?) We can also agree that words and names are incredibly powerful. Words can create categories to help us better understand the world and each other. (Before we knew what dyslexia was, kids like my grandmother were just called "stupid.")

Accurately describing something is good. But people misuse language when they take a *descriptor* and turn it into an *identity*, an immutable "I am" statement that is outside their control. We submit our labels to Christ; we don't submit ourselves to our labels and expect God to rubber-stamp whatever follows. Proclivities and preferences do not change our identity in Christ, and the end goal of our identity is holiness, not individualism. We affirm these legitimate points queer theorists have brought to the forefront, and we say thank you! But what are some of the lies that have snuck in?

Compositional Fallacy:

Wrongly assuming that what is true of *some* things in a group is true of *all* things in a group.

Example:

A: Some norms are oppressive.
FC: Binary gender is a norm.
C: Therefore, binary gender is oppressive.

Lie #1: All Norms Are Oppressive

Are some norms obnoxious, unnecessary, and constricting? Totally. Are *all* norms? No. (This is a called the compositional fallacy. Just because something is true for *some* things doesn't mean it's true for *all* things.) Some norms *should be norms*, whether you like them or not. Don't take your socks off on an airplane. Change your underwear regularly. Save sex for marriage. Take care of your body.

Lie #2: All Norms Are Socially Constructed

This is another compositional fallacy. Some norms are socially constructed, and some are not. And when it comes to family, we *should* have norms because no other institution in all of history has ever been zable to replace family in terms of creating a stable society.[28] And God's commands for Christians? Yup.

Those should be norms *for us.* He's the Designer, and He knows how we work best.

Lie #3: There's No Real Difference Between Men and Women

Does every man, woman, boy, or girl have the exact same kind of differences? No. But are the two sexes *generally* distinct from each other? Yes. (We'll go into this more in chapter 13.) Let's not toss millennia of observation out just because some people are exceptions to the rule.

Lie #4: You Can Support Queer Theory and Be an Orthodox Christian

Um...no. If queer theory is all about norms, then we need to identify which norms are biblical mandates. In order to know what is healthy, you must first know how something is *designed* to function. To believe in design is to believe in a creator. To buck against design (and the norms that go with it) is to reject the idea of a Creator who has the authority to tell us what is healthy.

ARGUE for a Healthier Approach

Thankfully, many of these lies are easy to combat when we mix in some biblical truth and good old-fashioned common sense.

1. Redefine the "Authentic Self" in Gospel Terms

When we define authenticity as "what comes naturally," then all we're left with is our sin nature. And if we are in Christ, then we are a new creation; the old has gone, the new has come (2 Corinthians 5:17). We have a new authentic self—the person we were created by God to be—made in His image, reflecting His image. Encourage people to live their *new self* in Christ! That is what it means to ground your identity in Him.

2. Understand the Role of Norms and Stigmas

It's rough to be on the receiving end of judgment for being different. Nobody likes to feel "othered." But some things are stigmatized because they are innately unhealthy.[29] Stigmas have historically reinforced healthy behaviors and discouraged the unhealthy. Unbridled freedom is a recipe for chaos.

3. Some Norms Are Biblical and Healthy and Some Are Not

It is important that we help our little bears understand the difference between biblical, healthy norms versus norms that are culturally constructed. We cannot lump all norms together as barriers to be destroyed. (Don't tear down a fence until you know why it was put there!) Rather, we should uphold and embrace norms that promote biblical values and result in physical, social, and emotional health.

REINFORCE Through Discussion, Discipleship, and Prayer

1. Identify some "norms" of your household, such as: "Don't talk over people when they are talking to you," or "Wait until everyone is seated before you start eating." Ask your kids how norms can be ways of loving each other.

2. Pick out some healthcare norms, like eating, exercising, and brushing your teeth. How can disregarding these norms hurt you? Remind your kids that some norms are for their benefit.

3. Talk to your kids about what "healthy" means. Remind your kids that we can only define health if you know how something was *created to function*, and that requires a creator. Whenever your kids hear people talk about things that are healthy, ask them: "What do they mean by 'healthy'? Does what they're describing match how God created us to function?"

4. Differentiate between biblical norms and societal norms. Play the "Society or the Bible?" game. Whenever you think of it, point out a norm, like driving on the right side of the road. Ask your kids: "Is that from society or the Bible?" (Duh, society.) What about learning from your authorities? It's absolutely biblical. Parents are called to train up their children in God's commands (Deuteronomy 6:6-7). Pastors and elders

are called to teach based on their ability to recognize sound doctrine and refute those who oppose it (Titus 1:9).

5. Reinforce the difference between real and make-believe. Queer theory often turns innocent play (like dress-up) into an immersive identity, so it's important that our kids know the difference between real and make-believe. You can reinforce this distinction by being intentional in how you talk about playing pretend—for example, you can ask: "Are you pretending to be a kitty?" instead of simply, "Are you a kitty?" This reinforces the goodness of make-believe without accidentally introducing the idea that they can change identities.

PAWS for Prayer by Julie Loos

PRAISE God for Who He Is

We praise you for being the perfect Designer. You design with purpose, value, and worth. You are the Potter, and we are the clay. We don't have to invent our identity or rebel against it because Your ways are perfect and good and best for us. When others think Your molding of male and female are limiting, confining, or constraining, we know it is freeing. As the created, we gladly submit to the Creator.

ADMIT Where We Have Fallen Short of His Standard

There are times, Lord, we all buck against norms because in our flesh we don't want to submit to You. We want to be our own authorities. Forgive us. Forgive us also for not standing up against man-made norms that are truly unfair. Even so, Lord, we are dismayed and even righteously angry about this alternative worldview that rebels against Your design and authority. It even rebels against language and tries to take on Your role as Creator by inventing language. You are the *Word*. Your *Word* is *Truth*. Those espousing this theory (Isaiah 29:16) turn things upside down—as if the Potter is anything like the clay!

WORSHIP WITH THANKSGIVING for the Things He Has Done

Nevertheless, Lord, we thank You that when we submit our identity to Your Lordship, we then can be holy as You are holy. We can find true joy only in becoming who You intended us to be. We praise you for how You created and formed man, an individual complete in body and spirit, and that when You created woman You fashioned and formed her in such a way that they could become one flesh—fitted together by Your design.

SUBMIT Yourselves and Your Requests to God

Deliver those caught up in this worldview from a rebellious spirit. Turn their hearts of stone into hearts of flesh, submissive to You and Your design. If they are going to rebel, let them rebel against the sin nature that indulges the flesh. The root of rebellion is pride. "For everything in the world—the lust of the flesh, the lust of the eyes, and the pride of life—comes not from the Father but from the world" (1 John 2:16). Release them from the grip of the world. In their pride they do not seek You; in all their thoughts "there is no room for God" (Psalm 10:4). May they make room for You—and in so doing, find that their "authentic self" is the new self, found in Christ.

DISCUSSION QUESTIONS

1. **Icebreaker:** Everybody has their own kind of weird. What's yours?

2. **Main theme:** *Queer theory seeks to rewrite humanity by undermining every concept of normal—from gender to sex, to education, and even to mental health.* Why should this concern us as Christians? Do some norms need to go? Which ones? Are there some norms we can't afford to lose? Which ones?

3. **Self-evaluation:** Queer theory is obsessed with people looking inward to discover who they "truly" are. Do you find yourself consumed with "discovering" yourself? Are there things you excuse in yourself because they are "how you are"? How are we to submit even our personalities

to God? Are there any ways you've seen this kind of self-focus infiltrating the church?

4. **Brainstorm:** Make a chart comparing the biblical worldview with queer theory. Answer the following questions for each: Created or evolved? Where is ultimate truth found? What went wrong in the world? How do we fix what went wrong? How do we define good and evil?

5. **Release the bear:** What is your kid's weird? Tell them how much you love it! Remind them there is a difference between how God made them in terms of quirks and how God made them in terms of their humanity and gender. It's okay to defy the norms when it comes to quirks and personality. It is not healthy to defy the norms in terms of God's design for humanity, marriage, gender, sex, and family.

Things That Are Tripping Everyone Up

PRAYER OF LAMENT

Ask Boldly

LAMENTATIONS 3:40-42; EZEKIEL 11:19-20; 13:10-14; JUDE 12

Let us test and examine our ways, and let us return to the Lord. Let us lift up our hearts and our hands and then with them mount up in prayer to God in heaven. Give us ears that are sensitive and responsive to the touch of our God, that we may do what You say. The seducers of the age have built flimsy walls and covered them up with whitewash. But we say, by Your power, Lord, these whitewashed walls will fall—bring them down to the ground, Lord, so that the foundations will be exposed and all shall understand and realize that You are the Lord. Help us contend for the faith. Expose the hidden reefs, the elements of danger, in our midst.

Father, we need Your help, and we need it now. Give us eyes to see evil and courage to call it what it is. Give us ears to hear the voice of the enemy, no matter how beautifully disguised. Show us the boundary lines to set for our families, and incline our kids' hearts to not straddle them. Help us shine light in the darkness and bring hope to the hurting. Sanctify our children in the truth; Your Word is truth. You, O Lord, have delivered Your people before. You have brought justice and punished the wicked. You have preserved a remnant. What You have done before, You can do again. Do it!

CHAPTER 10

Purity Culture

When Our Best Efforts Went Kablooey

AMY

Not too long ago, my Twitter feed blew up with news articles covering a book launch for Pastor Nadia Bolz-Weber. Normally this sort of thing wouldn't have made the nightly news, but Weber wanted to celebrate her tell-all exposé of the failings of purity culture by commissioning a very unique statue...of a golden vagina.[1] The statue was crafted out of purity rings donated by former adherents to the True Love Waits movement. Bolz-Weber believes the statue was metaphorically crafted by the evangelical church when purity culture launched in the spring of 1993, and thousands of hearts were sacrificed to the golden calf of virginity.

The purity movement was not an unmitigated success, too often inadvertently sending the message that sexual sin was the one sin God couldn't forgive. As shame-filled testimonies came to light, Christian parents were called to stop the cycle of hurt by abandoning the toxic message of chastity. Instead, Christian sexologists like Dr. Tina Schermer Sellers said that what we should be teaching our children is that, as long as you are committed to your partner, you are modeling God's intent for love regardless of who they are or when you sleep with them—something Sellers calls the "New Covenant Sexual Ethic."[2]

Did you feel your discernment alarm going off just now? Yeah, me too. That's because Sellers and other liberal Christians are using the abuse of the chastity message to advocate a humanistic view of sexuality. This message has just enough Jesus to make premarital sex sound biblically supported and morally right.

Our kids deserve the truth—that God's plan for sex starts with marriage—but when the truth has been abused and twisted by the people we trust most, it no longer looks attractive...and can seem downright terrifying. We don't abandon truth because of its abuses. We correct the abuses and stand firm in the truth. The sexual revolution of the '60s championed the sex-positivity that we just discussed in chapter 8. So like all movements, it started a whiplash response by evangelicals...but things went terribly wrong. Sure, it worked for some people. But as we saw in the story above, others were so browbeaten into shame that they would rather toss any semblance of morality than return to being compared to chewed-up bubble gum. A lot of things are tripping people up with reguard to sexuality. So let's start by looking at ourselves in the mirror first and tackling what went wrong in the purity culture that a lot of us grew up in. To get off on the right foot, we'll first look at what was actually being taught and preached to teens.

The Original Message

In 1992, Dr. Richard Ross and Jimmy Hester first sketched out the ministry that would eventually become True Love Waits (TLW).[3] Their goal was to speak over the voice of the sexual revolution and advocate the superiority of the biblical sexual ethic to teens and singles. To be effective, though, this message required more than just a fatherly "Don't do it." They believed Christians needed to present truth while making the message appealing, practical, and rooted in the redemptive power of Christ. And they couldn't do it alone; they needed parents.

You read that right. No more passing off "the talk" to the middle school health teacher. (Seriously, they suffer enough.) Instead, parents were called to take the lead role as primary sexual educators to their children and were invited to attend training classes. These trainings explained the TLW curriculum and offered written materials to help them have meaningful discussions about sexuality at home. Youth leaders would then reaffirm these "home chats" by teaching that God designed sex to be shared exclusively between a husband and wife.[4]

Now, it didn't take long for teens to get all philosophical about what *actually* counted as sex. So, to avoid any confusion, TLW leaders advocated purity instead of just abstinence. This broader emphasis better communicated the biblical standard for holy living while rejecting potential gray areas like pornography, impure touching, lustful thoughts, and inappropriate banter. Teenagers were told they were not slaves to their raging hormones. They could avoid STDs and unplanned pregnancies and remain "pure" until marriage by relying on Christ, maintaining an active support base, and setting healthy boundaries between themselves and the opposite sex.

These boundaries were most recognizably outlined in Joshua Harris's book *I Kissed Dating Goodbye*.[5] In it, Harris told teens they could avoid the heartache of superficial relationships—those made without any intention of commitment—and the temptation to compromise their moral convictions by giving up the "selfish" pursuit of a boyfriend or girlfriend. This didn't mean they couldn't hang out with friends in groups—only that intimate dating should be avoided until a couple was ready to head to the altar. In the meantime, teens were encouraged to protect one another's purity as well. Guys were told not to mislead girls into thinking the relationship was more than it was in the hopes of luring her into the bedroom. Girls were encouraged to dress modestly, as a guy's mind easily wandered when revealing clothing left little to the imagination. Both were advised to seek friendship rather than romance first, as it is a person's character, not an emotional state, that withstands the stresses of marriage. If the good-looking hunk of creation they admired didn't want anything serious, teens were encouraged to move on. It wasn't worth the risk of giving a piece of themselves to someone who never intended to stay in the first place.

But what if this message came too late? What about the teens who had already gone too far? Were they beyond redemption? Not at all. Christ's death and resurrection meant they were no longer slaves to sin. They could find forgiveness and love in Him. But the Jesus who said, "Neither do I condemn you," also said, "Go now and leave your life of sin" (John 8:11). This meant that some teens needed to avoid one-on-one situations, install Internet and TV restrictions, and refrain from certain conversational topics. For others, it meant their relationships had to end so they wouldn't fall back into impure habits. No book, ministry, or speaker said it would be easy, but all the teachers, pastors, writers, and speakers agreed that pursuing God's design was always the best choice.

Many churches held a form of commitment ceremony to help families and teens unite around God's design. For some this was a simple affair of signing a pledge form at the back of a workbook or buying a purity ring. Other churches pulled out all the stops and had formal pledge ceremonies and purity balls for girls. Pledge ceremonies were typically held before the church and involved the whole family (or at least the parents and the child) committing to protect the purity of the child as they entered the dating sphere. Purity balls, on the other hand, were like a Southern debutante ball, complete with gowns, fancy dinners, the works! (And yes, in some places, they still go on today.) Instead of being presented to society as a woman of marrying age, however, girls pledged to be chaste until marriage, and their fathers vowed to cover and pray for them. As one attendee reflected, "Purity balls are a symbol telling people that this is what I'm doing...Making a promise to myself and to God that I will stay pure until I get married."[6]

Purity balls were often a special time for parents and children to come together in mutual commitment before God, encouraging each other to stand against cultural pressure to have premarital sex. They were fun events that many girls looked forward to. (Who doesn't like an excuse to dress up?)

What Went Wrong

If what you just read sounded totally different from your purity culture experience, you aren't alone. In the original curriculum, truth and grace were fairly balanced. By the time this message reached youth groups, however, things often went sideways.

For starters, the movement itself wasn't perfect. Stories, skits, and metaphors in the leader guides devalued the human body while seemingly idolizing virginity. Students who weren't virgins were compared to chewed-up gum, half-eaten lollipops, juice that someone had already spit in, flowers without petals, and used pieces of tape. There were even group activities to emphasize these points. For instance, a student was handed a rose and encouraged to touch it, smell it, crush it, and pass it along to the next person. After the whole youth group had manhandled the rose, only a few bruised petals were left clinging to the stem. And then the leader would ask, "Who wants the rose now?" (And leaders never gave the right answer: Jesus. Jesus wants that rose.)

Kids, too, often felt pressured by pushy parents or friends to make a pledge they weren't ready for or didn't fully understand. They knew they didn't want to let their youth pastor or mom down, so they played the part...until the boyfriend or girlfriend came along, that is.

These activities were supposed to be analogies for what happened during premarital sex, but overly zealous church leaders made virginity their primary focus, neglecting the redemptive work of Christ. Some even ignored the original design of the curriculum by excluding parents, refusing to be transparent about what was being taught, or by integrating their own perverted twists to the lessons.[7]

Then you had the more legalistic parents. These folks were so committed to keeping their kids on the straight and narrow that they barely told them what sex was. After all, you can't desire what you don't know exists, so sex ed was avoided like the plague. (I mean, seriously...what could *possibly* go wrong?) By the time these students reached adulthood, they'd received so many legalistic or false teachings that they found themselves struggling with intimacy in their marriages. They were ashamed of their bodies or thought their sexual development and attraction toward others was a threat to their salvation. Talk about unintended consequences!

As a result, women harbored such resentment toward the traditional teaching of chastity that here we are now—with "Christian" teachers now encouraging parents to avoid these "shame-filled messages." And, to be fair, some of the messages really were poorly thought-out. Let's look together at the most damaging ones that came out of 1990s purity culture and see if we can't clear the air, dispel the myths, and offer a more biblical approach.

ROAR Like a Mother!

RECOGNIZE the Message

As we saw above, the original purity message was biblically accurate, but a lot of damage was done under the banner of biblical sexuality. We here at Mama Bear Apologetics have no problem admitting when the church made some missteps, and we're going to look at three big ones that have caused many people to walk away from the church and God's teaching about biblical sexuality for good. Spoiler alert: They're all fixable!

1. Purity Is the New Holiness

When a former classmate shared his experience with purity culture, one of his greatest frustrations was the legalistic teaching that purity was synonymous with holiness. As author Jessica Valenti scathingly remarked, "You can be vapid, stupid, and unethical, but so long as you've never had sex, you're a 'good' (i.e., 'moral') girl and therefore worthy of praise."[8]

Your worth as a person depended on who you *didn't* sleep with. The fragility of this worth was communicated through some powerfully black-and-white examples. One teacher had her class take turns spitting on an Oreo to illustrate a girl's undesirable state after she lost her virginity. Boys stuck tape to different pieces of construction paper to show how useless-as-unsticky-tape you became if you got too handsy with too many partners. At a TLW rally, a teen leader remarked that Christians who lost their virginity were like rumpled magazines that no one wanted to buy. Countless books referred to those who had slipped as "impure" or "damaged goods."

Once damaged, any spiritual blessings that came with marriage were out of reach. If you went too far, you could kiss your chance at a happy marriage goodbye! Who would want an apple other people had bitten into? And all the married sex that was supposed to be *a-maz-ing* once you walked down the aisle on your wedding day? Nope, that was only for the chaste couples. The best you could hope for was for some other non-faithful person to settle for you—two perfectly matched pieces of chewed-up, spit on, crumbled-up garbage living in mutual compromise. How romantic.

2. You Give a Piece of Yourself Away to Each Person You Date

In case you haven't read *I Kissed Dating Goodbye*, Harris retells a friend's dream in which she and her husband were joined at the altar by every woman he had ever dated. Even though he had broken up with these women years ago, they remained permanently connected because each possessed a piece of his heart. (Harris is not clear about what causes this piece to be joined to another. It could mean he was sexually intimate with these women, or that he fell in love with them emotionally. In his book, he implies both.)

Fifteen-year-old Elise made a similar reflection when interviewed for a magazine article. She said, "I think your life is kind of like a flower, and every time you have a relationship or a boyfriend or something, you're taking a petal of your flower and giving it to that person. So you're giving all these petals away. Pretty soon you're not left with anything to give your husband."[9]

For Harris and Elise, whenever you enter into a romantic relationship outside of marriage, your very self becomes fragmented and a piece is transferred to your partner. If you aren't careful, by the time you find Mister or Miss Right, you'll have run out of pieces to give.

But since virginity can only be lost once, it doesn't make sense to believe one can progressively give "pieces" away to different people. This ambiguity allows for a variety of interpretations, and Harris later implies that even falling in love with another person has the same effect. This line of thinking raises a host of questions regarding the nature of self. For example: If we gave every bit of ourselves away while simultaneously gathering bits from other people, who or what do we become? How can one's self endure while becoming fragmented? Must it remain whole to exist?

This flawed philosophy sent many people, the majority of them women, into a panic whenever they began dating someone new. *How far is too far? What if I get too close, and he doesn't turn out to be the one? How many pieces do I have left?* No one knew. What they did know was that they couldn't get those pieces back—and worse, a piece of each partner stayed with them too, so any future relationships only added to an ever-compounding orgy.

Is it any wonder that people felt as if they were in a legalistic trap? Like I said, it's a mess. Look, dating does not turn people into metaphysical vending machines because—surprise!—God made you in His image, not in the image of a PEZ dispenser.

After hearing endless stories of his writings being used as a hammer, Harris denounced his book and stopped further publication. Unfortunately, in 2019, he renounced his faith entirely.

3. Your Body Is His Problem

This lie was exclusively directed toward the girls of the group, and good grief was it a doozy. It wasn't just your actions that could be sinful; it was your *body itself*. In elementary school you were basically a ticking time bomb of temptation. Once puberty entered the scene, you exploded from a Shirley Temple into a Delilah looking for a Samson. A girl's figure suddenly became a threat to the souls of the boys in the youth group as well as to the faith of the girl herself.

This meant girls were totally on the hook if their brothers in Christ couldn't keep their eyes to themselves. And that womanly figure you had been waiting for your whole preteen life? You had better cover that up, because now that puberty had kicked your development into high gear, the body you were once told was fearfully and wonderfully made was now starting to make you look like a harlot. As author Linda Kay Klein put it, female bodies were "nothing more than things over which men and boys could trip," shameful stumbling blocks waiting to drag you and the boys who liked you away from God.[10]

Tucked within this body-shaming nightmare was the belief that guys just couldn't help themselves. They were wired to respond visually to girls, after all. If their imaginations started running wild, it wasn't their fault. That's just how they were made. And plenty of matronly women hovering around the church would happily clutch their pearls while pointing out all the different ways girls were going astray. "So you had best watch how you dress, or else!"

OFFER Discernment

It's no surprise that the purity fallout looks like it was inspired by the book *The Handmaid's Tale*, but that doesn't mean everything that was taught was unbiblical. There's a good amount of truth we can point to even in the mess, and no, we're not donning a proverbial white cap and a red dress by doing so.[11] This is just good old-fashioned discernment in action.

For starters, abstaining from sexual activity before marriage is God's design for biblical sexuality. (See Hebrews 13:4, 1 Corinthians 7:2, and all of the bride's warnings not to awaken love before it pleases in Song of Solomon.) It falls under the spiritual fruits of self-control and faithfulness (Galatians 5:19-24), and thus is a demonstration of holiness. Holiness calls for Christians to be set apart. Chastity—avoiding sexual activity before marriage—is an aspect of holiness, but it's not the whole measure of it, as many students were led to believe.

This important distinction was missing from much of the purity movement. TLW material was very clear that we are made clean through Christ. The problem was that kids who had already fallen were less likely to believe that message because of how virginity was often idolized. As one holier-than-thou teen put it, "I can be a non-virgin whenever I want, but they can never be like me."[12] Prideful much?

Since you can only be a physical virgin once, this meant there was no unringing that bell once it had been rung. Many students mistakenly thought their physical virginity was essential for salvation, making throngs of kids think there was no hope once they had gone too far.

Secondly, actively sinning *does* hinder your walk with God (Proverbs 15:8; 28:9; 1 John 3:9-10). And it's also true that having multiple sexual partners before marriage *can* cause emotional, physical, and spiritual harm. Studies have shown that marital happiness is higher between couples who have no previous sexual partners as opposed to those who do.[13] Promiscuity also brings an increased risk of STDs, which can result in infertility and transmission to the future spouse. Some couples struggle with guilt from having past partners.

Others feel compared to their spouse's past lovers—whether they are or not. All of this can be avoided if each partner chooses chastity.

Lastly, as much as our world loves to deny it, what we wear does convey a message. This is true of every culture and time. It's why you don't wear sweatpants to a job interview or on a first date. It's why so many professions have uniforms. What we wear communicates something about us.

For good reason, Paul encourages women to dress themselves in good deeds rather than pearls and braids. To say that our clothes don't communicate a message just doesn't make sense. For now, though, let's check out the most common lies within purity culture.

Lie #1: No One Will Want You if You Aren't a Virgin

Remember all those awful examples we read about? These illustrations tried to show the seriousness of losing one's virginity outside of marriage, but they ended up reducing the value of the individual to the state of their purity, leaving many feeling hopeless, dirty, and irredeemable.

This also caused immense confusion about sex. Some had the idea that sex was so wrong and dirty that marital intimacy was difficult or unappealing. Many women saw sex as more of a duty than a God-given pleasure, which caused tension within their marriages.

These illustrations were particularly damaging to children and teens who were survivors of sexual assault. Much of the TLW campaign completely failed to account for the spiritual and emotional needs of these young people. Even if their loss of innocence was through no fault of their own, they were still left with the impression that they had lost their purity, were offensive to God, and had no chance at a fulfilling marriage and sex life.

Metaphors and similes are invaluable tools when you're telling a story, but they are painfully inadequate when you compare the complex human person to a single-purpose inanimate object. What kids need to hear is that they are not objects. Their value isn't found in virginity, but grounded in a Savior who can make all things new.

Lie #2: Following This Formula Will Guarantee a Great Marriage and Sex Life

Oh yes, this was totally a selling point within purity culture. If you saved yourself for marriage, the sex was going to be better than anything you could imagine! Your marriage was going to be great! You and your spouse would be happier than those smiling families in the car commercials! Purity was *the* formula for marital and bedroom success.

Those teens grew up and got married. And far from mind-blowing, their wedding nights were awkward and painful. For some, intimacy felt anything but intimate with ten years of "sex is evil" messages ingrained in their heads. Some grew up in fundamentalist households and turned to pornography because they didn't even know what they were supposed to do! When purity failed to deliver on the promise of easy intimacy and perfect spouses, many couples felt lied to and ended up walking away from the church forever.

Using future sex to bribe teens not to have sex should never have happened. Great intimacy has to be nurtured, sometimes through Christian counseling, and it sure as heck has some awkward, fumbling, "I got a leg cramp" moments that never made their way into the highlight reel of the purity scene. God never promised mind-blowing bedroom skills for the chaste. He did promise that sex is good, pleasurable, and able to satisfy and sustain a husband and wife. It's not a person's virginity that nurtures a successful marriage, but the mutual and continued practice of the biblical fruits of love that enables a relationship to weather the storms of life.

Lie #3: The First Time Is the Only Time That Matters

This was the huge lie that green-lighted promiscuity among teens. Once they had crossed that bridge, there was no going back. Might as well enjoy some debauchery with the rest of the sinners! What was often missing was a proper understanding of chastity.

When we look at the Beatitudes, we see Jesus blowing the false binary of sexual purity out of the water. Matthew 5:27-28 shows that chastity isn't only a body issue but a heart issue. Virginity isn't just lost by those who got too carried away on prom night; it's any sexual act outside of marriage. This means that the virgin college student watching porn is just as guilty as the sophomore who sleeps with her boyfriend. The unmarried couple living together is just as broken as the guy waking up from a one-night stand.

When you really study it, chastity becomes like the law: revealing our brokenness and pointing us toward our need for a Savior. It completely leveled the sexual playing field, but no one knew it because all anyone seemed to care about was the wedding night, not the heart.

ARGUE for a Healthier Approach

If we want to raise our kids to have a healthy sexuality, we don't do it by ditching God's design—as many progressive teachers encourage. We do it by aligning what we teach with His Word. This starts by affirming the beauty and purpose of sexuality. Sex is good! It feels good! And it's a blessing to be completely vulnerable, intimate, and loved by one person for the rest of your life in the covenant of marriage. The most romantic moment isn't the first kiss; it's the one-millionth kiss from the wrinkle-faced sweetheart of your youth.

Redemption is possible for everyone. No amount of sexual brokenness can keep you from the healing power of God. Yes, physical virginity is a one-time deal, STDs have to be treated, and babies have to be cared for. But as a classmate once said, "If Paul, who persecuted believers and had them put to death, can be redeemed, so too can our broken past."

Next, our kiddos need to understand that chastity is faithfulness in body, mind, and heart, and Satan is going to attack all three. To be effective in the battle requires total dependence on Christ, honesty with parents, and a great support group of like-minded friends. Make no mistake, we cannot act like the world and expect to end up with all the benefits of godly obedience. Instead, we have to live counterculturally. We have to understand that dating isn't a hobby; it's the act of searching for a spouse, and it places you in a whole lot of tempting situations. Christian dating will mean setting healthy boundaries and honoring the other person like Christ.

This countercultural defense also involves how we dress and act. Now for guys, clothes aren't as much of an issue. Just the other day some radio jockeys were debating whether guys could have sexy outfits, and the best they could think of was unbuttoning an extra button on their shirts. The awful truth is that women are objectified through clothing more so than men. Just compare men's and women's Halloween costumes if you have any doubts.

For ladies, there is a lot more baggage here. Let's start off by saying no outfit justifies or will prevent abusive behavior. If a guy is going to be a creep, he's going to be that way whether you're dressed like a nun or wearing a miniskirt. And no, you weren't asking for it. Who would?

However, this doesn't mean that how we dress doesn't communicate a message. It does. We can't look like the world and expect to convey an other-than-worldly message. As affirmed by influencer Taylor Alesia, our clothing should reflect strength and dignity (Proverbs 31:25), even if the teen-pop icons disagree.[14] Seriously, gals, we're to the point where being "fashionable" requires having to walk with our hands over our backsides to keep from flashing our fellow church folk. That's a problem. When it comes to our closets, we need less Kardashian and more Christ.

So how do we walk the tightrope over the minefield that is dressing with dignity? By first recognizing that this may look differently for each family—you are not the church-fashion police. Prayerfully seek God for His guidance in your life and that of your family. And while there is no hard-and-fast rule, here are a few basics we can hopefully all agree on:

An outfit is probably too short, tight, or low-cut if....

- You have to take off your underwear to look good in it.
- You lean forward and expose what only a doctor or a nursing infant should see.
- You can't walk or pick something up off the ground without holding down your skirt because you'll expose yourself to the people behind you.
- Anything that would normally be covered by underwear is hanging out the bottom or the sides.
- You still look naked even with it on.

This isn't legalism or rocket science, people. It's just practical! To accompany clothes that might be a bit on the showy side, a camisole, a pair of bike shorts, or a long-waisted shirt are easy additions to affirm dignity without compromising style. Our goal is to encourage our kiddos to dress in a way that respects themselves while teaching them to be respectful of each other no matter what the other person is wearing.

REINFORCE Through Discussion, Discipleship, and Prayer

1. The word *purity* has been put through the ringer, and sometimes we have to concede when it might be too far gone to be saved. Instead, let me offer "sexual integrity" as an alternative. *Integrity* better encompasses the mind, body, and spirit unity that is comprised within discipling your child's sexuality; all these pieces are *integrated* in the Christian worldview. Because one can display sexual integrity before and after marriage, the term also dispels the legalistic pure/impure dichotomy so often found within the early purity teachings. *Chastity* or *sexual faithfulness* are also great choices.

2. Discuss with your child how you can honor God and foster sexual faithfulness within your home. For teens this may include things like avoiding shows about people having sex, dates where teens spend extended alone time together, and unsupervised media access. Parents can likewise model sexual faithfulness by avoiding sultry shows and avoiding alone time with members of the opposite sex—especially if you are a single mom or dad with a significant other. Make sure everyone is aware of the agreed-upon expectations—and that everyone follows them. Make sure they're reasonable, achievable, applicable, and fair. Discuss which boundaries will be in place and how you and your child will be accountable to them. Teens also need to know what steps are to be expected if these boundaries are violated.

3. Make sure you and your child have a support network that is outside of your family. Your child should seek friends and mentors that share their convictions and will ask the tough questions. Who are these people? Do they regularly meet? If you do not have an outside support network, we

encourage you to become involved in your local church and start making connections.

4. Encourage your child to pursue purposeful dating. This is counter to the world's approach to dating for entertainment, and it reinforces that the purpose of dating is to find one's spouse. The goal should be to get to know the person and see whether they would be a good ministry partner—since life is ministry! Activities could include volunteering together at the church, group trips, cooking together at home, and service projects. Pick activities that help learn each other's character, family background, and beliefs. Set boundaries for your kids that will help them avoid situations that could lead to unnecessary temptation, like being alone together. Remind them that if they are deliberately acting in a way which encourages sexual affection (stroking, making out, or looking for a dark, quiet place to be alone), they should find a way to restore boundaries (meet up with friends, change the activity) and, if need be, call it a night. Again, discuss these with your child so you can come to a sensible agreement.

5. Teach your boys how to ask a girl out, how to talk to her parents, how to behave on a date, and how to respect the girl's parents' wishes. Have mother-son dates where he can practice his gentlemanly and chivalry skills. Plan father-daughter dates where your husband demonstrates to your daughter how a gentleman is to behave.

Talk to your kids about the specifics of what is okay and what is not in a dating relationship. A guy or girl wanting your teen to break his or her convictions or send sexy photos is not okay. Make sure your daughter knows that she doesn't owe a guy *anything*, no matter how fancy the steakhouse.

If you don't feel your teen is mature enough to date, encourage him or her to demonstrate maturity by being respectful of your wishes. Offer to revisit the conversation later, reminding your teen that sneaking behind your back won't prove maturity.

And teach your teen how to end a relationship in a way that preserves the dignity of the other person. No social media bullying, shaming, or text breakups. Look the person in the eye and explain your reasons. Delete pictures, return sweatshirts, and be above reproach.

PAWS for Prayer by Julie Loos

PRAISE God for Who He Is

We praise You, Yahweh Nissi—the Lord, our banner. We lift Your name high because You have the power to overcome any enemy that comes against us. Not only are You holy and pure, but You are our Redeemer when we fall. No matter what we have done or failed to do, You are Jehovah M'Kaddesh—the Lord who sanctifies and sets us apart for holy use—our bodies included.

ADMIT Where We Have Fallen Short of His Standard

Forgive us for abandoning Your biblical standard for holy living. There are times when we have parented out of fear, peer pressure, and trying to make up for our own past mistakes. Intending good, Your church has made missteps in our teaching about sexuality. At times we have promoted legalism over love and have equivocated purity with holiness. Out of fear of communication, we may have turned our kids toward brokenness.

WORSHIP WITH THANKSGIVING for the Things He Has Done

We are so thankful, Lord, that You redeem the broken, turning ashes to beauty. No one is out of Your reach or Your loving repair. You have the balm that heals our loved ones' emotional, physical, and spiritual wounds. Gratefully, we come acknowledging that You foreordained male and female, marriage, family, and boundaries for our sexuality and for our good. Any discipline You bring on us is for our good and our sanctification.

SUBMIT Yourselves and Your Requests to God

Lord, as we try to guide our children in purity, help us balance truth and grace on the beam of Your Word. Help us model self-control and faithfulness for them. When they are tempted to compare themselves to others, help us guide them to use Your Word as their mirror. Protect them from the schemes of the evil one and his masquerading minions. May our children want to honor one another by setting boundaries and living above reproach. Help us train them in sexual integrity of mind, body, and spirit. If they give in to temptation, let them run to us and to You for help rather than hiding in shame or fear. May they purify their souls in obeying Your truth through the Spirit in sincere love of the brethren, loving one another fervently with a pure heart (1 Peter 1:22).

 DISCUSSION QUESTIONS 

1. **Icebreaker:** Did you go through a True Love Waits ceremony in high school? Do you know anyone who did? What was your impression of TLW? What did your youth group teach about sex? If you weren't in church as a teenager, what were your impressions about what Christians thought about sex?

2. **Main theme:** *The church tried to encourage chastity but used bad analogies that scarred some people for life.* In what ways did the church's attempts to teach sexual faithfulness backfire?

3. **Self-evaluation:** What are your thoughts about sexual activity for single parents? Do you think it's the same for them as for teenagers? Why or why not?

4. **Brainstorm:** Here is a fun thought experiment. Brainstorm together to make a list of every single social problem that would go away if people had sex only with their spouses. (Seriously...it's mind-boggling.)

5. **Release the bear:** This week, make a point of discussing integrity with your kids. If you need to correct behavior, ask them how they would have handled the situation if their thoughts, heart, and words were fully aligned with God's Word.

CHAPTER 11

Pornography

It's Not Technically Sex if You're by Yourself, Right?

AMY AND HILLARY

Jesus often used stories to illustrate the upside-down nature of the kingdom of God. Higher truths were communicated through everyday accessible characters and settings that made sense to the people at the time. But 2,000 years later, not all of us can relate to shepherds or oil-toting virgins. In our world, movies are the new parables, and one of the best examples I (Amy) have seen when discussing pornography can be found in an unlikely place: Disney's *Pinocchio.* Hold on to your crickets, folks, because you probably won't see this movie the same way again.

Pinocchio begins with a kindly wood-carver, Geppetto, whose visit from the Blue Fairy makes him the adoptive father of a wooden puppet. Talk about a modern family! Geppetto tries preparing the wooden boy for the real world, but temptation is right there with a slick hat and false promises. *Follow me,* says the creepy fox, *and I'll make you a real boy.*

The fox steers the young puppet to Pleasure Island. Here we watch Pinocchio happily riding on a wagon with rambunctious youngsters. On the ride, his buddy Lampwick tells Pinocchio how great it will be when they can do whatever they want. On Pleasure Island, no one will tell them what to do. A dream come true!

The boys clamber out of the wagon and disperse into the town, which is positively overflowing with cigars, delectable food, and rocks just begging to be thrown through windows. With all their newfound freedom, they don't notice the Coachman's shadowy henchmen locking the gates of the island so no one can escape. Only after it's too late do the boys realize they've fallen into a trap. They watch in horror as one by one the boys transform into donkeys and are crated up to be sold off. One boy who hasn't yet lost his voice cries out for his mother, begging the Coachman to allow him to go home.

"You've had your fun!" the Coachman growls, throwing the donkey-boy into a crate. "Now it's time to pay!" The boys thought they were just having innocent fun; they didn't know they were being forced into slavery.

If you were to rewind the movie back to the beginning of the scene, you would notice it wasn't horses pulling the wagon, but donkeys. Boys who were already lost to the lies of Pleasure Island were being used to drag the next batch to the same grisly fate.

Mama Bears, a similar crisis is happening in our culture. But instead of pool tables and smashed windows, our children are being lured into bondage with pornography.

The Scope of the Problem

If you haven't personally struggled or known someone who has personally struggled with porn, the issue might feel a bit distant. Like, you *know* it's a problem, but you don't really understand how big of a problem it is. So just how widespread is porn now, anyway?

In 2019, the world's largest porn conglomerate reported *42 billion visits*. So basically the entire earth's population times six visited their site.[1] That's double what they had a mere two years prior. And the amount of *new* content added to the site? Enough to watch porn all day, every day…for 165 years. And remember, that is just *one* porn site in *one* year. That doesn't even include the approximate 26 million other sites that exist, several of which *also* boast visits in the billions per year.[2]

This is where the numbers cap out, and it's not because the porn industry isn't growing. As noted by anti-porn organizations like Fight the New Drug, Pornhub was exposed by *The New York Times* for profiting off child exploitation and nonconsensual content back in 2020.[3] The result? Pornhub stopped reporting the amount of new content being added as well as top trending searches like "barely legal" and "teen." This way, they can fly under the trafficking radar while still profiting off the abuse of children and young women.

We would all like to think that porn is a "them" problem. Not *us*. Not *our* husbands. Not *our* kids. But we cannot afford to stick our heads in the sand on this one. According to Covenant Eyes, more than half of pastors have struggled with porn, and 57 percent of youth pastors "live in constant fear of being discovered" for their porn addiction.[4] When it comes to our kids' conception of porn, 90 percent of teens and 96 percent of young adults are *neutral, accepting, or encouraging* of porn consumption.[5] Yup, you read that right. Nearly every kid at school has no problem watching porn and will happily text their favorite videos to their friends so they can join in the fun.

Back in the day, the only way boys could get a peek at a pair of boobs was by swiping a dirty magazine from someone else's secret stash. Now our kids carry instant access around in their pockets. As for the grooming process? It starts with every screen in the house.

The Kaiser Foundation ran a study on the amount of sexualized content flashing across TV screens and found that 80 percent of TV programming and 60 percent of music videos had sexualized content or featured the objectification of women.[6] And that was 20 years ago!

Children's media now is especially concerning. In a survey of ten of the most popular children's shows, sexualization of female characters was present in *every episode evaluated*.[7] This was just in the most popular shows *for girls*. In content directed at boys, most commonly video games, 80 percent of female characters were sexualized, scantily clad, or looked like a supermodel, with a quarter of them being all three.[8]

With the rise of cell phones and social media platforms, the world has never had easier access to hyper-sexualized content. By the time our boys reach fifth grade, 90 percent of them will have been exposed to porn, with the lowball average age of first exposure being eight years old.[9] As Vicki Courtney reminds parents in her book *5 Conversations You Must Have with Your Son*, the question isn't *if* your son will encounter sexualized material, but *when*. Looking at the statistics above, the *when* can happen at almost every commercial break.

By the time our girls reach age 18, 60 percent of them will have been exposed to porn themselves.[10] And for the lucky 40 percent who haven't, more than likely they're dating guys who have or are regularly consuming it themselves.

Because the child brain is still forming, it can easily become wired in response to pornography exposure, resulting in lifelong consequences right as they are shifting into the "How *you* doin'?" stage of sexual development. The younger a child is when they are exposed to suggestive images, the more their brains are wired to seek instant gratification and pleasure. They're also less likely to perceive the dangers and consequences of what they're viewing because the good judgment portion of the brain doesn't fully develop until adulthood. They just see a hot chick, so they'll buy the video game, or watch the movie with the shirtless hunk, and click on the website to see more because it feels good. The adult entertainment industry knows this and is happy to meet their demand. In short: They're using our kids' brains against them, grooming them to be *sensual* consumers instead of sensible ones. How do they get them to be sensual consumers? By hijacking the brain and using its chemicals against them.

The Most Powerful Drug in the World

We talked in chapter 3 about how God made a pretty great design when followed, and especially what a powerful bonding agent sexual energy is when channeled toward one's spouse. But did you know research backs this up? While we appreciate the sentiment of Disney calling "true love's kiss" the most powerful thing in the world, neuroscience begs to differ. What is as powerful as crack cocaine? The almighty O.[11]

Several chemicals are released during sexual arousal and orgasm. We'll talk about three specifically here—oxytocin and vasopressin, which lead to bonding, and dopamine, which leads to both pleasure and potentially addiction. To understand why pornography is such a huge problem in our culture, we need to look at what is happening on a physiological level. One key thing to keep in mind as we look at these three chemicals is that all three are "value neutral," meaning they can't discern right from wrong, beneficial from harmful. They just do what chemicals do. Brains reward all kinds of behavior without distinction.[12]

Oxytocin and vasopressin are the main chemicals that contribute to bonding, both between sexual partners and between parent and child. As a Mama Bear, you can probably appreciate the power of oxytocin in bonding with your child. Just think of the feelings you had when you first held your new baby. Now hold that thought...Did you know that the same chemical is released during orgasm? It is. And our desires, motivations, and attractions become directed to whoever or whatever is around us when that burst of oxytocin hits our brains.

When we look at these chemicals from a Christian perspective, we can celebrate the way God made our bodies to reinforce our emotional attachments and emphasize that God created this chemical cascade. It's a great design—when used to enhance the bond between husband and wife. But what if these chemicals are released while watching porn? Yes, the human brain becomes wired to actually crave a two-dimensional image over the real thing—over a real person. We literally bond to a screen. This is actually one of the reasons porn usage *decreases* a person's likelihood to engage in real-life sex. And before your kid tries to rationalize that "porn helps them to save sex for marriage," just remind them: Sex with yourself is still sex. Porn is not a more "moral" alternative to sleeping around.

The fact that our bodies and minds are bonding to someone or something outside of marriage should be concerning, especially when we consider the devastating effects for future relationships. Neurologically, an orgasm causes you to prefer the person (or thing) to whom your orgasm is attached. Ideally, it causes you to seek their attention and affection for future sexual experiences.

So what happens when there isn't another person to seek or the image is constantly changing? Our brains get used to novelty or the bond-breaking process. We actually train the brain to think breaking the bond is normal![13] This makes it ever more difficult to actually bond with a real person. And even if we do bond, the bond is weaker because it's used to being broken.

So when we hear someone complain about how sleeping with one person for the rest of their life sounds boring, what they're really lamenting is the damage they have created in their own brain that's preventing them from being comforted by the breasts of the love of their youth (Proverbs 5:18-19). They're not celebrating their freedom. They are actually mourning the scope of their own brokenness, and they don't even realize it. It's immensely tragic, but through God's grace, fixable.

The Pleasure Chemical

The next chemical involved is dopamine. This little molecule is the reason why porn is so addictive. Dopamine is the reward chemical in the brain. We get little shots of it when we eat something tasty or see a piece of art that we like...or when someone "likes" our photo on social media. The problem with porn isn't that it releases dopamine; it's the *amount* it releases. Our body can only handle so much.

Dopamine does nothing for our moods unless there are dopamine receptors in our brains for it to bind to. What happens when you flood your brain regularly with too much dopamine? Your body says, "Oh! I guess we don't need all these dopamine receptors. Let's get rid of a few." So your body actually *desensitizes itself* to pleasure. A person is less able to experience pleasure with normal things like time with friends, a good meal, or a great concert. This also explains the link between porn usage and depression.[14] A person has altered their brain to the point they are unable to feel joy without porn. To get the same "high" or feeling of happiness, a person now needs *more* dopamine because they have fewer receptors. And here's where porn use can turn into porn addiction. Not-so-fun fact: It's the exact same neurological pathway and mechanism as a crack cocaine addiction—and because of the added "learning" through oxytocin and vasopressin (which makes you crave that which follows the orgasm), it's even *more addictive.*

Porn and Violence

As mentioned above, regularly viewing porn decreases the dopamine receptors in a person's brain—which means, as in all addictions, that the person has to increase their consumption in order to get the same amount of euphoria. When it comes to pornography, it is not the amount of pornography but the *type* that changes. The more habituated users are to watching the act of sex, the less sexually stimulated they become. This causes the user to crave ever more shocking and even violent forms of sex to become aroused.

This is where violent porn comes into play. I want to be gentle with my Mama Bears here, but at the same time, you need to know what is out there. Common in the *milder* forms of violent porn are men slapping, hitting, and choking women. The women are portrayed as *liking it.* And remember, *what a person orgasms to is what they will crave in a real-life partner.* As University of Michigan law professor Catharine MacKinnon states,

> The catharsis hypothesis—the notion that the more pornography men use, the less abusive sex they will seek out elsewhere—has been scientifically disproved. Closer to the reverse has been found: it primes the pump. As women have long known, use of pornography conditions consumers to objectified and aggressive sex, desensitizing them to domination and abuse requiring escalating levels of violence to achieve a sexual response. Use of pornography is also correlated with increased reports by perpetrators of aggressive sex and with increased inability to perceive that sex is coerced. Consumers thus become increasingly unable to distinguish rape from other sex.[15]

The link between real-life sexual violence and viewing of violent porn has been shown repeatedly in the scientific literature.[16] Not only is this trend hijacking our kids' sexualities; it is affecting how they interact with one another in real life and through social media.

Groomed to Consume and Groomed to Perform

Girls don't wake up one day and suddenly decide they're going to swing naked on a wrecking ball, but they certainly can be groomed to. Remember dopamine? Yeah, that's the same chemical that gets released when our girls see that someone has liked their social media posts. The creators of platforms like MySpace and Facebook initially included this as a way to encourage positive interactions. Yet in the documentary *The Social Dilemma*, the creators admitted that they had no idea it would morph into what it is now—fuel for addiction and depression, especially among teen girls. Each platform has an addictive little feature called the "like" button that blasts the user with a hit of dopamine every time their phone dings. To keep the reward juices flowing, kids (and adults too, mind you) will often tailor their social media feeds to get the most attention—the most likes and the most dopamine. The more attention, the more likes, the more dopamine.

For most of their childhood, our girls will be in the "observer" role of the sexualization of women. They'll play with seductive-looking dolls and watch kid characters twerking like pop stars. Then they're given a cell phone, and all of a sudden, their role shifts from "observer" to "performer." And believe me, it is a performance. Most girls enter social media with no intention of degrading themselves for public approval. Yet when they notice that girls who act suggestively get more attention, some will start to compromise.

The boys are being conditioned to like what they see in porn, and the girls are being conditioned to perform to these boys' likings. And back and forth it goes.

The effects are not just limited to social media. One of the saddest pieces of research we came across involved interviews with a group of girls who were fed up with what porn had done to the guys at their school. One young woman in an article lamented that having sex was the only way to get her boyfriend to *watch a movie with her*.[17]

So not only are these girls having sex at younger ages, but they aren't even doing it for their own sake. Due to the effects of porn, girls' primary worry is now *how they look* during sex. Girls are increasingly learning that their value changes according to their ability to turn a guy on and perform according to pornographic standards. Knowing that their boys consume so much porn, these girls have adapted their behaviors to give "the porn experience." Gynecological surgeons like Dr. Naomi Crouch report that girls as young as *nine* are contacting her for labiaplasties because they are "distressed by the appearance" of their vulvas.[18] (We didn't even know what a vulva *was* at nine, let alone that it could be unattractive.)

Kids spend an average of 6.5 hours a day plugged into social media.[19] While guys are more likely to record themselves playing sports or doing some moronic challenge, girls are more likely to fall victim to the comparison game and feel pressured to produce sexualized content to "stay relevant." Photo filters and superficial highlight reels of another person's life have them focused on achieving beauty standards that don't exist while hating the reality that does. Instead of seeing themselves as wonderful creations of God, they base their value and self-worth on the number of followers they have and likes they receive. This can lead girls to engage in increasingly risky online behavior (like posting nude photos and more) all to appear valuable and stay relevant online. Actions that the American Psychological Associate described as "self-objectifying behavior."

So What Exactly Does It Mean to Objectify Someone?

When talking about pornography, the two most commonly used descriptors are *objectification* and *dehumanization*.

Here's a thought experiment: Think about anything you use in your house—say, a pair of scissors, a computer, or a paperclip. Some objects have many functions (a computer) and some have few (a paperclip). The only reason you interact with these objects is because you want them to perform a function to improve your life in some way—entertain you (like a TV) or make something easier (like a calculator). What happens when it can't perform its function anymore? You get rid of it and get a new one.

Objectifying something doesn't necessarily mean you don't love it. You can love something you objectify; it's just not the kind of love we should have for our fellow human beings. I love my computer. I decorate it and keep it in a fun case! I protect it and get it fixed when it is wearing down. But ultimately, its value is not intrinsic. At the end of the day, if it doesn't do exactly what I want it to do when I want it to do it and at the speed I have grown accustomed to, then it's time to replace it. That is how we treat objects.

Girls do not realize that this is what awaits them at the end of the objectification process. Many girls mistake *attention* for *attraction*, assuming their skimpy outfits and sexual wiles will attract a great guy. She may even find a guy who treats her well, buys her flowers, and takes her to dinner—for now. But at the end of the day, if she doesn't perform the duties he came to her for (a hot body and great sex), she is as useless to him as a broken stapler.

Spot the Faulty Logic

A: If a guy acts interested in me, that means he likes me.
FC: When I wear skimpy clothes, guys act interested in me.
C: Skimpy clothes will help me find a good guy who likes me.

What About Dehumanizing?

Dehumanization is when you strip a person of their human rights or qualities. Men and women were created in the image of God, with free minds, free choices, and free emotions; they carry an inherent worth other creatures do not. When we dehumanize someone, we do not recognize their inherent dignity or even consider that they may have thoughts, desires, or emotions that are different from our own (or at least ones that should matter to us). Historically, most of the evils perpetrated against humans have been preceded by a dehumanization campaign. During the Holocaust, Jews were depicted as bugs or animals, an infestation needing to be purged. Same thing for our Black brothers and sisters during chattel slavery. And now, in our supposedly progressive society, we do the same thing to babies in utero. People don't even like calling them babies. They are just "a fetus," and killing them is just "terminating a pregnancy." Very clinical. Very sterile. Pay no attention to the human being at the end of the suction stick.

Dehumanization, in general, is an exceptionally dangerous road to go down. The scariest part is that people usually don't even realize the shift in their thinking. The women in porn are always in the mood, just like my calculator is always "in the mood" to calculate for me. The men are abnormally well-endowed, always perform on cue, and never interact with the woman beyond her body. Pornography teaches boys that girls exist for the purpose of bringing them pleasure. And the girls learn to perform in whatever role will get the most attention from the boys. Nobody asks the porn star what her major is; she is there for one reason only. In porn, everyone is an animal doing what animals do. *De*humanized.

ROAR Like a Mother!

RECOGNIZE the Message

As you can see, porn is absolutely destroying our kids' sense of what it means to be human and what healthy sexuality should be. If it sounds like we're losing the battle against pornography, it's because we are. We have underestimated the enemy and wandered onto the battlefield totally unarmed. But God has brought forth victory in worse circumstances. We must anticipate how the porn industry is reaching our kids, debunk its lies, and equip our boys and girls to stand firm against a porn-saturated culture. So what are the messages inherent in porn?

1. Women Are Always in the Mood for Sex

The television show *Friends* addresses this in the episode called "The One with Free Porn." After discovering that Monica and Rachel's apartment has accidentally been hooked up to the porn channel, Chandler and Joey refuse to let anyone turn off the television for fear that the channel won't come back. So enraptured are they by the free porn that they barely eat or sleep. By the end of the episode, we see them having a conversation about how "weird" their day was. Chandler went to the bank, and the super-hot teller didn't want to have sex with him in the bank vault. Joey recounts, shocked, how the pizza delivery girl just took his money and left. After an awkward pause, they both decide that maybe it's time to turn off the porn.

2. Women Enjoy Being Degraded and Treated Like Sex Objects

The women in porn are almost always portrayed as *liking* everything a man is doing to them, no matter how violent or degrading. According to Robert Jensen, a main propaganda message of porn is that "any woman who does not at first realize [that she likes] this, can be persuaded by force."[20] Imagine taking that belief into your dating life or dating a guy who holds that belief. Or trying to convince yourself that *all the other girls like this stuff.* Our kids are in the "monkey see, monkey do" modeling stage up until their twenties. And when you have a powerful reinforcer (like an orgasm), this "observational learning" can become permanently seared in their psyche.

Spot the Faulty Logic

A: Women wouldn't do things they don't enjoy.
FC: Women choose to do porn, even with sexual violence.
C: Women enjoy sexual violence.

3. Porn Sex Is Normal Sex

According to a recent study in the UK, more than half the boys (53 percent) and a large number of the girls (39 percent) were under the impression that the acts depicted in porn *reflect how sex is in real life*. Even more disturbing was the number of children—more than a third of young teenagers—who responded that they'd like to "try out the behavior they had viewed." As the study's coauthor, Dr. Elena Martellozzo, put it,

> If boys believe that online pornography provides a realistic view of sexual relationships, then this may lead to inappropriate expectations of girls and women. Girls too may feel pressured to live up to these unrealistic, and perhaps non-consensual, interpretations of sex. This is clearly not positive for developing future healthy relationships.[21]

Not to mention that consent, STDs, or condom use rarely occur in these skin flicks. Obviously, our kids need to learn about sex from *us*, not online videos featuring Fabian the well-endowed pool guy.

OFFER Discernment

While nothing (and we mean nothing) is inherently good about pornography, we should still grapple with the reasons people watch it. Most people immediately point to the sin of lust, but that's a bit too simplistic. Yes, lust is occurring during the viewing, but it's what happens right before that is more telling.

Porn usage can often be due to a person trying to meet a legitimate need in an illegitimate way. In order to have victory, a person must identify the real issue. If we treat pornography as the main issue instead of as a symptom, we can miss the root cause.

In the book *Sex and the Supremacy of Christ*, contributor David Powlison recounts a story of a man named Tom who struggled with pornography and masturbation. Through just a little digging, Tom and his counselor discovered that his problem wasn't lust; it was anger at God for not giving him a spouse.

Desire for intimacy is often at the top of the list for girls and women who view porn. Once the physical act of masturbation comes into play, however, they may experience the same level of addiction as the boys, but their desire was originally fueled by a need to connect. A desire to connect and be known is a God-given desire, one we shouldn't dismiss.

Likewise, there has been a noted link between pornography and feelings of loneliness, depression, and anxiety.[22] Now, which is the chicken and which is the egg has yet to be determined. (Do the negative emotions cause the porn usage, or does porn usage cause the emotions? It's likely both.) And, furthermore, it doesn't take some fancy study to show that girls are often more comfortable talking about their feelings than boys. When our boys are experiencing extreme discomfort, they often can't even identify it, let alone admit to it. So they turn to something that makes them feel good without having to talk it out.

In conversations I've personally had with people who are honest about watching porn (and who are self-aware enough to describe what happens right before they stumble), frustration with some aspect of their life was at the top of the list. In other words, they weren't necessarily looking for sex. They were looking to…not feel so crappy. We are wired for intimacy and connection. And like any drug, a person's porn-viewing habit can start out as a form of self-medication. That doesn't make it okay, but it should help us better understand how to help.

And yes, lust is going on as well. We are wired to respond to visual sexual stimuli. Song of Solomon wasn't shy about the beauty of the male and female body. Breasts like two fawns, drinking wine from her navel, blowing on her garden? Yup, that's all in Scripture. Our bodies are beautiful and desirable, and depictions of sexual expression are attractive to us because that's exactly how sex was designed! Being aroused by them is totally normal, and it's something to be fostered between husband and wife.

Being attracted to visual displays of nudity isn't just a guy thing either. Girls also like to see some skin, which is why Team Jacob never complained when their werewolf heartthrob from the hit teen series *Twilight* couldn't find himself a shirt. Finding an ancient vampire coven? Piece of cake. But a shirt? Total mystery. So, yes, we get it. We're all sexual creatures, and porn recognizes (that is, exploits) that fact. Furthermore, there really are health benefits to orgasms. Scientifically speaking, orgasms release chemicals that lower blood pressure, decrease anxiety, and promote better sleep. But we are not just bodies, and even if something has some benefits, it doesn't make it moral.

Spot the Faulty Logic

A: We should choose healthy habits.
FC: Orgasms have health benefits.
C: It's healthy to pursue anything that gives me an orgasm.

Porn is evil, period. We don't even care if someone thinks their marriage is better because of it. I'm sorry, but having to get turned on by someone else so you can have sex with your spouse is not a net gain.

So what lies does porn tell? Too many to list here. But here are a few of the biggies that our kids are being duped by.

Lie #1: Porn Isn't That Big of a Deal

We've said it before and we'll say it again: Normal is not the same thing as moral. But unfortunately, that's what our kids think. It's part of the desensitization process. People experience shame over shameful things. You can tell when something has lost its shamefulness when kids openly talk about it. Both of us have heard young people (even Christian youngsters) loudly and openly discussing porn, which means they don't care who hears them. Why? *Because they aren't even embarrassed anymore.* They have forgotten how to blush (Jeremiah 6:15). Your kids may not talk to you about pornography usage because they expect that *you* think it is a big deal. But as we mentioned previously, upward of 90 percent of youth today do not. And why should they? Their brains aren't fully formed to understand future consequences. As Abigail Shrier states, "Try convincing a teenager that something she wants to do carries risks...It's a little like informing her the sun will burn out five billion years in the future."[23]

Lie #2: Porn Is a More Moral Alternative to Sex

If your kids are brought up in church and youth group, they will likely hear the youth pastor entreating them to save themselves for their future spouses. Unfortunately, we may have mistakenly given them the impression that if no other party is present, then it isn't really sex. If a girl watches porn, she assumes she has not given her heart away to someone other than her future husband. If a boy watches porn, he may justify it to himself as technically "following the rules" because he hasn't deflowered any of the girls in the youth group. If it's just you and a screen, then nobody is getting hurt, right? They truly see porn as obeying the directive laid out by biblical teaching. But sexual faithfulness isn't just abstaining from sex with another person. As we've seen in the research above, a huge number of relationship issues are caused by porn usage—issues they will take into their future relationships.

Spot the Faulty Logic

A: Sex outside marriage is immoral.

FC: Porn helps me control my sexual urges around my girlfriend or boyfriend.

C: Porn is a better alternative to sexual immorality.

Lie #3: Porn Is Harmless

This is a lie from the pit of hell. But often people aren't motivated to quit something until the harm hits them where it hurts. So let's explain this in terms that males will especially understand: *Porn is creating erectile dysfunction even for guys in their teens and twenties.*[24] In short, porn is rewiring brains and impeding people's ability to connect with other humans. So basically, if you want to be anxious and depressed and ruin your future sex life, then by all means, watch porn. But I'm guessing you don't and neither do your kids. We don't always have to make everything uber spiritual. Sometimes good common sense will do the trick.

Lie #4: Porn Can Be Empowering

A common argument is that porn allows a woman to take control of her own body and use it as she wishes. But women in the sex industry disproportionately have histories of abuse and are often victims of violence and poverty.[25] If you know a woman in the sex industry who is emotionally healthy and fulfilling her childhood dream of being paid for sex, please introduce me. I would like to hear her story. And if you think sex workers are into what they do, I suggest you follow Fight the New Drug on social media to hear from the sex workers themselves. The life of glamour they tried to portray was a far cry from the drug-addicted life they were actually living.[26]

Just because you choose to be exploited does not mean you are not being exploited. This is basically saying, "A guy can't take it from me if I give it up willingly." Ask the question: Can someone be empowered and degraded at the same time? We say no. Wielding sexual power may *feel* empowering in the short run, but it's a sleight-of-hand trick of the enemy. These individuals may be completely unaware of how their sense of self-worth is slowly being siphoned away until there's nothing left. By the time they come to their senses, the industry is done with them, ready to move on and suck the soul out of the next wide-eyed ingenue. Thanks for playing; your services are no longer required.

Lie #5: Porn Can Promote Healthy Sexuality

This is a huge problem within secular psychology because many sex therapists recommend porn to their clients. But remember, much of their counseling training is based off teachers like Wilhelm Reich, Alfred Kinsey, Sigmund Freud, and others who held a materialistic worldview, which states that we are only bodies. Their worldview isn't based on objective morality or a high view of the body, so their "treatment" will also reflect the culture's view of sex, not God's.

Spot the Faulty Logic

A: Better sex makes better marriages.
FC: I have better sex with my spouse after watching porn.
C: Porn is good for my marriage.

Lie #6: Porn Can Be Ethical

Ethically sourced is a buzz phrase, especially for today's Gen Zers. Just like diamonds and your favorite chocolate, some porn is now being touted as "ethically sourced." Ethical porn (sometimes called feminist or fair-trade porn) means all participants are willing and fairly paid...and often paid *really* well. So, consent plus fair wages equals ethical. Our kids assume that if someone is making a good wage off their work, then they aren't being exploited—so no harm, no foul. And even the word *work* is being twisted. Porn stars refer to having sex as their "job," their "art," or their "business." Phrasing like this can be confusing to our kids when they hear us talking about the importance of getting a job. Why would they do one for $15 an hour when they could get a job paying $200 an hour? Work is work, right? (#linguistictheft)

ARGUE for a Healthier Approach

Porn is basically a cheap counterfeit for the beauty of God's design for sexuality. It uses our God-given sexuality, lures us away from the beauty and goodness of God's design for sex, and exchanges wholeness for brokenness. (What a deal!) One of the best ways to help combat pornography is to help our children distinguish between the real thing and a counterfeit. Though not guaranteed, there are generally lasting benefits that come from adhering to God's design.

As mentioned above, porn often hijacks real needs and seduces the individual with the promise of fulfilling them. Acknowledge those needs with your kids. Make a habit of helping them voice their needs. Kids are notorious for acting out when they don't understand a negative emotion. If your son or daughter is having a hard time voicing their emotion, maybe get them an emotion chart where they can point to how they are feeling. The more they learn to articulate a need, the less likely they'll need to express it in other ways.

Sex isn't just some act between bodies or screens but a powerful testament to the goodness of God that bonds husbands and wives spiritually till death do they part. It nurtures the entire family unit. And you can bet your bottom dollar that this same power is equally destructive outside of God's intended use.

Every aspect we have talked about shows how powerfully reinforcing the sexual act is, whether done in front of a screen or with a person to whom you have pledged your life. God created the act of sex for husbands and wives to recommit to each other bodily and to connect with one another in a way that transcends logic or reason. It is an incredibly powerful chemical bond, and not one you want to make with a person who has not pledged their lives to you in front of friends and family (or at least in front of a justice of the peace!).

As we saw in our discussion on purity culture in chapter 10, a lot of well-meaning teachers tried to get this point across to us—but it's a tricky message to share without inducing hopelessness in a person who has fallen shy of the ideal. As in most things in Christianity, we need a both/and approach. Who (or what) you share your orgasm with matters, *and* God has promised redemption to those who have fallen. There will likely be some emotional (and physiological) consequences, *and* God can make all things new.

The younger a child starts with porn, the harder the effects will be to reverse.

It doesn't happen overnight, and there will likely still be lingering memories, but healing can happen. As Paul wrote in Philippians 3:13-14, "Forgetting what is behind and straining toward what is ahead, I press on toward the goal to win the prize for which God has called me heavenward in Christ Jesus." We don't want to forget the lessons we've learned in the past, but neither can we let our past failures dictate how much we strive for God's best in the future.

REINFORCE Through Discussion, Discipleship, and Prayer

As we've seen, the reasons for watching porn can be varied. But there are a few things that we can do as parents that can help mitigate the issues.

1. Get a filter on all your and your children's devices. Net Nanny, FamiSafe—take your pick. Parental settings on your streaming services are also a must. It's reckless not to have these.

2. No phones or computers in the bedroom or the bathroom. We know you'll get pushback on this, but it would be like having a door connecting your house to a porn theater and refusing to lock it. Nearly all experts, regardless of faith, agree that it's a bad idea for kids to have smartphones or computers in the privacy of their own rooms. There's even a growing number who are against smartphones, *period.* We understand each family is unique, so we leave this up to the parents. But if you need a little encouragement to be countercultural, remember what your mom always told you: Just because all your friends have one does not mean you have to. Part of being set apart as a Christian is making wise and healthy decisions. If our kids feel that giving up a smartphone is a cross too big to carry as a disciple of Jesus, you *might* have just uncovered a bigger spiritual issue that needs attention.

3. Prepare your kids for what to do if they accidentally see a pornographic image or if a friend tries to show them one. Talk to them about how it rewires the brain to crave things that aren't real.

   For girls, explain the prevalence of anxiety and depression associated with porn usage. Most girls want to avoid these emotions like the plague.

They also need to know that a godly woman's identity is in Christ. She doesn't need to base her self-worth on a boy's reaction to a saucy social media post. She's too precious for that. Help her to be countercultural so she can encourage her friends through her behavior to reject the lies that exploit them.

Boys will need an escape plan as well as encouragement to know they aren't weak or emasculated for choosing not to look at pornographic images when their friends are crowded around a screen. Part of being a godly man is protecting the men and women around them. Walking away from porn is one way to do that. Another is not asking for sexy pics from their girlfriends or sending and posting ones themselves.

4. Help your kids foster healthy *in-person* relationships. We are in a digital world, and while our kids are more connected than ever, they are also lonelier than ever—an emotion that can lead to porn usage. Make your house the one where kids want to congregate. Usually this is the house with the best snacks and where the parents are always up for a loud, rambunctious gaggle of teens to take over the living room TV till the wee hours. Yes, it's noisy and your food bill goes up, but it's a small price to pay for peace of mind and a connected kid.

5. Practice what you preach. We love you, Mamas, which means we're not going to lie to you. The average TV show geared for adult audiences has made porn a regular plot point. Don't be fooled; shows like *Bridgerton*, *Outlander*, and *Euphoria* are porn with a better storyline. What we (and our children) need to remember is that being a believer is going to affect our Netflix subscription, but I promise that your faith walk and witness to your children is worth this minor earthly sacrifice. Check out Vid Angel, an amazing app that allows you to choose which junk to filter out in TV shows and movies.[27]

Spot the Faulty Logic

A: Sex is for married people.

FC: [TV show] depicts sex between a married couple.

C: Watching the sex in [TV show] is okay.

PAWS for Prayer by Julie Loos

PRAISE God for Who He Is

Father God, You are the lover of our souls. You are faithful and jealous for our love. You designed us and made us wonderfully. You are wise in Your creation of man and woman, of the attraction and bond of husband and wife. Because You are an intimate and personal God, You made us for connection and intimacy as well. El Roi, the God who sees, knows everything; nothing is hidden from You. Yahweh Shammah, the Lord is there; there is nowhere we can go from Your presence.

ADMIT Where We Have Fallen Short of His Standard

Forgive me when my eyes have looked upon and my mind has entertained things not pleasing to You. Forgive our culture for allowing everything to be sexualized—for not making You the object of our worship but rather objectifying men and women who are made in Your image. We have not protected our young from the prowling lion who seeks to kill, steal, and destroy. We have idolized instant gratification and pleasure—even domination, abuse, and violence—as poor substitutes for love. We have confused attention for attraction. Forgive us for losing the ability to blush.

WORSHIP WITH THANKSGIVING for the Things He Has Done

Thank You that our desire for intimacy is rooted in our desire to know You. You developed our minds and our bodies with intricate stages of development, with the ability to foster good judgment, with a need for bonding. Where we have allowed burning desires to be kindled by inappropriate means, You offer beauty for ashes. We are grateful that how we look in Your eyes is of much more worth than how we look in the eyes of others. There is no amount of shame You cannot erase with Your grace.

SUBMIT Yourselves and Your Requests to God

Release us, we pray, from the bondage of pornography. Show us where and how to draw a line in the sand. Guide us as we teach our children to recognize dangers and realize consequences. Lead us to be sensible consumers and not sensual ones. May our desires and devotions be aligned under Your doctrine and not to our evil devices. To have eyes only for You and Your way. Expose the root causes leading loved ones, friends, and strangers to this quicksand of habits. Lord, we ask that You help us obey all Your commands so that we and our children may prosper forever as we do "what is good and right in the eyes of the Lord" our God (Deuteronomy 12:28). May we set our sights on You.

 DISCUSSION QUESTIONS 

1. **Icebreaker:** Did you remember the Pleasure Island scene from *Pinocchio*? What are some other movies you remember as a kid that were a lot darker when you watched them as an adult? (*Fox and the Hound*, anyone?!)
2. **Main theme:** *Pornography takes the beautiful design of sex to bond a husband and wife together and instead addictively bonds the porn user to a revolving door of different "partners."* What statistics about pornography in the chapter shocked you the most? Did you have any idea that porn was that big of a problem?
3. **Self-evaluation:** Have you ever struggled with watching things you shouldn't? What were your motivations for seeking them out?
4. **Brainstorm:** What are some ways you can prioritize in-person relationships for your children at your house? What might be some of the warning signs your child is experiencing loneliness?

5. **Release the bear:** Take this week to put all the advice into practice. Put filters on everyone's devices. Disable notifications for social media. Move computers out of bedrooms, and make sure no screen in the house is difficult to see from other angles. Treat your home like you are battle-proofing for the war on porn!

Same-Sex Attraction

Hurting People to Be Loved

HILLARY

It should come as no surprise that having a family member or close friend who identities as gay has been closely linked with Christians reevaluating the Bible's stance on homosexuality. And there is a lesson to be learned here: If we do not have any same-sex attracted people in our family or circle of friends, we may have missed the legitimate pain that is taking place within this demographic. It is unwise to allow personal pain to reinterpret the truth of God's Word, but it should inform the way we treat this very delicate topic.

I (Hillary) have often said that the homosexual community has been treated as the scapegoat for all of the church's sexual sins. What do I mean by *scapegoat*? Originally, the concept of a scapegoat referred to a ritual element in the Jewish holiday Yom Kippur (Day of Atonement). Leviticus 16:20-22 gives a picture of what is going on:

> When Aaron has finished making atonement for the Most Holy Place, the tent of meeting and the altar, he shall bring forward the live goat. He is to lay both hands on the head of the live goat and

> confess over it all the wickedness and rebellion of the Israelites—all their sins—and put them on the goat's head. He shall send the goat away into the wilderness in the care of someone appointed for the task. The goat will carry on itself all their sins to a remote place; and the man shall release it in the wilderness.

When applied to people who identify as LGBTQ+, no actual atonement is going on but rather a twisted and hypothetical transfer of guilt, as if people's zeal for the *one* sin of homosexuality could replace their collective guilt for the rampant sexual immorality going on in their own fellowship. A colleague of ours recalled a time when, after speaking at a conference, a woman approached him asking what to do with her son who had just confessed same-sex attraction. She lamented to our friend, "Why can't he just be like his sister? She is engaged to a nice boy, and they are about to have their first child."

Hard stop. Did she just say she wished her same-sex attraction son could be *more* like her daughter who was living with a man she was not married to and was now pregnant by? That situation was preferable?!

Church, this is not okay. We can't act like one type of sexual sin is worse than another. Sexual immorality is sexual immorality.

A Long History of Hypocrisy

Hypocritical Christians have existed within the church at every stage of church history. (John and I used to live by a church with a sign out front that said, "We're not full of hypocrites! There's room for you too!") If we were to take an honest look through church culture over the last 100 years, I'm pretty sure we'd recognize that people who struggle with LGBTQ+ attractions are not the first group to be hypocritically targeted.

In my grandparents' generation, divorce was the scapegoat. You could be a gambling, alcoholic, abusive monster, but as long as you weren't divorced, you were still welcome in polite society. But the church lost that battle when no-fault divorce became the law of the land. What was once the unforgivable sin is now so prevalent in our churches that pastors rarely preach on divorce anymore (for a variety of reasons we don't have time to explore here).

Then it was out-of-wedlock pregnancy. Boys and girls could do whatever they wanted in the back seat. As long as there was no concrete proof, it was treated as a "don't ask, don't tell" situation. Once upon a time, babies were irrefutable evidence that such an act had taken place. You could only hide a baby bump for so long. Unfortunately, after Roe v. Wade, there arose a really destructive social pressure within the church to get an abortion and hide the evidence of sexual immorality. I personally know women whose moms took them to the abortion clinic just to save face at church. Many churches realized this was the culture they were fostering and thankfully shifted by supporting ministries for unwed mothers so these girls could freely choose life for their babies without shame.

And now, it seems, many Christians have set their sights on the *next* big sin—the battle we've lost in the culture but not yet in the church: homosexuality.[1] You can have three kids from three dads or have as many baby mamas as you like, but as long as you aren't gay, you are still welcomed in the fellowship of believers.

Christians: We. Need. To. Stop. This.

If we truly believe that acting on homosexual desires is sin, then the church needs to be *the place* where people can be honest about their struggles.[2] We cannot swing wide our doors to those struggling with pornography, addiction, and promiscuity but then get all shy and prudish with homosexual desires. No wonder those with same-sex attraction have run for the hills! And like the scapegoat, they were driven there by people claiming to speak on behalf of God.

Can we put ourselves in the shoes of a Christian who experiences same-sex attraction? I've talked with counselors who describe the pain that their clients have gone through. Some have been treated like pariahs by their church small group or rejected by their families. Some are under the impression that the mere presence of same-sex desires makes them an abomination—as if homosexual feelings or practices are the unpardonable sin. Isn't that exactly what the enemy would like us *all* to believe about ourselves? That there is something about us that disqualifies us from coming before the throne of God, cutting us off from the very One who desires to see us walk in freedom? So let's dispense with that nonsense now.

Same-sex attraction is not the unpardonable sin.

The gospel is not about "making gay people straight."

The gospel is about transforming sinners into obedient Christ-followers.

How Should We Respond to Same-Sex Attraction?

A huge mistake we can make as Christians when it comes to homosexuality is confusing people for the agenda, mistaking captives for rebels. Are there some people who flaunt their homosexual practice, have no desire to change, and try to destroy anyone who even hints at a Biblical sexual ethic? Sure. Is there a concerted global movement seeking to rewrite sexual morality? Also yes. Read Gabrielle Kuby's *The Global Sexual Revolution*. It's an eye-opener. Has there been a concerted effort in the West to normalize homosexuality through music, movies, advertising, and any other means possible? You've seen it yourself. It's not a big secret. Two gay-identifying journalists give step-by-step instructions in their 1986 article "Overhauling Straight America." Read it for yourself and decide if their plans have succeeded or not.

So yes, we need to recognize the spiritual battle afoot—one that is trying to distort the image of God as seen through gender, sex, marriage, and family. But please hear me when I say there are many more people than we realize who find themselves with same-sex attractions and have no idea where to turn because the loudest voices they hear at the church potluck are the ones railing against radical gay activists. We must clearly and vocally distinguish people struggling with same-sex attraction from those who militantly embrace and promote homosexuality. Not doing so can have disastrous repercussions.

If the moral law of God is written on our hearts, then we can expect that same-sex attracted individuals will already feel a degree of confusion over their attractions. When shame is already involved, it's easy for these strugglers to mistake the church's warnings against the radical homosexual agenda as being directed at them *personally*. And we have kids in our church whose hormones are just kicking in, who have always felt "different" and who are being told by activists that if they feel "different" then it's probably because they are gay or transgender. These kids know what the church teaches, and so they fearfully hide their feelings and confusion. And that's what we call a perfect storm for the enemy to come in and continue whispering his lies.

Our kids are constantly told by media that homosexuality is normal and healthy. And as I have said ad nauseum, familiarity is not easily distinguished from truth. So I'm going to make a contentious suggestion: Maybe it's time to *start* with the assumption that our kids will, at some point, question their gender or sexuality (especially if they struggle to fit in with their peers). Why? Thirty years ago, if you concluded that you were gay, it wasn't because the idea was suggested to you so many times that it finally sounded true. The same cannot be said today. We as a society are being bombarded with the ongoing *celebration* of homosexual and transgender individuals for "bravely speaking their truth." Kids model what they see heroized. It's not rocket science. If your child never struggles with same-sex attraction or gender identity, great! But if they do, you'll be prepared.

When Your Child Struggles with Same-Sex Attraction

If your child comes to you saying they are gay, it is important to *not freak out.*[3] If they've watched the YouTube activists, they've been told to expect "persecution" and rejection—especially from family. Some kids are legitimately terrified their parents will reject them. Others are hoping for it. Either way, don't go there. Listen to them. Ask questions. Remind them that you love them no matter what, even if you disagree with them. What we want to make absolutely clear is that *same-sex attraction does not define them*, nor does it separate them from the love of God. Yes, desires matter—but more important is what we do with them. Crucify them. Die to them. Don't identify *as* them (even if you don't plan to act on them).

Avoiding Extremes

I said previously that homosexuality is an ideological battle that we've lost in the culture, but not yet in the church. Unfortunately, this issue is literally splitting churches apart. Many Christians find themselves at an impasse, caught between the false dichotomy of truth and compassion. (And yes, this is a *false* dichotomy!) On one side are people who say, "Marriage is between a man and a woman. The Bible said it, I believe it, that settles it." On the other side is the self-titled "affirming churches." In their zeal to love their (gay) neighbor, they stand in solidarity with something the Bible says is not part of God's design. In essence, they are raising themselves up to be more merciful and more loving than God Himself—often leaving biblical inerrancy in the dustbin as they go.

We cannot fall prey to either of these extremes, Mama Bears. We have to be the generation to disciple our children to truly love and understand their same-sex-attracted peers while maintaining a commitment to biblical truth about marriage. Because as we saw in chapter 3, if we mess with the picture God gave us through sex, marriage, and gender, we mess with people's ability to see God accurately. Who among us is willing to stand before God and say they encouraged people to remain in bondage to a distorted view of Him when it was His desire for them to walk in freedom? We cannot afford to get this one wrong, Mama Bears.

The Scientific Complexities of Same-Sex Attraction

Sexuality is a difficult subject to study from a scientific perspective. There are some who feel either uncomfortable or ill-equipped to discuss same-sex attraction from a theological perspective, but they are more than ready to discuss the supposed science behind it. After all, *surely* science can provide a more clear-cut, less polarizing answer. I posit that this is a dead end too, for a few different reasons.

Scientific Difficulty 1: No Clear Separation Between Demographics

A lot of research claims to study the differences between heterosexuals, homosexuals, and bisexuals, as if these are nice, neat categories with no overlap. The problem with this methodology is that you if you recruit test subjects based on neat, clean categories, wonder of wonders, you'll find nice, neat, clean categories. Sociologist Lisa Diamond discusses the problematic nature of these "identities" in her presentation on sexual fluidity (which I highly recommend you watch).[4] When comparing data in the tens of thousands of randomly selected individuals—in studies spanning multiple time periods and multiple countries—a lot of overlap and discrepancies occur between peoples' self-identified orientations and their attractions and behaviors.[5]

Simply put, there are a whole lot of self-identifying heterosexuals who report fantasies *toward* and sexual activity *with* people of the same sex. There are also self-identifying homosexuals who report fantasies toward or sexual activity with people of the *opposite* sex. The idea that our attractions are fixed and immutable is generally not true.

The point is, if you can't clearly identify and separate your subjects, you cannot study the differences between them. Sorry, folks. If you are waiting for science to settle this issue, you might be waiting awhile.

Scientific Difficulty 2: What Exactly Do We Mean by "Sexual Orientation"?

The most common argument is that our sexual desire is somehow intrinsic, like the title *sexual orientation* suggests—as if we were born with a sexual compass pointing toward men or pointing toward women. We now realize that sexual attraction is much more fluid than that. As we saw previously from the Lisa Diamond meta-research, most people who experience same-sex attraction are not exclusively same-sex attracted. Less than 2 percent of the men and even fewer women report unwavering, exclusive same-sex attraction. So we can't say that *no homosexuals* are "born that way," and we can't say *all homosexuals* are "born that way."

And even if people were consistent, the question of orientation is not as simple as "Which gender are you attracted to?" because of the *why* factor. *Why* do we experience the sexual desires we do? And what constitutes a sexual desire?

There is a whole field of research devoted to *attachment theory.* Attachment theory teaches that humans have an internal drive to attach to both the same and opposite sexes for different reasons. The most unique perspective I've ever heard regarding attachment and homosexuality is done by Ricky Chelette, executive director of Living Hope Ministries.

In short, Chelette teaches that children need three A's from each parent (attention, affirmation, affection). They also need a certain level of attachment to same-sex friends growing up. As Chelette describes, failure to progress through these attachment phases can leave a person craving the attachment they missed, thereby *influencing* future sexual desires—whether directed toward same-sex or opposite-sex.[6] For example, if a sensitive boy yearns for the rough-and-tumble masculinity that he feels he lacks (or that he admires in other boys), his admiration can be twisted into (or confused with) sexual desire once those crazy puberty hormones kick in.

Thirdly, we have amassed enough research (not to mention anecdotal evidence) suggesting that sexual trauma can also play a role.[7] As we discussed in chapter 11, pleasure and orgasm are powerful reinforcers that can direct our future sexual desires. What happens when a child's first exposure to sexual stimulation is with someone of the same sex? What happens when they have a traumatic experience with someone of the opposite sex? Both situations can affect a person's sexuality. The problem arises, though, that if part of their orientation is nurture instead of nature, then it cannot be considered merely an inborn orientation.

As you can see, until we can clearly differentiate between groups, we cannot form concrete conclusions about what the science does or doesn't say. If you would like to see a summary of research, I recommend starting with the executive summary published in *The New Atlantis* by researchers Lawrence Mayer and Paul McHugh.[8] If nothing else, it will keep your child busy when they come home claiming that science is "conclusive" about anything regarding homosexuality.

Theological Arguments

There are no mainline churches (that we know of) who use the Bible to argue for the acceptance of sex-positivity or pornography. The same can't be said for same-sex attraction. In the last several years, gay-affirming and progressive churches have begun making what they believe to be a biblical case in support of same-sex relationships.

Six main passages in Scripture address homosexuality. These passages are often referred to as the "clobber verses" by progressive Christians because they supposedly "clobber" everyone into a single interpretation of Scripture. These passages are found in:

1. Genesis 1–2 (original creation)

2. Genesis 19 (Sodom and Gomorrah)
3. Leviticus 18:22 and 20:13 (Jewish laws regarding homosexual behavior)
4. Romans 1:18-32 (basically the decline of a culture from all sorts of sexual sin)
5. 1 Corinthians 6:9-10 (the list of people who won't inherit the kingdom)
6. 1 Timothy 1:8-10 (the list of the unrighteous sinners)

There are two main camps when it comes to interpreting these verses. They are commonly referred to as the traditional view and the revisionist view (also sometimes called the non-affirming and the affirming views). For the purposes of this chapter, we will use the words *traditional* and *revisionist* because the main issue discussed here is textual interpretation, not the affirmation of same-sex-attracted individuals.

The main thesis of the revisionist is as follows: The Bible has nothing to say about committed, monogamous, same-sex relationships. The cluster of arguments supporting this thesis was made famous by Matthew Vines in his 2015 book *God and the Gay Christian.* According to Vines, homosexuality was considered in biblical times to be a "manifestation of normal sexual desire *pursued to excess*"[9] (emphasis mine). Vines argues that all the biblical prohibitions against homosexual sex are in terms of lust, not orientation. As to the reason Sodom was destroyed? Inhospitality only.[10] As to Paul's condemnation in Romans 1, Vines argues that Paul makes "no mention of love, fidelity, monogamy, or commitment...Do [Paul's words] apply to all same-sex relationships? Or to only lustful, fleeting ones?"[11] Vines concludes: "While I could act on my sexual orientation in lustful ways, I could also express it in the context of a committed, monogamous relationship."[12]

Vines also argues that the concept of homosexuality as an orientation didn't exist in biblical times, so the Bible couldn't possibly address it. When the Bible does speak of homosexuality, it is not in the context of relationship. Rather, it is in regard to gang rape (Sodom), pederasty (man-boy sex), sex with slaves (which degraded the slave), and other cultural practices. The word *homosexual* wasn't originally in the Bible, argues Vines.

His argument regarding fruit has also been readily embraced by churches eager to right the wrongs of the past. This line of reasoning was ultimately what convinced popular progressive Christian author Jen Hatmaker to change her stance on homosexuality. In an interview with Peter Enns, she said:

> It was actually Jesus' teaching on fruit that locked us in hard... When I looked to the fruit of the non-affirming Christian tree, the fruit was so universally bad. It was suicide. It was broken families. It was folks kicked out of their churches. It was homeless teenagers. It was self-hatred and self-harm and depression, crushing loneliness, separation from God...If we are being honest, the fruit of the tree is rotten.[13]

These and other arguments have been used to say that the Bible's teaching regarding same-sex relationships is ambiguous at best. It is important for us to teach our children what the Bible has to say about marriage and same-sex relationships. But if people are undermining the interpretation of Scripture, we can't just make a positive case to our kids and stop there; we have to help them see *why* all the attempts to circumvent the clear reading of Scripture fall flat. We could reinvent the wheel here and answer each of these in-depth, or we could point you to Kevin DeYoung's book *What Does the Bible Really Teach About Homosexuality?* It is a short book and answers all these questions and more!

ROAR Like a Mother!

RECOGNIZE the Message

Out of all the topics we're covering, perhaps same-sex attraction carries the most baggage. It is probably the chapter people will flip to first. Messages about homosexuality come from all directions—scientific, philosophic, psychological, and even theological. We cannot address all of them, but we can address some of them.

1. Born That Way...and God Doesn't Make Mistakes

The message here is that sexual orientation is considered a fixed, immutable part of a person. Therefore sexual preferences are something over which one has zero control. It would be like asking them to change their eye color. Furthermore, if it can be shown that an individual was born with unalterable same-sex attractions, and God doesn't make mistakes, then trying to change orientations is actually going *against* God's design.

Spot the Faulty Logic

A: God doesn't make mistakes.
FC: I was born gay.
C: Being gay is how God made me.

2. Love Is Love

This can be interpreted in two different ways. It usually means that romantic love between two people of the same sex is not different—no better or worse—than romantic love between people of opposite genders. But I think there's another issue at play: Our kids are getting confused as to what romantic love even *is*. A child I know came home claiming to be "pansexual" because they "love everyone." Y'all, my nephew wanted to marry my mom when he was a kid. It's a shame we only have one word for love because our kids are getting super confused. (See page 138.)

3. My Sexuality Is My Identity

One of the biggest charges leveled at the Christian church is that not affirming homosexuality is an attack on a person's very identity. According to activists, you don't *have* same-sex attraction. You *are* homosexual. It doesn't just describe an aspect of you; it is your unchangeable core around which everything else revolves.

4. The Bible Has Nothing to Say About Long-Term, Committed Homosexual Relationships

This is the crux of Vines's argument. If one can "prove" that homosexual practice does not contradict what the Bible says, then there is no reason to treat it as sin. Homosexual relationships would be bound by the same parameters as heterosexual relationships—two people in a monogamous committed relationship for a lifetime.

OFFER Discernment

As stated in the beginning of the chapter, those who identify as LGBTQ+ have some legitimate grievances against the church for treating their struggles as worse (or less redeemable) than other sexual struggles. Feeling that they didn't choose their attractions, they wither in despair; why even try if they're already condemned and hopeless? This is not the message we should be sending.

Spot the Faulty Logic

FC: The Bible says gay sex is an abomination (Leviticus 18:22).
FC: I have same-sex attraction.
C: I am an abomination.

Furthermore, while we can't scientifically make predictions about every gay individual, we can make observations regarding LGBTQ+ identifying individuals as a demographic. Psychological suffering is a hallmark of those who identify as a sexual minority; we can't ignore it. If there is one facet on which all the research is consistent, it is the prevalence of a whole bunch of other issues—depression, anxiety, suicide, body dysmorphia, substance abuse, and more—plaguing this group.[14] And don't even get me started on the loneliness epidemic.[15] We must recognize these issues as we seek to minister to hurting individuals—individuals whom God made to be loved. At the same time, we must acknowledge the lies that have snuck in.

Lie #1: I Have to Follow My Desires

Sexual desire has been given center stage when it comes to a person's identity. The assumption is that if a person is "wired" a certain way, then not following the way they were wired is inauthentic or oppressive. But what we need to remember is that *we are all wired to sin.* My sin may be different from yours, but we shouldn't claim that something isn't sin just because it comes naturally. Just watch how any two-year-old behaves "naturally."

Lie #2: If You Believe Homosexuality Is Sin, You Hate Homosexuals

I can't say this enough: The enemy is here to steal, kill, and destroy (John 10:10), and that includes relationships. What better way to extinguish any hope for relationship between God's church and a sinner than to convince the sinner they are hated? Mama Bears, we have to fight for the category of "I love you, but your actions do not reflect God's image." These are *not mutually exclusive*, no matter how many people argue that they are. Without that category, none of us could have a relationship with God.

Lie #3: The Bible's Silence Can Be Tacit Permission

Revisionists make a fair point that Scripture doesn't specifically talk about long-term, loving, same-sex couples. But where things get wonky is when they try to use this logic to argue that same-sex relationships must then have God's approval. This is called an argument from silence. It's a slippery slope, trying to determine what God *might* have meant *had He said something.*

What we do know is that everywhere homosexual sex is mentioned in Scripture, it is condemned. We cannot, in good conscience, assume that there must still exist another unscathed subset of homosexual practice, unmentioned in Scripture, that is morally sanctioned by God. The revisionist is reading *into* Scripture rather than just reading Scripture.

Spot the Faulty Logic

A: Same-sex behavior and orientation are different.

FC: The Bible only talks about same-sex behavior.

C: The Bible is silent on same-sex orientation.

Lie #4: "Good" and "Bad" Fruit Refer to the Consequences of Ideas

Many gay-affirming individuals will reference the "fruit" of holding to a traditionalist view—the depression, homelessness, and the other things Hatmaker cited. Might I posit that bad fruit grows on all sides when we deviate from Christ's love or Christ's truth?

Fruit, according to Luke 3:8, is behavior that reflects repentance. When we see people continuing in a sexual relationship that is outside God's design, that is bad fruit. When we see people trying to shame individuals into obedience, that, too, is bad fruit! No one side produces bad fruit. Good fruit comes when we lean into God's love, submit our desires to Him, and allow Him to transform our desires like we never thought possible. If you want to read about what good fruit looks like, read Jackie Hill Perry's *Gay Girl, Good God*, Rosario Butterfield's *Confessions of an Unlikely Convert*, or Christopher Yuan's *Holy Sexuality*.

ARGUE for a Healthier Approach

We cannot be divided anymore. When we begin to embrace God's truth, healing and wholeness can begin. Here are a few things to keep in mind.

Truth #1: We Must Submit All Parts of Ourselves to Christ, and Our Sexualities Are Not Excluded from this Submission

So many voices in culture are telling people that submitting their sexuality to God's design is "being inauthentic" or "living a lie." Sorry to be the bearer of bad news, but it is much worse than that. Obeying Christ means *dying to ourselves and our desires* (Galatians 2:20; Colossians 3:5; Luke 9:23). Faith comes in when we trust in the goodness of God and believe that His commands really do bring life! If a person is not convinced of the goodness of God, they will never be convinced to deny such a powerful part of themselves.

Truth #2: A Person's Sexuality Is Not Their Whole Identity

Our society has elevated sexuality to the point of it being the preeminent expression of a person...and our kids will hear this belief repeated so regularly that they won't even question it. So we must reinforce the truth that our sexuality is *not* our entire identity. If a Christian believes it is, they have already denied Christ as their primary identity. At the foot of the cross, all other identities fade into the background. In light of our true identity, living a life according to the desires of our flesh is the most *inauthentic* thing we can do.

Truth #3: Having Proclivities Is Not the Same as Sinning

Remember: Satan is equally pleased to conquer you through sin as he is to conquer you through shame. It's okay to admit, "I have attractions that I didn't ask for and don't want," instead of pretending that said attractions don't exist. (That rarely works.) Rather, treat all sinful desires the same: crucify them (Galatians 5:24), and submit them to God. They may keep returning, but— when we don't allow them mastery over us—they usually return with less power. When we say, "I want my sin but I want Christ more," Satan is defeated! He is defeated on the sin level, and he is defeated on the shame level! Booya! (And just as a side note, sin didn't enter the world when Adam and Eve were tempted; it entered when they disobeyed.)

Truth #4: We May Not All Be Called to Celibacy for Life, but We're All Called to Sexual Faithfulness

This is a nonnegotiable for the follower of Christ. All of us. As we saw in chapter 1, sexual faithfulness is always how Christians have been set apart from culture. And as much as we would love to be the ones to define what counts as sexually moral and immoral, we do not have that power. God alone, the Creator of sex, is the One who defines how His good gift is to be used—between husband and wife in marriage.

Truth #5: Marriage Is So Much More than Sexual Attraction

The erotic part of marriage is wonderful, but it's not the only thing (or even the main thing!) that keeps a marriage together. Being able to trust, to be vulnerable, to love, to forgive, to laugh, to fight, and to repent—these all happen in a happy marriage. There are millions of people in marriages who struggle with sexual dysfunction, and every one of them—when they are committed to Christ and to their spouse—have had to learn other ways of being intimate. *Sex is not the only means of intimacy*. Furthermore, the beauty of marriage is that you don't have to be attracted to an entire gender—just your spouse. There are numerous examples of individuals who formerly identified as same-sex attracted (SSA) who have married many of whom still struggle with SSA *in general.* Did they suddenly "become heterosexual"? Nope. But they were able to find *someone* of the opposite sex to whom they were attracted! You only need one. We're not saying this is God's path for every same-sex-attracted individual. But as followers of Christ, we need to at least leave that option open.

REINFORCE Through Discussion, Discipleship, and Prayer

1. If you are married, make "This is why I married you!" a regular household phrase between you and your spouse. Many of our kids think sex and compatible personalities are the main reasons for marriage. Let them see your friendship, your banter, your laughter, your prayer, your service, and your forgiveness. Whenever you are appreciating aspects of your spouse, remind them (in front of your children), "See? This is why I married you."

2. When you discipline your child, make sure to tell them: "I love *you*, but not what you just did." This will help distinguish between the categories of identity and behaviors.

3. Remind your children that part of loving like Jesus is to find those who are on the outskirts and invite them into fellowship. Encourage them to look for kids in their classes who might not fit in or are lonely, and

invite them over for playtime together. Emphasize how this is what it means to love others like Jesus did.

4. Talk to your children about identity. What makes them who they are? Which parts of them are unchanging? (Their ethnicity, their gender, their relation as your son or daughter, their status as children of God.) Which parts of them might change? (Their likes or dislikes, food preferences, favorite activities, clothing styles, and hobbies.) Remind them how a true identity is something that doesn't change, but it's okay to express their identities in many different ways. Teach them that there are many ways to express themselves while not confusing these expressions as part of their unchangeable identity.

5. Remind your kids of the different kinds of love. When they say, "I love [XYZ]," ask them regularly, "Which kind of love do you mean?" (Prepare for eye rolls the more you do this.) We want to instill over and over that not all love is romantic love. For more information, listen to episode 97 of the *Mama Bear Apologetics Podcast*, "The Four Types of Love and Why Our Kids Need to Understand Them."[16]

PAWS for Prayer by Julie Loos

PRAISE God for Who He Is

O God! Jehovah Rapha, You are the Lord who heals. And we all need Your healing. We run to You, our refuge from hurt, our shield from deception, our fortress for protection, our dwelling place away from the sexual firestorm that bombards us. You heal the wounded and forgive the wounder.

ADMIT Where We Have Fallen Short of His Standard

First, Lord, we, Your church, ask forgiveness for the times we have inflicted pain on those who identify as LGBTQ+. Forgive us when we have rejected them, called them unredeemable, labeled them unpardonable, treated them as untouchable. We realize we have not always comprehended the depths of the hurt of sexual trauma that can push people away from Your design for their affections. At the same time, forgive us when we have reinterpreted Scripture through the lens of our own pain over the sexuality of a loved one. When our knees have buckled under the weight of the right thing to do in hard situations, and we have not stood tall for Your truth, forgive us, Lord.

WORSHIP WITH THANKSGIVING for the Things He Has Done

Thank You for hearing our cries. When we abide in You, we can confidently draw near to Your throne of grace and "receive mercy and find grace to help us in our time of need" (Hebrews 4:16). When that need is for transformation—You give us power. For fleeing temptation—You give us self-control. For standing firm—You give us faithfulness. When we surrender to You, we become attached to the true vine. As Your branches, our identity is grafted in Christ alone.

SUBMIT Yourselves and Your Requests to God

Help us see this one true fact. We are all born *this* way: sinners. And we are all offered the same rescue plan: by faith alone in Christ alone with our sin atoned. Give us eyes to see those who struggle. Help us clearly and lovingly show that one is so much more than one's sexual identity, and that to deny that is to sell oneself way short of God's glorious purpose. Let us teach our children to be faithful disciples submitting all their desires to You. In this world of so much confusion and so many evil darts targeting our children, we pray as You prayed for Peter: "I have prayed for you, [child's name], that your faith may not fail. And when you have turned back, strengthen your brothers" (Luke 22:32).

 DISCUSSION QUESTIONS 

1. **Icebreaker:** Do you have any friends or family who identify as gay? What was it like when they shared this? How did other people react? How did you react?

2. **Main theme:** *Same-sex-attracted individuals are people to be loved, but that doesn't mean we affirm the lie that God approves of sexuality outside of a husband-and-wife relationship.* Read through Romans 1:18-32. Based on this passage, why do you think Scripture places such an emphasis on the sexuality of Christians?

3. **Self-evaluation:** Have you ever found yourself treating homosexuality like a worse sin than other sexual sins? Have you ever been tempted to compromise what God says about same-sex activity out of a desire to love someone? How might this be you trying to be "more loving than God"? What is a proper balance?

4. **Brainstorm:** We are called to love as Christ loved without affirming lies. Brainstorm ways to include and love the same-sex-attracted people in your life without compromising on truth. If you don't have any in your life, get a plan in place so that if and when you *do* discover a friend with SSA, it doesn't throw you for a loop. Distinguish between activities that affirm a lie versus ones that affirm a person. (Example: My friend in California tried to "love" his gay friends by going to a gay bar with them. I loved his heart but counseled him that maybe that wasn't the best approach.)

5. **Release the bear:** With your kids, as appropriate for their ages, read the article "Overhauling Straight America," which is available online.[17] The article should not change the way your children interact with their same-sex-attracted peers, but it should open their eyes to what is going on in the media so they don't blindly absorb its messages.

CHAPTER 13

I Identify as a [Fill in the Blank]

Understanding Gender Identity

HILLARY

Were I to summarize the main thrust of adolescence, it would be in one single word: *identity*. Prior to adolescence, children don't really think about who they are or why they do things. You've found your kid smearing cream cheese all over the dog and ask, "Why the heck did you do that?!" What do kids say—like, every time? They shrug and mumble, "I dunno." Because *that's kids*. They rarely know why they do anything! Like the Joker in *The Dark Knight*, they just *dooo thiiiiings*. Not until adolescence do they reflect upon the *why* behind their choices.

So, why *do* we do things? We talked about worldview in chapters 2 and 9. Worldviews filter a lot of our unconscious behavior, but what about the things we're intentional about? Our careers? Our clothes? Our overt likes and dislikes (or at least the ones we share)? How we present ourselves to society comes down to not only who we are, but also *how we want people to perceive us*. Yes, it's that ever-elusive concept of identity.

What does it mean to discover your identity? Do you remember when you were trying to figure it out? I do. Vividly. Everyone was supposed to have their "thing." What kind of girl were you? Were you sporty? Artsy? Goth? Were you into band or 4H? Theater? As a youth group leader, I watched one girl reinventing herself every year. She went from giggly freshman cheerleader to disgruntled grungy sophomore, then to sporty snowboarder her junior year. Each year a different persona. That's to be expected from teenagers. They try on different identities, asking, "Does this feel like me? How about this one?" But in recent years, this process has gone terribly wrong. Identity has gone beyond hobbies or personality, and instead, kids are now primarily identifying by how they are different from "the norm" (#queertheory).

In terms of mental health norms, kids are clamoring for the best and newest disorder. They more quickly self-identify with a diagnosis than a hobby *because diagnoses now ascribe status and even perks*.[1] Same thing for identifying as LGBTQ+. Labels make them interesting, as long as they aren't a boring, straight, cisgender, mentally healthy cyborg. The result? They barely have time to figure out their actual identity because they are so focused on labels. Are they a guy, a girl? Agender? Nonbinary? Genderqueer? And what if it changes on a regular basis (genderfluid)? Extracurriculars? Pshhh...Who even has the time? I need to figure out my pronouns for the day.

Can you imagine trying to navigate this new landscape, Mama Bears? *As a teenager?* Going through puberty has always been hard, no matter the culture. If we look back at our middle and high school days with rose-colored glasses, we forget the hormone-infused misery that defined many of our adolescent experiences. Bodies were changing; emotions were raging. And brains? Fuhgeddaboudit. Some days they worked, and other days they didn't; whoever lived in there might've been really smart...but they were rarely home. The pubescent mind and body are unpredictable, awkward, and uncomfortable. Swirl that in with a whole demographic of other people in the same turmoil (and all vying for social dominance), and you've got a *lot* of existential angst going on—and that's before kids had to figure out if they were a boy or a girl!

How in the world can we help our kids grow into men and women of God if they aren't even sure what it means to be a man or a woman? Or if they even are one? Adolescents today are being taught that gender is on a spectrum and the possibilities are endless.

Gender used to be this beautiful no-brainer. It was a tiny sliver of certainty in a sea of hormonal confusion. Questioning our gender never even occurred to most of us—at least for 99.982 percent of us.[2] But our kids are in a different boat, and we, Mama Bears, need to be ready to counter the identity attacks being leveled at this next generation of image bearers.

My Personal Gender Story

As we saw in the queer theory chapter, kids are now being taught that their biological sex and their gender identity are two separate things. It's a manufactured, ideology-driven division—untestable, unproven—and it's making an already tumultuous time that much more chaotic. Praise God I didn't have to deal with that as a kid! Had I been raised in today's world, I'm not quite sure how I would have turned out.

Based on pictures, I started out as a typical little girl playing dress-up and imagining myself with long flowing hair...but that stage didn't last long. Somewhere along the line I started hating dresses with a passion. And I didn't just hate to wear them because they were restrictive (I couldn't show off my gymnastics moves!) but rather because of what they *represented*—all the other little girls I didn't fit in with.

I wasn't able to articulate my disgust with my gender until sometime in high school. I finally realized that I hated everything feminine because I equated being a girl with being weak, stupid, irrational, and illogical. Movies like the *Indiana Jones* series didn't help, where the supposedly "strong" female characters weren't strong; they were just brassy, loud, and annoying. And they *still* had to be constantly saved because of their own stupidity! If that's what a "strong woman" looks like, then you can keep her too! I'll be over here, hanging with the dudes.

Thankfully, I never questioned *if* I was a girl (probably because I was five-foot-one and 80 pounds soaking wet). All I knew was that I didn't want to be *that* kind of girl—the stereotypical, irrational kind who cried at movies, weddings, and babies. Though I enjoyed hair and makeup, I shunned femininity. Secretly, I thought that if I could prove to be like a guy in every other way, I'd be more attractive than all those frou-frou girly-girls that guys loved to complain about.

I even convinced a psychologist that I "thought more like a guy." After several sessions with me, she actually agreed! I vividly remember her saying: "Oh, wow...you are right. You *do* think more like a guy."[3] I considered it the highest of all compliments and relayed her conclusion to other people as proof that even the professionals agreed! And I did all of this into my late twenties...until I met the man who would later become my husband.

John and I fell in love with each other's minds before anything else. Our shared love of theology, apologetics, and philosophy put us in #nerdlove from the beginning. The week we made our long-distance romance official, I got sick and had to stay home from work for a whole week. Then I promptly got pink eye...and was home alone for *another* week. You do not want to see what happens to a chronic overthinker when you isolate her for two straight weeks. I spent every waking moment of that time analyzing exactly where my relationship with John was headed. When the pressure finally got to me, I sent John this long email, demanding a fuller DTR (define the relationship) than what we had already DTR'd.

He responded with the gentlest email possible. It was super short, along the lines of, "I already told you where I stand. Be at peace. God's got this." I sat there and let those words sink in for about ten minutes, and then I started to cry.

And it wasn't just a little cry. It was a big one, as if a lifetime of crying was suddenly coming out all at once (which, in some ways it was, since I hadn't cried in like ten years). I wasn't disappointed at his answer; rather, God revealed something to me in that moment. I can't quite describe it, but I got a picture of the woman inside of me who had been bound, gagged, and hidden. At that moment, with that email, it felt as if that woman had been released and was coming into the light, blinking in shock, dirty and disheveled...but free. My crying wasn't for *me* me. It was for the part of me—her—that I'd buried all this time. It was like for the first time, it was okay for her to come out because I had found a man with whom it was safe to be vulnerable. I bawled for about 45 minutes out of grief for what I'd done to this poor woman inside me.

The change wasn't immediate, but I can say with certainty that I have gotten girlier and girlier the longer I've been married to John. It hasn't affected my core personality. I'm still very logical, systematic, and blunt. And to this day, I'm more comfortable in a room full of guys than girls; they feel safer and more predictable. What *has* changed is that I have fun with my femininity now. I embrace my weaknesses. And crying? OMGosh...I'm a total crier now. (Be careful what you make fun of. God turns you into it!)

I've had to learn an entire other language of femininity, and I still have trouble fitting in with the average girl. But you know what? That's okay. *There is room in womanhood for a woman like me.* I don't have to fit some stereotype. Had I been born 20 years later, I might have never been able to discover all these parts of myself because I would have been taught that my gender identity was different from my biology.

A Brief History of Gender Identity

Prior to the 1950s, the terms *gender* and *sex* were mostly synonymous. The differentiation mostly mattered for specific disciplines (like Romance languages) where words are gendered (masculine and feminine) but not biologically sexed.

In 1966, a doctor named John Money popularized the phrase "gender identity" while advertising for his clinic at Johns Hopkins University.[4] Money was the researcher who pioneered gender theory—the idea that a person's gender identity was different from their biological sex. But how could he prove it? In 1965, a perfect test case dropped into his lap.

In 1965, Ron and Janet Reimer gave birth to identical twin boys, Bruce and Brian. Sadly, there was a mishap during baby Bruce's circumcision, and his penis was burned beyond repair. Dr. Money convinced the parents that all it would take was a surgery, some hormones, and a little encouragement in the right direction, and Bruce could easily be raised as Brenda.

This was the moment Dr. Money had been waiting for! Identical twins?

Raised as separate sexes? In the same household!? It was a researcher's dream. He saw the twins yearly until they were in their teens, publicly touting the experiment as a smashing success. But this all came to a crashing halt in 1997 when researcher Milton Diamond decided to investigate Money's claims.

What Dr. Diamond uncovered should have discredited Dr. Money forever: sexual abuse, pedophilia, voyeurism, and a kind of (ahem…) "sexual role reinforcement therapy" that is too graphic to describe here. Far from seamlessly adapting to life as a girl, "Brenda" grew up miserable and was bullied by classmates for "her" masculine proclivities. After the Reimer's finally admitted to "Brenda" what had happened, he immediately reassumed his male identity and lived the rest of his life as David. Unfortunately, too much damage had already been done. By 2004, both David and his twin brother were dead from suicide.

So, where did Money get the radical idea that sex and gender were separate to begin with? Historically, we've agreed that people who produce sperm (men) and people who produce eggs (women) are different, but what we've disagreed on is the *extent* and *origin* of those differences. Exactly how different are the two sexes? Have these differences always existed, or have they been imposed over time?

Physically, women are generally smaller and weaker than men. Emotionally, women are often more in tune, but can have a harder time compartmentalizing.[5] Unfortunately, these general differences were often used to justify treating women as not only physically but intellectually inferior. We were denied access to university education, prohibited from participating in mainstream professions, and lost all property rights upon marriage. Regarding the first feminist convention in 1848, political scientist Charles Murray states, "Women were rebelling not against mere inequality, but near total legal subservience to men."[6]

Instead of saying that men and women tend to gravitate toward certain spheres, people started acting like women were incapable of doing things that were traditionally masculine, and that men were exempt from doing things that were traditionally feminine. However, as Nancy Pearcy argues in her book *The Toxic War on Masculinity*, what we now think of as "traditional" gender roles have only been around since the industrial revolution. A majority of earth's history consisted of agrarian and trade societies where men and women worked side by side. The women often ran the home and managed the family business; the men did the heavier, manual labor; both parents contributed to rearing the children.

When mass production demolished the family business model, it took the most intellectually stimulating tasks out of the home—along with the men. Is it any wonder that second-wave feminists fought against these rigid gender roles? Wanting to be included in the "male" sphere of business and intellectual life, many feminists erred on the opposite extreme by denying *any* inborn differences between the sexes. Enter activists such as philosopher Simone de Beauvoir, who taught that "one is not born, one is made a woman,"[7] and anthropologist Gayle Rubin, who argued that "gender is a socially imposed division of the sexes."[8] It's as if women got so tired of all the baggage that came along with being called "woman" that they just threw it all down and demanded to start from scratch. Gender is just a construct! And if it was constructed, then we can *deconstruct* it and reconstruct it however we like! Enter intellectual Judith Butler, who taught that gender is "produced" through a "stylized repetition of acts."[9] Translation: Gender is determined by what you *do*, not who you *are*. That brings us to now, where feeling, dressing, and acting like a female is what makes a person a woman.

Spot the Faulty Logic

A: Gender is what you do.
FC: I can change what I do.
C: I can change my gender.

Keeping It Simple

If we want our kids to understand what is going on, we need to take them back to the beginning—like how to define gender. Often, the word itself reveals how it was intended to be understood. The root word of gender is *gen*—which means "produces" or "causes." Our *gen*der (that is, sex) describes how we, as humans, *gen*erate other humans. Women produce eggs and men produce sperm, both of which are necessary to re*produce.* Therefore, linguistically speaking, our gen*der* is what kind of produc*er* we are—egg or sperm. *This is a binary we cannot escape.* (Binary means only two options with nothing in between.) And this binary is very real; we have never witnessed any kind of functional egg-sperm hybrid.[10]

The binary of male/female is almost a dirty word now though, as seen by how popular the label "nonbinary" has become, especially with our youth. But what does it mean to be nonbinary? Before we can know why kids are bucking against the binary, we need to figure out what their beef with the binary is to begin with. And that leads us right to the feet of the great boogeyman, gender stereotypes.

Stupid Gender Stereotypes...Where Did They Even Come From?

It's interesting how gender theorists simultaneously rage against stereotypes while also making them the foundation for their entire theory. Come on, y'all: Either stereotypes are evil and need to be tossed, or they are the fixed, absolute, center around which our gender identity and expression revolves. You can't say "Both boys and girls can like playing with dolls" one moment and then "If you like playing with dolls you are more of a girl" the next. Pick one or the other, folks. You can't have both.

A gender stereotype is a preconceived idea about how the different sexes act, feel, behave, etc. (And as Amy often says, "Gender stereotypes describe many but define none.") As we saw in the Genderbread chapter, gender identity and gender expression are how a person *identifies in their mind* and how they choose to act out that gender *in their personal style.*[11] In essence, separating sex from gender places someone's fundamental identity on the shifting sands of gender stereotypes—stereotypes which may differ depending on the culture. And therein lies yet *another* problem: There is no set definition of masculine and feminine.[12] Some stereotypes have changed drastically over time and vary depending on location. Are we talking about the Wild West where manhood rested on a dude's ability to build a house with his bare hands, or are we in revolutionary France, where an aristocrat's man-card was contingent on rocking a pair of heels, kabuki-like makeup, and a giant powdered wig? Time and location matter.

But here's the issue: Gender theorists and LGBTQ+ advocates have convinced an entire generation of students, teachers, medical professionals, and researchers that sex is different from gender identity, and that gender identity is determined by gender stereotypes (like personality, interests, and aptitudes). *And then* they rabidly preyed upon people who already struggled to fit in or felt isolated.

Mama Bears, our kids need to know that their personality, interests, and aptitudes (or preferred clothing for that matter) do not determine their gender identity. Each of these aspects can change over time. We get new hobbies. We acquire new job skills. Goodness knows the twentysomething version of you has a different *everything* than the mom-of-three-kids version of you. (Do I even like parties anymore?! I just want to stay home in my fleece pants.) We should all have the freedom to discover, explore, and change, without worrying about it *redefining our gender*. I can't imagine the existential crisis that arises for kids who think they have to have this all figured out in their teen years.

I've thought long and hard about how we can demolish this flawed thinking *before* it wreaks havoc on our little bears. The best explanation I can come up with involves a boatload of graphs. Y'all ready to get nerdy?

Dismantling the Gender Spectrum One Graph at a Time

As we saw in the Genderbread chapter, gender theorists often use a very simple graph that "helps" kids determine their "gender identity." It looks something like this:

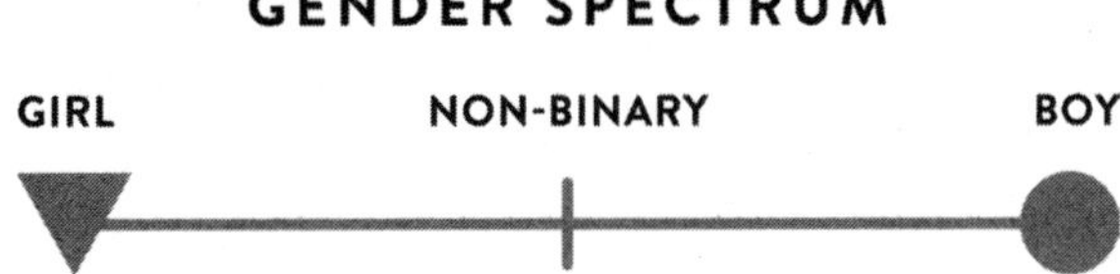

Theorists pick a trait, determine the "feminine" and "masculine" ends of the spectrum, and then ask a child where they land. (And since so few people are at the extreme ends, everyone ends up sounding a little nonbinary; it's built into the system.) So we need to ask where these "masculine" and "feminine" stereotypes originally came from and if they are as deterministic as the LGBTQ+ lobbyists claim.

To explain gender stereotypes to our kids in a concrete way, we first need to understand what a distribution curve is (because gender stereotypes involve two overlapping distribution curves). A distribution curve is essentially a bar graph put to a curve. It shows how certain traits are distributed in a population. The horizontal line represents the spectrum of the trait. (Aha! *That's* where spectrums come in!) The vertical height of each bar represents the number of people who fall into that portion of the spectrum. Think of it like this: *On a scale of 1–10, how much do you like cooking?* When we analyze the *distribution* of a trait, we can uncover what "most" people are. See the graph below. Whatever the trait is, there is a *norm.* (Gasp! Oppression!) The "norm" is the area into which "most" people fall. But you also have people who land on either extreme, *and that's okay*. We love diversity here at Mama Bear!

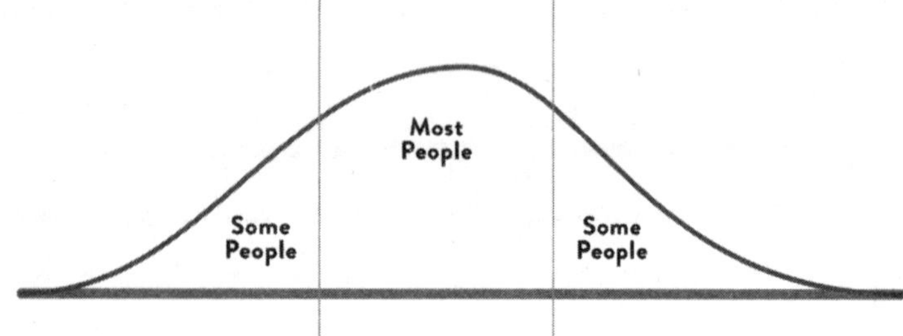

And guess what? When studying the traits for different genders, there can be a distribution unique to each sex. There are certain traits that most men identify with, but they can be extreme on one end or the other. Same for women. So what happens when we overlap these two graphs for any particular trait? Well, that's where you can see if there are *general* gender differences (aka stereotypes).

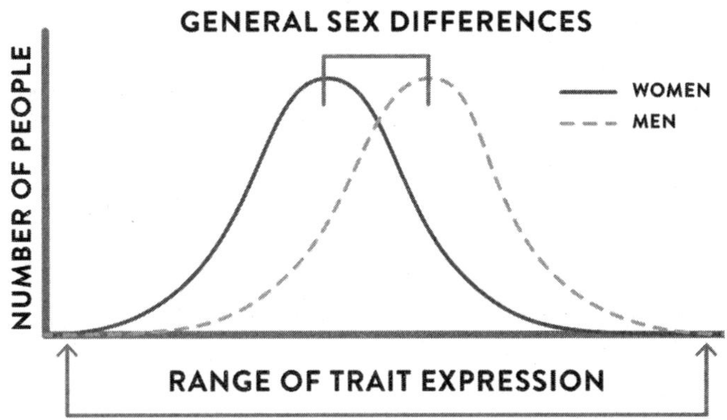

Let's start with something simple to understand, like height. Here's a graph that shows how height is distributed between men and women.

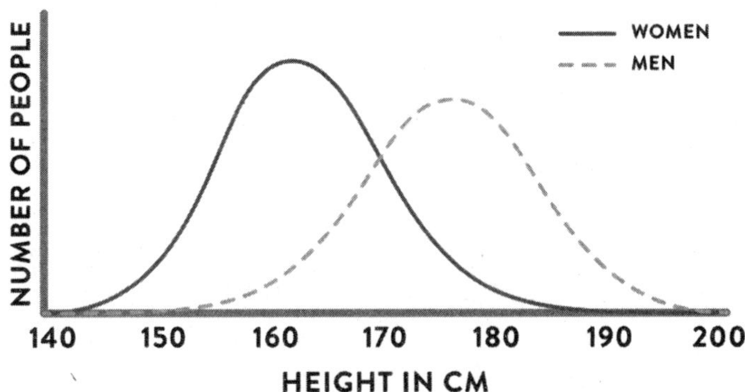

Theoretically, the two ends of the spectrum (the horizontal line) would represent the shortest person in the world and the tallest person in the world. Everyone else is in between these two extremes. If we were to compare height between men and women, we'd notice that men are *generally* taller than women, but there is a lot of overlap. Some women on the tall end are taller than men on the short end of the spectrum. Nobody would determine the male or female in a relationship based on height, even though men are *generally* (i.e., stereotypically) taller than women. This kind of spectrum is one that kids can easily understand. So let's look at how this applies to gender stereotypes, specifically regarding personality, interests, and aptitudes.

Pick any gender stereotypical trait. For example, how much does a child enjoy wrestling with other people? If we were to survey a few thousand boys and girls and chart it out, we'd probably discover that *in general*, boys like roughhousing more than girls.

However, there will be girls who love wrestling just as much as your rowdiest boy, and there will be boys who *hate* wrestling as much as your prissiest girl; there's plenty of room on the spectrum for all of these boys and girls. Let's see how that looks on the overlapping graph which includes separate male and female curves:

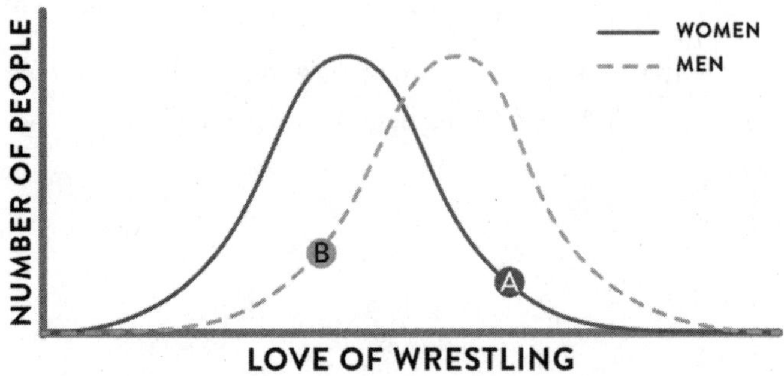

Nothing wrong so far. There is room for a girl who likes wrestling on the girl spectrum and boy who hates it on the boy spectrum.

Now let's pretend we're looking at the curve from above. Instead of seeing the two overlapping curves, we'd see a single line with where the boy and the girl land.

Holy cow! That looks waaaay different! Suddenly our girl is more of a "male" and the boy is more "female." Congratulations—your child has just discovered they are either trans or nonbinary. Science proved it.

Here's the problem, Mama Bears: This is how the gender theorists are presenting the data to our kids! They are reducing a two-dimensional diagram into a single dimension, and the results look a whole lot like a bunch of gender-confused kids!

So How Do We Combat This?

I can't say this enough: Get your kids familiar with these graphs as soon as they can understand graphs. You want them to hear over and over again "personality, interests, and aptitudes are on a spectrum...gender is not." And if they ever get confused because they feel like they're on the "masculine" or "feminine" end of the spectrum, break out our two-dimensional model which has that beautiful range of expression for both boys and girls. Ask, "Where do you think you fall on the spectrum for [trait that is making them confused]." Find it on the graph, and ask, "Is there still room for a [boy or girl] like you on this graph?" Of course there is! Remind them that the world is in fact *richer* for a boy like him or a girl like her! We have so much freedom in our biological bodies, nobody has to fit some preconceived notion of "masculine" or "feminine" in order to know their gender. Don't believe me? Take a look at Amy's blogs on the Mama Bear Apologetics page discussing men and women in the Bible who defied their gender stereotypes—and were often praised for being godly!

Our kids need to know that they do not answer to God for how well they fit into a stereotype. They answer to God for how well they lived *as He created them to be*. And Mama Bears and Papa Bears, we need to make sure that we are not accidentally tacking things onto what it means to be a godly man or woman. A godly woman can enjoy motorcycles, rolling in mud, and wearing boots. A godly man can enjoy dancing, rom-coms, and knitting.[13] Breaking the confusion surrounding gender identity starts with us, and it starts by reminding our children over and over and over again that there is room for a boy like him or a girl like her—and that she will one day find a rockin' husband who loves her exactly for what she brings to the table, and he can find a wonderful wife who prefers his sensitivity over machismo.

We also need to be instilling not only a healthy gender identity, but also healthy sexuality by reminding them that bucking the norm of stereotypes does *not automatically mean they are gay*! I have personally known many feminine men and masculine women who didn't start out same-sex attracted, but ended up declaring themselves gay after enough people told them that they were "gay and just didn't know it yet."

Remember what I've said before: The brain has a hard time distinguishing between the familiar and the true. And if the most "familiar" message a kid hears is "having this trait means I'm gay and just don't know it yet," that lie eventually worms its way into their minds, plants seeds, and births questions about their sexuality that they might otherwise not have asked. It needs to stop *now*, and it stops with us, Mama and Papa Bears! If there was ever anything to roar at, it's that—convincing kids that their gender and sexuality depend on their mannerisms or interests. According to Matthew 18:6, a person telling the gentle, sensitive boy that he is gay should have a giant millstone attached to their neck and thrown in the sea. Seriously, y'all…me and Jesus feel very strongly about this.

ROAR Like a Mother!

RECOGNIZE the Message

Now that we see what is currently going on within gender confusion, let's talk about how to roar through it! (I recommend going back and refreshing yourself on the queer theory ROAR on pages 170-174. Many of the same points could be used here, but we'll keep these a little more practical.)

1. Be Your "Authentic Self"

You'll hear the phrase "authentic self" a lot within gender ideology, where it's seen as constraining and oppressive to equate gender with biological sex. Doing so "forces" people into an unnatural box and prevents them from being who they really are.

2. Try Out All the Identities to Figure Out Who You Are!

When gender theorists say this, they mean you should try transgressing all the gender norms to see if another gender identity "fits" you better. If it does, then you might be transgender. They also mean try out all the sexualities, as we saw in the NSES guidelines in chapter 6.

3. I Identify as a [Fill in the Blank]

According to gender theorists, your gender is how you, in your head, identify. Do you feel more like a boy? A girl? Neither? Something in between? There is even a whole vocabulary for "nonbinary" people who don't fully identify as either gender. These identities often refer to how much (or how often) a person skews toward masculine or feminine.

4. My Pronouns Are...

Kids are no longer able to exist as boys and girls by default. If they haven't thought about it, then they need to figure it out so they can tell the class which pronouns to use on the first day of school. And if he/him/she/her/they/them are too limiting, there's always a whole list of "neopronouns" like ze/zer[14] or even nounself neopronouns like frog/frogself or (and I'm not kidding) demon/demonself.[15] No matter what, they must have a label.

OFFER Discernment

Before we address the lies that have snuck in with these messages, let's first affirm what modern gender theorists get right. The main grievance we can heartily affirm is that gender stereotypes have been unnecessarily rigid.

This is a particular problem for boys. What is a *positive* male parallel to the female category of "tomboy"? I'll wait. Can't think of any? Maybe that's because there really aren't any. Since at least the 1980s women have been accepted for (and encouraged to have) traditionally masculine traits; the same cannot be said for boys. Feminism has meant that our rough-and-tumble, soccer-playing, UFC-watching girls have had lots of freedom to explore the many and varied nuances for feminine. But our ballet-loving, beauty-creating, quietly-playing, aggression-averse boys still risk being called a "sissy." I cannot even fathom the damage that has been done by making our boys' manhood contingent on whether they liked to play tackle football. If David could dance in his underwear, cry regularly, and play the harp while still being considered a manly man after God's own heart, then so can our sensitive boys.

But let's not leave our girls out either. They've been sucker-punched by society's wildly unreachable beauty expectations—especially in terms of sex appeal. (Kids weren't meant to think about sex appeal!) But now, being sexy (or wanting to be) is a non-negotiable for our girls. Many feel that their worth is dependent on their ability to compete with a five-foot-seven, hundred-pound, stiletto-wearing glamazon whose clothes leave little to the imagination. Some girls feel so far from this "ideal" that that they figure, "Maybe I'd be better off as a guy?" You know, why even attempt a losing game? It's no wonder that in recent years, as Abigail Shrier says, "The girls fled womanhood like a house on fire."[16]

And when it comes to fitting into a box, I'm sorry to say that the church shares some of the blame as well. We've meant well, but our men's and women's ministries are often so stereotype-laden that the men and women who don't fit those molds mistakenly get the message that they are not man or woman enough *for God.* I realize that we can't please everyone, but let's just be very careful that we're not subtly reinforcing a faulty understanding of what a "Christian man" or "Christian woman" is like by putting the same *type* of man or woman up in front all the time. We just don't have that luxury in this gender confused culture.

So, I get it. I heartily understand how the separation between sex and gender identity has freed *some* people from hurtful stereotypes. However, it has not ultimately freed them *to truth,* but to lies. Let's talk about a few of them.

Lie #1: Gender Stereotypes Determine Gender Identity

Probably the biggest lie of gender theory is that it "frees people from gender stereotypes," but that's just not the case. Using stereotypes to determine a person's "gender identity" reinforces the very thing activists claim they're trying to destroy—gender stereotypes! As we've seen, stereotypes are a poor foundation for identity because they change depending on time and space. True identities don't change. An apple can't stop being an apple, a dog can't stop being a dog, and I can't stop being a woman, no matter how much I prefer facts to feelings. I can act or dress differently based on context or mood, but it doesn't change my identity. Just keep it simple, y'all: Bring whatever you've got to the table as the gender you were born. There's lots of room for a man or woman like you!

Lie #2: I Can Know What It's Like to Be Someone Other Than Me

When people say they "identify" as a male or female, it assumes that they know what a [fill in the blank identity] *is*, and what it feels like to be one. Can someone "identify as a woman" because they "feel more like a woman"...or a man? How does that work? I don't know what it feels like to be *anyone* other than me, let alone a whole other gender.

Lie #3: My Feelings Are Truer Than My Body and Determine My Identity

Even if we could theoretically know what it feels like to be the opposite gender, when did our feelings become more immutable than our bodies? You can only have one fixed standard, one foundation around which to build your gender identity. Once the psychological "gender identity" becomes a bigger kahuna than biological sex, the body becomes secondary—nay, an enemy! The thing preventing me from living my "authentic self." Mama Bears (and Papa Bears), we only get one body in this life, and how we treat it matters. If someone were to punch me in the arm, I wouldn't ask, "Why did you punch my arm?" I'd ask: "Why did you punch *me*?" And at the same time, I don't cease to be me if I have that same arm amputated. We cannot be "freed" from our bodies as if we were just ghosts in a meat machine. The separation of a person's psyche/soul from their body has a name: death. Without both soul and body, we cease to be human, and humanity is not up for revision.

Lie #4: I Can Control How People See and Treat Me

If a person won't admit that their "gender identity" is based on stereotypes, they must at least grapple with admitting why they want others to see them as the opposite sex or androgynous (nonbinary). Are they avoiding an implicit expectation? Do they prefer the way the opposite sex is treated by others? No matter what the reason, it ultimately comes down to "I don't like the way I am treated as a [male/female] and need to be seen as the opposite before I'll be treated the way I want to be treated.

Spot the Faulty Logic

A: Men are treated with respect.
FC: I don't like how I'm treated as a woman.
C: If I become a man, I'll get more respect.

Mama Bears, I wish there was some formula that would guarantee we're all being treated the way we want to be treated, but there's not. We can be respected or disrespected for any number of reasons. Some people will expect too much from us, or some, too little. We answer to God for what we do with what we've been given. Maturity means taking responsibility for what's within our control and releasing the results to God. Anything else is an endless rat race fueled by discontentment.

ARGUE for a Healthier Approach

1. Interests, Aptitudes, and Personality Are on a Spectrum...Gender Is Not

We can't just say "there is no spectrum," because there actually *is* a spectrum...of *traits*, like interests, aptitudes, personality, or even style. A person may have interests or mannerisms that are more traditionally masculine or feminine, but that doesn't determine whether they produce sperm or eggs. Our ability to *fit in* with others of our gender does not determine our gender! And as a side note, get used to not fitting in: That's part of the job description of being a Christian in a fallen world. We are to be *set apart* from culture, no? *Not* fitting in is our jam.

2. Gender Stereotypes Are Not Biblical Mandates

Most of the lies within gender and transgender theory are predicated on masculine and feminine roles, but stereotypes *are not how God describes men and women.* As we saw on pages 130-131, the Bible's stories depict a wide range of masculinity and femininity. Furthermore, when it comes to the distribution of spiritual gifts, nowhere does Scripture say that there are male gifts and female gifts. The Spirit gives generously to *all* (1 Corinthians 2:7-11; Romans 12:6-8). Though there is debate within the church on *roles* for men and women, these are not based on personality characteristics or aptitudes.

3. You Can't Identify as Something You Can't Define

In 2022, the web erupted after Judge Ketanji Brown Jackson refused to define what a woman was, stating "I am not a biologist."[17] In order to identify *as* something, you need to know what *it is*. I could walk around saying, "I identify as a flurpadurp." What is a flurpadurp? It's anyone who identifies as a flurpadurp! Clearly, this reasoning doesn't work. We can't assume that people know what something is while simultaneously *redefining it* (that is, a woman is anyone who identifies as a woman). It doesn't work for flurpadurps and it doesn't work for men or woman.

REINFORCE Through Discussion, Discipleship, and Prayer

1. Talk to your kids about what it's like to fit in or not fit in. Remind them that we all have our own special kind of weird. Reflecting Christ means reaching out to those who don't fit in and welcoming them into the group. Ask your kids on a regular basis: "Who felt left out today that you were able to include?"

2. If your child has a gender-nonconforming interest or aptitude, remind them ad nauseum how they will "bring to [hobby] something that [other gender] never will." For example, if you have a boy who dances, remind him that he can dance as a boy in a way no girl ever will; if you have a girl who loves erector sets, get excited about how she'll bring an eye to construction that no man ever will. And then also get excited about how their future husband or wife will love this aspect of them! Our kids are being repeatedly told by society that if they are outside their gender box, then they are either in the wrong body or gay. They need to

hear *from us* (and as many people as possible) how their gender-atypical interests are a unique part of how God created them as a boy or girl.

3. Recognize the difference between a child being *drawn to* gender atypical activities and one who is *backing away* from gender typical activities. Both root causes can show up as gender atypical behavior but have very different reasons behind them. If your child has gender atypical interests, *find out why*. A friend of mine's son wanted to wear dresses. After digging deeper and asking some questions, my friend discovered that his son was upset because his sisters wouldn't let him play dress up with them—in their mom's clothes. So dad showed him the special daddy-dress-up clothes and suddenly the boy's fascination with dresses disappeared. This little boy was concerned about *fairness*, not fashion. He didn't give a hoot about dresses; he just didn't like being told he couldn't do something because he was a boy. Or, sometimes, a kid has been so hurt by other kids of their gender that they seek refuge with the opposite gender—like I did. Kids often don't have the words to express what they are actually feeling, and it manifests as them trying to act like the opposite gender.

PAWS for Prayer by Julie Loos

PRAISE God for Who He Is

You are Creator God, designing us male or female. You created us in Your image, (Genesis 1:27) by design, with purpose. The genesis of our identity is in You. And since You are not the author of confusion but of peace (1 Corinthians 14:33), we can be at peace with the way You made us.

ADMIT Where We Have Fallen Short of His Standard

Forgive us when we have unduly burdened your definition of male and female with connotations of what that does and doesn't mean. Forgive us, the church, for not celebrating the breadth of expression of masculinity and femininity within our own men's and women's ministries. We also admit our own lack of understanding over how confused others are when things seem so clear to us. It clouds our compassion. Forgive our culture for wrongly letting fickle feelings rule over reality.

WORSHIP WITH THANKSGIVING for the Things He Has Done

We thank You that You have attributes that are seen in both men and women—like a father, a husband, and even a mother (Isaiah 49:15; Matthew 23:37). From fierce protection to tender care. We are grateful that because You are not changeable and because our identity is grounded in You, *our* identity is unchangeable. Thank You that we were born male or female with freedom to express our personalities, abilities, and interests in a wide range of ways.

SUBMIT Yourselves and Your Requests to God

We pray for those caught up in the confusion of gender identity issues. May we empathize with their struggles without perpetuating the lies of the evil one. We remember that at one time we gratified the cravings of our flesh and followed its desires and thoughts (Ephesians 2:1-3). Deliver the confused. Convict those who are darkened because of suppressing Your truth (Romans 1:18). Show them, Father, that "wonderful are your works" and that their souls can know that very well (Psalm 119). May their bodies and souls speak truth to their feelings. May they come to know the God who does not lie, who is the way out of confusion, the truth about their identity, and the life they are truly seeking.

 DISCUSSION QUESTIONS 

1. **Icebreaker:** Growing up, were you a girly-girl? A tomboy? Somewhere in between?

2. **Main theme:** *The world is telling our kids that their personality, interests, and aptitudes determine their gender.* Why is this problematic?

3. **Self-evaluation:** Have you had overly rigid ideas of what boys and girls

should be like? Have you been guilty of steering your kids away from interests because you worried that they weren't "gender typical"? Are you shepherding your kids to be godly men and women the way *God* created them to be, or are you sometimes trying to mold them into who *you* think they should be? Ask the Lord to reveal any expectations you have of your kids that are undermining His unique calling on their lives. (See prayer #86 in *Honest Prayers for Mama Bears.*)

4. **Brainstorm:** There will always be kids who buck the gender stereotypes. What are some ways you can encourage these kids to embrace their God-given interests and talents while still affirming their God-given genders?

5. **Release the bear (1):** What gender stereotypes have your kids already absorbed? Ask you kids what they think it means to be a girl or boy (or man or woman) and *listen to what they say.* Are there any misunderstandings that need to be corrected? Discuss the ones that need correcting, and emphasize the freedom found within the Bible for both men and women to be how God created them to be without having to identify as another gender.

6. **Release the bear (2):** Practice explaining the gender trait graphs to each other. Use the graphs to explain *general* gender differences, then roleplay what you would say if your child came home thinking they were nonbinary or a different gender because of a personality trait, interest, or aptitude. What might your child's "graph" look like (that is, what trait might be causing them confusion)? It will take practice to be able to reinforce this concept. Practice on each other first!

CHAPTER 14

*Trans*cending the Gender Cult

When Birds Identify as Bees

HILLARY

Chloe Cole is mad. And she has every right to be. At the age of 12, she began experiencing (what she perceived to be) a disconnect between her body and her "gender identity"—a medical diagnosis called gender dysphoria. By age 13, she was approved for puberty blockers and then testosterone, a cross-sex hormone. At age 15, she underwent a double mastectomy, and by 16 she realized that she'd made a terrible mistake.[1] All the problems she'd been trying to outrun were still there. But now she also had a deep voice, the inability to ever breastfeed (*if* she can even have kids), and a whole lot of regret. The surgeries that had promised her freedom did not deliver. Since detransitioning from her male identity back to a girl, she has devoted her life to holding the medical establishments accountable for fast-tracking kids through procedures that are neither safe nor reversible.

Gender Ideology as a Cult

Chloe is not alone. Identifying as transgender—a once-rare phenomena that affected around 0.1 percent of the Boomer population and prior—has increased 2300 percent for Gen Z.[2] Some hail this as a victory made possible by the transgender trailblazers that came before. Others, like author and journalist Abigail Shrier, psychiatrist Miriam Grossman, and physician-scientist Lisa Littman, are not so sure.

One thing is for certain though: A disproportionately large amount of political discourse has focused on mainstreaming what used to be a fraction of one percent of the population. This group is now so "protected" that they are virtually untouchable. Say anything remotely critical of the LGBTQ+ ideology, and you'll be labeled a hateful bigot. It's like a cult!

Okay, maybe not "like" a cult; it *is* a cult—with all the tell-tale signs. Most cults have similar steps, which take an individual from "recruit," to a card-carrying member who would rather die than leave the tribe.

And yes, you may be wondering: Is using the term *cult* too strong? I don't think so. According to *Encyclopedia Britannica*, a cult is usually a "small group devoted to a person, idea, or philosophy."[3] Additionally, *The Free Dictionary* includes this definition: "*Obsessive,* especially faddish, devotion to or veneration for a person, principle, or thing."[4] Even better is *Psychology Today's* definition:

> What exactly is a cult? Destructive individuals and cults use deception and undue influence to make people dependent and obedient. A group should not be considered a cult merely because of its unorthodox beliefs. It is typically authoritarian, headed by a person or group of people with near complete control of followers. Cult influence is designed to disrupt a person's authentic identity and replace it with a new identity.[5]

So when I say that gender theory is a cult, this is why—and I'm not the only one making this argument.

The Family Research Council, an evangelical organization that upholds biblical family values, headlined a six-part series of articles titled "The Cult of Transgenderism."[6] Also, a writer who was formerly part of a political sect compared the characteristics of cults with what trans activists are doing, and observed that "today's trans activism bears similarities to a cult." She said though she uses the word *cult* "with mixed feelings...I've decided to use it anyway. Because if I had to distill my objections to trans activism into one bite-sized morsel, it would be that it denies people the language they need to express reality. I use the word 'cult' not as an insult, but because it fits."[7]

Dr. Az Hakeem is a psychiatrist in the United Kingdom. He has worked psychotherapeutically with gender dysphoria patients for nearly 25 years and is the author of *Trans: Exploring Gender Identity and Gender Dysphoria*. He says, "Gender ideology is made up. It's a social construct. It's a cult belief."[8]

So yes, I (and others) view the gender ideology movement as a cult because it behaves like a cult. So how exactly does this show up with gender theorists?

1. Identify and Recruit the Vulnerable

Cults prey upon people who are hurting because they are more vulnerable to being manipulated by the promise of clarity and relief. As the *Psychology Today* article says, "No one joins a cult voluntarily; they are recruited into it."[9] Kids who already feel like they don't fit in are yearning for a community to belong to. In a leaked audio file from a California teacher training, we can hear the presenter, Kelly Baraki, say,

> So we started to try and identify kids. When we were doing our virtual learning—we totally stalked what they were doing on Google, when they weren't doing school work. One of them was googling "Trans Day of Visibility." And we're like, "Check." We're going to invite that kid when we get back on campus... Because that's really the way we kinda get the bodies in the door [of the LGBTQ clubs]. Right? They need sort of a little bit of an invitation.[10]

2. Create an Existential Crisis, and Then Swoop In to Solve It

As Logan Lancing and James Lindsey say in their book *The Queering of the American Child*,

> When the cult can't find vulnerable people to bolster recruitment, it creates them. The cult is very good at convincing ordinary people that society has mistreated and abandoned them...by pointing at the "oppressive" society and blaming normal people and normalcy itself for causing [the] feelings [of shame and alienation].[11]

Who hasn't felt shame over some aspect of themselves? Who hasn't felt alienated? Either the cult finds kids who already feel that way, or they *create* that feeling—then claim they can "solve" the problem. As Maria Keffler shows in her book *Desist, Detrans & Detox*, kids are being shown PowerPoints on "gender dysphoria" claiming it can manifest as anything from depression to social awkwardness.[12] Gender theory to the rescue!

In the new comprehensive sex education classes, kids are introduced to topics (like sexuality) *far* outside their ability to process, which *creates* feelings of disorientation and crisis. Then, the cult swoops in with the "solution" for all these feelings of angst—the ones they just created! It's like pushing someone toward a cliff and grabbing them right before they fall and claiming: "I just saved your life!"

3. Love-Bomb the Recruits

Once a cult has found (or created) a person who is disoriented, hurting, and confused, they draw them in with extravagant displays of affirmation and acceptance. *You finally belong! We're your family! You are one of us!* The feeling of "unconditional" acceptance is the proverbial carrot that keeps the recruit coming back time after time, no matter how abusive the cult becomes. We see this happen in gender ideology when kids who have always felt "different" are treated as special, protected, affirmed, and even celebrated for coming out as a nontraditional sex or gender identity.

4. Isolate the Recruits from Friends and Family

The pivotal stage of cult indoctrination happens when recruits are separated from their family, friends, and other support systems. We see this happening as schools across the country paint parents as a "barrier" to be overcome.[13] Counselors promise students secrecy from their parents, allowing them to change names and pronouns and telling them, "If your parents aren't accepting of your identity, then I'm your mom now!"[14] Anyone who doesn't affirm the child's "new identity" is deemed "toxic," and nobody got time for toxic relationships! Purge those haters from your tribe!

5. Demand Total Obedience

Once a recruit becomes a full-blown member, the cult does what all cults do—demands total obedience with a zero-tolerance policy for critique. Step out of line, and the member will be slandered, disciplined, or even disfellowshipped. Listen to any detransition story and you'll hear about how quickly the person's "glitter family" rejected them as soon as they began questioning their transition. And by now, the member has cut all ties with anyone outside the cult, making it much harder to leave.

Mama Bears, this is a small sampling of how gender ideology functions as a cult. In the following pages, we'll talk about which kinds of kids are preyed upon, how to recognize signs your child has drunk the Kool-Aid (and what to do if this happens), and then ROAR through the broken promises they may have believed. Let's start with identifying risk factors.

Risk Factors for Gender Ideology

If there's one phrase that summarizes almost every story I've heard from people who have been in the gender cult, it's: "I always felt different." These individuals are vulnerable to believing that their otherness is a symptom of gender dysphoria[15] when in actuality it may be other factors like:

- *Neurodivergence*—Multiple studies note the link between neurodivergence (like autism and ADHD) and transgenderism.[16] One study (with over a quarter of a million data points) found that trans-identifying people are four times more likely to also have been diagnosed with Autism Spectrum Disorder (ASD).[17] There are a few theories on why this is the case. First, kids with ASD/ADHD tend to have obsessive tendencies; once they hyper-fixate on to a topic or idea, it is hard to get them to drop it. So if they do start down the gender theory rabbit hole, it can be difficult to convince them that gender dysphoria is not the root cause of their angst.

Secondly, kids with ASD/ADHD often struggle to understand social cues or unwritten rules of engagement. Neurotypical kids aren't quite sure what to do with them, so they just avoid them or bully them. Mama Bears, weird things happen when we feel disconnected from others. LGBTQ+ advocates are more than happy to provide these hurting kids with the community they so desperately crave…for the low, low price of total acceptance of gender dogma! (And as an autism side note, one author hypothesized that the "emotional relief" autistic girls feel from chest-binding might be the calming effects of compression garments on ASD individuals.[18])

- *Intellectual Giftedness*—Functioning at a *higher* level than one's peers can also leave a kid feeling like there is something "different" about them. It's no surprise that almost half (47 percent) of Lisa Littman's research subjects who reported rapid-onset gender dysphoria were on the gifted spectrum.
- *Co-occurring Mood or Psychiatric Disorders*[19]—When you feel like you are in a black hole, you'll take any hand that reaches down promising relief. And make no mistake, gender ideologues are *promising* these hurting kids that once they get in their new bodies, all their angst will magically disappear. In some cases it does… for a little while. Testosterone has been shown to help with anxiety and depression.[20] But if the person doesn't address the *root cause*, the problems just come back. Or, the person may subconsciously

reason, "Being me is painful. If I can just be someone else, I won't feel like this anymore."

- *Prior Trauma*—Closely linked to the issue of anxiety and depression is the prevalence of childhood trauma like physical, emotional, and sexual abuse.[21] This kind of abuse can leave individuals (especially girls) desperate to escape a gender that they perceived to be the root cause of their abuse.
- *Early Porn Exposure*—Over half of internet porn videos feature violence toward women with the women portrayed as enjoying it.[22] Some research shows that the earlier the exposure for girls, the higher the prevalence of gender dysphoria.[23] Many of these girls cannot articulate that their disgust with womanhood traces back to porn's version of sex, but as one detransitioner noted, the idea of sex *as a woman* was terrifying because of how "degrading" it looked.[24]

Having one or more of these traits doesn't guarantee that your child will come home with new pronouns, but it does make them more susceptible to these predatory ideas and gender-cult proponents.

A Very Brief History of Transgenderism (the Short, Short Version)

We know from Deuteronomy 22:5 that cross-dressing has been around since at least prior to Moses. But in what context? Mama Bears, I maintain that there is *something spiritual* behind the transgenderism movement, and not in a good way. I don't think it's a coincidence that most ancient cultures regarded these individuals as "chosen by the gods," often assigning them priest-like roles as a symbol of their sacred status.[25] Transgenderism was even codified into the religion for ancient Mesopotamians. An ancient prayer to Inanna (one of the sex cults[26] referenced on page 27) states, "To turn a man into a woman and a woman into a man are yours, Inanna."[27] The priests of Inanna were men who, in the role of their priestly duties, donned women's clothes, took on a woman's name, and did roles that were traditionally for women.[28]

Although gender confusion appears to have existed across many cultures in history, at no point was this practice ever considered compatible with Judaism or Christianity—hence the explicit command in Deuteronomy 22. And if all distortions in our sexuality (including gender) are related to distortions in our understanding of God, then we should expect to see evidence of distorted sexuality and gender at every point in history, and especially within pagan societies.

We're going to skip the ideological mudslide that paved the way for gender transitions (since we already beat that horse dead in chapters 9 and 13) and skip to the medical history. Gender Identity Disorder (GID) was officially added to the Diagnostic Statistical Manual (DSM) in 1980 and was defined as an "incongruence between anatomic sex and gender identity."[29] However, the real kick in the teeth came in 2013 when it was reclassified from a *disorder* to a *dysphoria*.[30] As per the name, a *disorder* assumes there is a proper order, and if *disordered*, should be corrected. A *dysphoria* merely states that someone is experiencing distress, and hence "emotional relief" is the goal. But might I point out that there are a lot of unhealthy ways to temporarily relieve distress? Isn't that essentially what most addictions are? This type of therapy assumes that someone can be undistressed while in a disordered state.

Spot the Faulty Logic

A: Positive feelings are healthy.
FC: My biological sex/gender causes me to have negative feelings.
C: I need to change my biological sex/gender to be healthy.

Different Types of Transgenderism

If your child comes home telling you that they identify as trans, it's important to know that there are a lot of different varieties. The most honest definition I've found so far is this: "'Trans' is an umbrella term for individuals whose inner sense of self (gender identity) or how they present themselves using visual or behavioral cues (gender expression) differs from the expected stereotypes (gender) culturally assigned to their biological sex."[31] Thus, "trans" can mean a lot more than just a man who wants to be a woman or vice versa. Here, we'll give a brief summary of the three main types (though there are more).

Classic Gender Identity Disorder (GID)

Classic GID usually manifests in young males (between two and four years of age) who—even before they can talk—are very confused about being a boy and who insist that they are girls.[32] While most of these cases resolve on their own after puberty, there is a subset for whom this kind of dysphoria rarely goes away (if ever) without *extensive* therapeutic intervention.[33] This phenomena is documented in a wide range of cultures, and almost exclusively in males.[34] For the purposes of this book, *please set this demographic aside in your head* for most of our conversations. Before God, I maintain that there is something we don't yet understand going on with this group and we, as Christians, do not need to add judgment on to their confusion. We need to lovingly walk with them as they attempt to follow God and allow *Him* to do the healing. And yes, while classic GID is still a *result* of the fall (as all things outside of God's design are), it is not necessarily a result of the *person's sin,* nor their acceptance of an unbiblical ideology. This doesn't change our stance on what God says about gender, but the way we interact with this group must reflect God's heart.

Rapid-Onset Gender Dysphoria (ROGD)

Rapid-onset gender dysphoria (ROGD), coined by researcher Lisa Littman, describes a gender dysphoria which manifests suddenly in adolescence and with a child (usually a girl) who has no prior history.[35] Before 2012, gender dysphoria was so rare in females that we didn't even have statistics on them. Fast forward to 2017 and suddenly 70 percent of all referrals to gender clinics were for girls.[36] Not only was there an unprecedented influx of girls expressing distress with their bodies, but this phenomenon was happening in *groups,* leaving Littman to conclude that this new gender dysphoria was a type of social contagion—a diagnosis that seemed to spread between individuals in a peer group.[37]

These first two types of gender dysphoria are very different and *should not* be treated the same. I'm not saying the distress for ROGD isn't still very real; it is. It just doesn't have the same root cause, nor the same prognosis as classic GID. Individuals (like Chloe Cole) with ROGD usually need therapy for other unrelated issues (like the ones listed on pages 269-271).

Nonbinary

Of all the identities, nonbinary seems to be trending right now. Nonbinary means a person doesn't fully identify as a boy or a girl. Most of the gazillion gender identities you'll encounter could technically be under the umbrella of nonbinary because they describe people who feel like they are a combination of both genders, neither gender, or a gender that can change (gender fluid).[38] As we saw in the previous chapter, if there's some extreme stereotype that we have to fit into, then we're all a little nonbinary. But kids now feel the need for a label, and nonbinary allows them to identify with the ultra-accepting (and "cool") LGBTQ+ crowd without having to permanently alter themselves (although some choose to). This particular group is often emphatic about using they/them pronouns. (They/them pronouns were originally used to refer to a hypothetical individual without having to say "he/she" or "his/her" a thousand times. Today, people also use "they/them" to refer to themselves if they prefer not to identified as either "he" or "she.")

Genes, Hormones, and Intersex Conditions

In the previous chapter, we discussed the concept of gender, but we didn't get into what constitutes a biological sex. We know there *is* a biological binary that we cannot avoid (i.e., sperm and egg producers), but it's not always as simple as a mere "XX = girl" or "XY = boy," so please don't perpetuate that myth. When it comes to biological sex, the two most pertinent things to know are the function of the SRY gene and the role of testosterone.

SRY Gene

The SRY gene is basically what gives a boy his boy-parts. If there's no SRY gene, the fetus's reproductive tissues will turn into ovaries by default. Since the SRY gene is normally on the Y chromosome, XX usually means girl and XY usually means boy. However, when a person's body makes eggs and sperm, it shuffles the genes around so that there is variety. (This is why biological siblings can be so different from one another!) The SRY gene is usually located on the Y chromosome, but it can occasionally jump ship during the shuffle and attach itself to an X chromosome. In this rare case, a person has the intersex condition called XX male syndrome where his chromosomes are XX, but he physically develops into a boy—because the SRY gene is still present. In other cases, the SRY gene is damaged, or the baby's androgen sensors are blocked. In this case, they've got the SRY gene, but it doesn't affect the baby's body like it should, so the boy-parts don't develop.

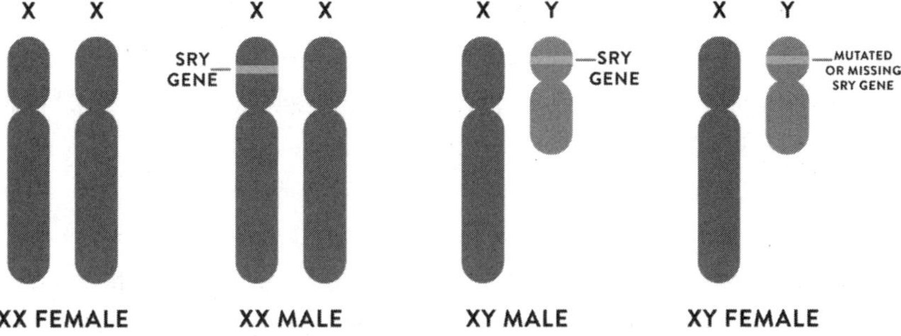

There are dozens of such conditions, which can leave no discernable trace.[39] The phrase "intersex conditions" can be misleading (which is why some sources—including the previous edition of this book!—cite a 1.7 percent prevalence in the population). When it comes to true intersex conditions where chromosomes and genitals do not align, the prevalence is about a hundred times less, accounting for *less than a fifth of one percent* of the population.[40] But again, there is no separate (or third) sex because our bodies are either egg factories or sperm factories (or neither)—but never both. Even if some of the biological *machinery* has malfunctioned, we can still (usually) tell what kind of factory it was intended to be.

It is very important to distinguish between intersexuality and transgenderism. Intersexuality is all about sex organs and chromosomes. It is an objective trait about which a person has zero control. Transgenderism is all about how a person *perceives* him or herself. If there was anyone on this earth who had the right to say that there might be more than just two genders, it's people who are born intersex, but the Intersex Society of North America does not think this is wise or helpful.

Testosterone

Testosterone plays a large continuing role in forming the rest of the boy-parts initiated by the SRY gene. But testosterone doesn't just affect the giblets. While there are no formal studies involving humans (as such studies are unethical), studies involving other mammals show that changing prenatal levels of testosterone can affect "gendered behavior." In rats, high levels of testosterone have been shown to increase aggressive play (considered masculine behavior) and lack of testosterone has been linked to less aggressive behaviors.[41] *This was true whether the unborn rat was male or female.* So, based on prenatal testosterone levels, you could have feisty female rats or calm and gentle male rats. Nothing wrong with either of them; they both sound like fun.

The same has been observed in humans, with levels of prenatal testosterone seeming to play a role in play type and toy selection.[42] If you're like me and loved roughhousing as a kid and didn't care much for dolls, maybe good ol' Mom had some heightened testosterone while you were a bun in her oven. And you know what? *There is nothing wrong with that, and it doesn't make you less of a girl.* Conversely, if you were a boy and your uterine environment had low levels of testosterone, you might enjoy playing quietly by yourself, *not* imagining yourself as a Tyrannosaurus rex or attacking every person in sight. And you know what? *There is nothing wrong with that either, and it doesn't make you any less of a boy.* So both genetics and other hormonal aspects can play a role in anatomy and gendered personalities. And guess what? There is room for all within biblical manhood and womanhood! Jacob liked cooking and Esau liked hunting, and God picked Jacob as his fave. The opposite was true of Cain (who sacrificed veggies) and Abel (who sacrificed meat); there's no formula to God's love, other than what's in our hearts (1 Samuel 16:7).

What Does the Science Show?

So what about brains? This could be a really short section or a really long section. We'll keep it short: It's inconclusive.[43] By inconclusive, I mean there are a gazillion studies on whether people's "brains" align with their birth sex or gender identity.

Basically, you can prove whatever you want depending on which study you use because there are factors that many of these studies don't account for which can affect a person's brain. Is the person already on hormones? Have they been living as the opposite sex already? Since these factors can literally change brain function, studying the brain *after the fact* doesn't tell us anything. So, if your kids come home saying that "science affirms transgender brains," show them the bibliographies of the two sources mentioned in endnote #43. It is, indeed, inconclusive.

What Does the Bible Say About Transgenderism?

Let's reaffirm the notion that we don't need to fit into a gender stereotype to be comfortable as our biological sex. That being said, there is a caveat according to Scripture, but it's pretty small. The only real, hard-and-fast rule I can find when it comes to gender identity is in regard to people who are *trying to look like the other gender*. Deuteronomy 22:5 says, "A woman must not wear men's clothes, nor a man wear woman's clothing." In biblical times, clothing was so specific to the genders that the clothing you wore communicated your gender.

This is still true in today's world. People may not accept that a man wearing women's clothing is actually a woman, but they will at least conclude that he wants to be seen as one. Here is where cultural norms actually matter. When it comes to the clothing we wear (other forms of gender presentation), a deviation from cultural norms sends the world a message: *I am dissatisfied with the gender God created me to be and I'm trying to trick you into seeing me as the opposite gender*. When you purposefully try to blur gender norms and boundaries, you aren't just being edgy; you're being subversive, and that doesn't really fall within the purview of Christian freedom. Basically, just respect what the Designer gave you (your body/sex/gender); be who you were created to be when it comes to personality, interests, and aptitudes; and let your kids know they won't always fit into society's boxes—and that's okay. Ephesians 2:10, y'all!

Preparing for Our Ministry to Detransitioners

Before we get any further, we need to bring everything back to our first ministry: people. As argued above, gender theory is a cult and is making promises it cannot keep. The church needs to be prepared for an influx of confused (and medically complicated) people who have nowhere else to turn, because the gender cult (like all cults) will not tolerate dissenters. And if the only thing this demographic has heard from the church is a mocking voice saying, "We told you so," they won't come near us with a ten-foot pole. We need to be the place they feel that they can turn when all their hopes of relief are shattered.

So what are some of the baby steps that we can take? First off, we must listen to those who are struggling. Are you ready to walk a mile in the shoes of someone navigating gender confusion and distress? If you're not sure, then pray this prayer:

Lord God, I confess that I don't understand the thinking behind gender ideology. God, I can arrogantly assume that I arrived at my conclusions because I'm a better thinker, less emotional, or less prone to deception. Remind me that all the problems I see could just as easily have been me, had I been in different circumstances, experienced different hurts, or been born with a different personality. God, show me the areas where I have believed utter lies and where people have given me grace as I grew in the knowledge of the truth so that I can extend this same gentleness. Convict me when I respond to the transgender issue with anger, condescension, or hyper-intellectualization. Remind me that I am interacting with people, not just ideas. Teach me to rage against sin, evil, and bad ideology without letting those emotions explode onto those who have fallen captive. May all I do be done in love. Amen.

Now, there's another group of you for whom the empathy comes naturally. You want to kiss all the boo-boos, wipe away every tear, and calm every fear, protectively guarding the gender-confused struggler against well-meaning (but ultimately damaging) "crusaders of truth." If that is you, then I have a prayer for you too:

Father God, I see [person] and the struggle [he/she] has had with their gender identity. I see the ways [he/she] has been wounded, and I feel so angry at those who have inflicted this harm. Lord, You are the Great Protector, not I. I want to help, love, and comfort. But Lord, protect [person] when my misguided compassion is getting in the way of your liberating work. It is not my job to alleviate the pain caused by the Great Physician. Where I am tempted to step in too much, forcibly remove me. In those times, may I remind [person] of my presence from afar, trusting them to your care. Show me when to act and when to release. Amen.

Let's get our hearts right, Mama Bears, before we combat the lies!

Correcting Through the Lies

This is a Christian book, but let me let you in on a little secret: We don't always need to punt to biblical authority when good old-fashioned common sense will suffice. This is especially true when talking to non-Christians who couldn't care less what the Bible says. In regard to gender transition, we just need to agree on what counts as 1) healthy/unhealthy and 2) physical harm. European countries have already acknowledged the lies below and are correcting course—even shutting down their pediatric gender clinics. The medical community in the United States, unfortunately, still seems to be going full steam ahead with gender ideology's unhelpful, "affirming" treatment. Here are some of the lies you'll hear from the governing bodies and how you can combat them.

Lie #1: Gender-Affirming Care Is Evidence-Based

Reality: After independently reviewing the available research, a meta-analysis concluded that there was a "a paucity of high-quality guidance for gender minority/trans people...largely limited to HIV and transition, but not wider aspects of healthcare, mortality or [quality of life]."[44] Translation: There aren't any good quality studies showing that "gender-affirming care" actually helps patients in the long run (and the ones that do exist are all centered around HIV).

Furthermore, when the Endocrine Society made 22 recommendations regarding gender-affirming treatments, they openly admitted to the "quality of research" on which they based each statement. Want to know how many of their recommendations were based on "high quality" research? *None.* Nineteen of the recommendations are based on research ranked as "low" or "very low quality."[45] So much for "evidenced based..."

Lie #2: Puberty Blockers Are Safe and Reversible

Reality: This is the claim that's been repeated ad nauseum, but there was literally *no way* to back it up since this "treatment" was still experimental. As we now know, these "safe and reversible" procedures are neither safe nor reversible. In terms of safety, girls who underwent puberty blockers entered a state of early menopause, especially in terms of bone density.[46] Kids put on puberty blockers experienced a greater risk of brain swelling and even loss of vision.[47] As for "reversible," puberty blockers stopped the growth of the male's penis at whatever age he began blockers, leaving him with a micropenis for the rest of his life, even if he decided to later go through male puberty.[48]

When it comes to cross-sex hormones, it gets even worse. Girls are permanently left with a deep voice, facial hair, and sexual dysfunction (including infertility and an inability to orgasm). Can you imagine making a decision when you were 13 that left you infertile and unable to orgasm for the rest of your life?[49]

Lie #3: Gender-Affirming Surgery Is Healthcare

Reality: How are these people defining healthcare? Correct me if I'm wrong, but shouldn't healthcare refer to fixing something that is broken so that a person can take *fewer* medications and experience *fewer* health complications? We see the exact opposite with gender-affirming surgeries (GAS), strapping people to medical wagons that they can't unhitch.

For males, the neo-vagina is seen as an open wound that the body continuously tries to heal. To prevent closure, they must daily (and often painfully) dilate the opening...forever. One meta-analysis reported "overall complication rate of 32.5 percent and a reoperation rate of 21.7 percent for nonesthetic reasons." Translation: Over a third had complications and over a fifth needed further surgeries to function properly.[50] Twenty-nine percent had difficulty achieving orgasm.[51] Over a third had "stress incontinence" (meaning they pee themselves).[52] In one long-term study, almost a fourth of the participants were "never satisfied with their sexual function," and that was 16 years post-operation.[53]

For the girls, one meta-analysis of 39 studies concluded that over three-quarters of the patients experienced surgical complications, many requiring further surgeries. Over a third developed urethral fistulas (meaning that there is an adhesion or connection between the urethra and another organ). For example, some fistulas might make a person dribble urine through their vagina. One-fourth reported urethral stricture (which makes it difficult or painful to urinate).[54] In one study with over 1200 patients, almost 20 percent reported *worsened* mental health following gender affirming surgery.[55] In worst case scenarios, the faux-genital can lose blood flow, die, and fall off. And don't forget all the tissue removed to construct this new body part—a procedure that leaves girls' forearms with severe scarring and nerve damage. Does this sound like healthcare to you?! It sounds like health destruction to me.

Lie #4: Very Few People Regret Their Transition

Reality: Fifty-five thousand people on Reddit's detransition board beg to differ.[56] According to research conducted by Lisa Littman, 76 percent of detransitioners did not report their regret to their providers.[57] The doctors who *do* follow up with their patients don't report on the nearly 30 percent of patients who fail to respond. So even if we wanted to have research, the detransitioners seem unlikely to admit their regret anywhere but in online forums. Furthermore, when detransitioners *were* studied, the average time between transition and detransition was five years or more, so any studies including only a five-year follow-up fail to account for the phenomenon.[58]

Lie #5: Gender-Affirming Care Improves Mental Health

Reality: There are too many parents to count (including Elon Musk) who were emotionally manipulated into gender affirmation for their kids by being asked: "Would you rather a living son or a dead daughter?" Yes, it's true that kids who identify as transgender have a greater risk of suicidality. But does puberty suppression or gender-reassignment surgery improve their distress? In general, no.[59]

Some studies do show trans individuals faring better (psychologically) after transition—but in most of these studies, subjects were only followed for one to five years post-operation.[60] A recent 35-year Dutch study evaluated whether gender-affirming surgery decreased suicidality over the long haul. They found that over the course of 35 years, there was no statistical benefit in a person medically transitioning.[61] In another long-term study in Sweden, transitioners were also followed for up to 30 years. Right around the ten-year mark, all hell broke loose in terms of increased deaths—often death by suicide (20 times higher than the control group!).[62] If nothing else, this should at least give us pause to consider that *just maybe* sex reassignment surgery has a honeymoon phase and is a temporary fix for a more persistent underlying issue.

What to Do If Your Child Has Been Sucked into the Gender Cult

For some of you, this is hypothetical. For others, the pain is all too real. You've seen the cult at work, and you've seen your child descend into the rabbit hole. What is a parent to do? While these suggestions aren't guaranteed to work on every child, here are a few things you can try.

1. Get Children off All Social Media

Many parents reported that their son or daughter's fixation on transgenderism was preceded by extended binge sessions on social media.[63] This is not a "limit your screen time" kind of situation. This may be a "hand me your phone and we're canceling all internet for the whole house if we have to" kind of situation.

2. What Is Up with Anime?!

I don't have any formal research to point you to, but every time a parent approaches me about their kid identifying as trans, the first question I ask is, "Are they into anime?" I have yet to have a parent say no. I don't know what is going on there, but something spiritually dark is connected to anime. Do with that what you will.

3. Limit Video Games

Part of the transgender brainwashing involves kids becoming dissatisfied with what they see in the mirror. In video games, you can identify as whatever you want through your own unique avatar. The more a kid plays video games, the more they get used to interacting as a fictional version of themselves. Eventually reality cannot compare. Furthermore, a lot of video games are now promoting transgenderism by introducing random LGBTQ+ characters who give a backstory completely unrelated to the video game. Remember from chapter 6, y'all: Normalize through repetition.

4. It's Okay to Keep Using Their Real Name and Pronouns

In order to deny reality, one must have an ever-present echo chamber drowning out objective facts. Parents can serve as a valuable source of keeping their children tethered to reality, as seen in the article "What I've Learned Rescuing My Daughter From Her Transgender Fantasy."[64] Don't be antagonistic about it, but—as one of my Mama Bears with a transgender child recommends—tell your kids something like this:

> I love you so much. You will always be my child. You've had a lot longer to process this than I have. I am hurting here too. Will you allow me to go through this at my own pace, just like you have gone through this transition at your pace? That would mean so much to me.

This is such a reasonable request that only the most far-gone kids can resist an appeal to your own pain.

5. Pull Them Out of School If You Have To

In drastic situations, a complete change in environment may be necessary. Parenting is ultimately about choosing your hard. It's hard to have a child who continues down the transgender road, and it's hard to uproot your life in order to save them from this ideology. Pick your hard. Remember, if you successfully extricate them from a lifetime of hormones and surgical complications, they will look back on your sacrifices as an adult and be very, very thankful. Be willing to endure their anger now, while they are under your roof. That's part of being a parent.

Discussion, Discipleship, and Prayer

Mama Bears, we find ourselves, in this moment, unable to help people see what is clearly in front of their faces. What are we to do when in conversation with our kids and with others?

1. *Ask the question: "What do you mean by healthcare? How many medical complications should we accept as reasonable before calling an elective procedure unhealthy*?" Don't try to push your thoughts on them. Just hear what they have to say and let them listen to their own answer. If they want more information, have a ready-to-go email or document that summarizes some of these points from the chapter. You can just forward it to them along with a personal message at the beginning. They are more likely to read your email than a whole book that you recommend.

2. *Be prepared to love on detransitioners.* Cult survivors need extra support—especially those who now have irreversibly harmed their bodies. For more on this, see the blog on the Mama Bear website titled "Our Coming Ministry to Detransitioners."[65]

3. *Familiarize yourself with the Cass Review.* The Cass Review is the recent report that was commissioned by the NHS in England, which used an independent third-party reviewer to decide where the research *actually* is regarding gender treatment for minors. It highlights the lack of quality studies or evidence of health or psychological benefits. It also cites the now known dangers of puberty blockers and cross-sex hormones, and the need to explore *other* possible causes of self-reported gender dysphoria.[66]

   Sadly, how did our *American* Academy of Pediatrics respond to the Cass Review? They doubled down, claiming to be all "research based," but didn't provide the research.[67] The American Endocrine Society put in their official announcement that they "stand firm in [their] support of gender affirming care," ironically claiming that "medical evidence, not politics, should inform treatment decisions."[68] (Ummmm...agreed? And didn't they already admit that the available research was all low or very low quality? See page 279.)[69] Countries like Britain, the Netherlands, and Sweden are finally concluding that the emperor has no clothes; the American medical establishment, however, is still praising the fashion show.

4. *Don't shield kids from all pain and suffering.* A major problem in our society is that people think that suffering is avoidable. It's not. We don't need to make our kids miserable, but we *do* need to let them suffer setbacks and wrestle through suffering without always jumping in to save them from it. They need experiences that teach them: "I overcame (things) before, so I can overcome (puberty) now."

5. *Guard your words.* We should not have to speak lies to be "hospitable."[70] When it comes to transitioning classmates, tell your cubs to use first names only. And practice!

6. *Be part of the solution.* There can be two different responses depending on the situation: If everyone else is applauding a classmate for their transition, refuse to participate. If all the youth group kids are mocking a kid who is confused, then befriend the kid—*and don't get these backward.* Teach your cubs to look for the outcast and "marginalized" kids who don't fit the box and include them. It's amazing how just a little love and acceptance can preempt an issue before it starts. That's being the hands and feet of Jesus.

The beautiful thing about the biblical teaching on gender and sexuality is that it is so simple and coherent (but not always easy). We don't have to appeal to a thousand different "what if" cases. We can take it back to the beginning: God created us in His image as male and female, and we are to separate from our families to unite with our opposite-sex spouse—or remain faithfully single. Are we fallen creatures whose desires wage war against us? Yup. Can we win this war? On our own, no, but the Holy Spirit in us can! We do not wage war against flesh and blood, but against the rulers, against the authorities, and against the powers of this dark world, and against the spiritual forces of evil in the heavenly realms (2 Corinthians 10:3-5). We do not wage war as the world does! But we have been given all power to demolish strongholds set up against the knowledge of God and to take captive every thought and make it obedient to Christ. We have many who have been taken captive by the enemy and forced to do His bidding (2 Timothy 2:26). But as the prior verse says, maybe they will come to "a knowledge of the truth." This is your task, Mama Bears and Papa Bears, should you choose to accept it.

PAWS for Prayer by Julie Loos

PRAISE God for Who He Is

We praise You, Father, that You are the God who saves and delivers. You are the bondage breaker. You break through strongholds to bring freedom and clarity. You reveal "deep and hidden things" and know what lies in darkness because light dwells with You (Daniel 2:22).

ADMIT Where We Have Fallen Short of His Standard

Forgive us for not more readily and vocally calling out these false teachers who evangelize an unbiblical sexuality that follows their depraved conduct and brings "the way of truth into disrepute" (2 Peter 2:2). Those who are slaves of depravity "seduce the unstable" (2 Peter 2:14) and "promise them freedom" (2 Peter 2:19). Nor have we reached out to those who feel "different" to share the love of Christ and bring them into the family of God, so they don't seek fake family through cultlike ideologies and movements. Forgive us.

WORSHIP WITH THANKSGIVING for the Things He Has Done

We thank You for coming to free the captives no matter what or who imprisons them (2 Peter 2:19). We thank You that You can open eyes that are blind to biblical sexuality: to free captives from the prison of misguided affirmation and false belonging and release from the dungeon those who sit in darkness unaware of the light of Your truth about their sexuality (Isaiah 42:7; 61:1).

SUBMIT Yourselves and Your Requests to God

Give us eyes to see who is being held captive. Bring Your Spirit to bear in this situation, because where the Spirit of the Lord is, there is liberty, emancipation from bondage, and true freedom (2 Corinthians 3:17). Release them from the social contagion and peer pressure that pulls them into this prison of lies. Safeguard those who may be even more vulnerable due to emotional, mental, relational, or intellectual issues. Unshackle them from every kind of evil deception, which fools those on their way to destruction because they refuse to love and accept the truth that would save them (2 Thessalonians 2:10).

 DISCUSSION QUESTIONS 

1. **Icebreaker:** Have you ever known anyone who was part of a cult? What were the first signs of trouble in their involvement with the organization?

2. **Main theme:** *Gender ideology is a cult that preys upon vulnerable individuals, promises them relief, but ultimately delivers broken bodies on top of broken hearts.* How have you seen the gender cult exercising in our society?

3. **Self-evaluation:** It's easy to mock what we don't understand. Do you think a person struggling with their gender identity would feel comfortable talking to you about it? Why or why not?

4. **Brainstorm:** How would you respond if your child told you that a friend wants to use different pronouns? What advice could you give as your son or daughter navigates this relationship? Brainstorm ways to approach these conversations as you hold grace and truth with both hands.

5. **Release the bear:** Cultic teaching is pervasive and insidious. Discuss ways that unscientific thinking (to say nothing of unbiblical thinking) has been normalized and disseminated by our media.

CHAPTER 15

Taking Up Your Sexual Cross

Because We're All Born That Way

HILLARY

I was meeting with two high school students, Jared and Gina, at a conference several years back. I had just given a talk, and they both had further questions. Gina was a devoted Christian and intended to go into ministry. She just had one hang-up: What about abortion? She knew abortion was wrong, but she had a hard time condemning it in cases of rape. "What would happen," she asked, "if I were to be raped and get pregnant? I would have to give up college, delay my entire life. I didn't ask to get pregnant. There was no sin I committed. What then?"

I could tell she was waiting for me to go into a pro-life apologetic monologue, but I considered my audience. This wasn't a girl who needed to be convinced abortion was wrong. This girl was scared of being put in a difficult situation. And her fear was legitimate! She needed encouragement—and I mean *encouragement* the way the Bible means it.

A lot of people are confused about what it means to truly encourage someone. We use it to remind people that they're good enough, smart enough, and stable enough to conquer anything that comes their way. Or we (mis)use parts of Scripture written for someone else and assure our friends that God won't ever let anything bad happen to them. They will soar on wings like eagles in all situations (Isaiah 40:31)! The Lord has promised them freedom from pestilence and disease (Psalm 91)!

This stuff sounds *great,* but the problem is, it might not be true. *God does not promise us safety here in this life.* (Just ask the first-century martyrs.) Nor does God promise us health, wealth, or long lives. (Just ask the present-day martyrs.) Statements in the Bible that were made to individuals or to Israel are not necessarily promises that we can claim for ourselves and demand that God fulfill.

While ooey-gooey statements about conquering all our enemies and success in all circumstances might feel good, they are not necessarily encouraging—in the biblical sense. Encouragement literally means *to infuse courage.* We don't infuse courage by telling people there is nothing to fear when there is. We infuse courage by reminding them that whatever comes, they can face it head-on with God's help. We infuse courage by reminding each other of God's presence in the midst of our fear, pain, grief, and discouragement.

After a few moments of thought, I looked at Gina and said, "It comes down to this. We are all called to carry the cross of Christ. The unfortunate reality is that you and I, as women, may be called to carry a different cross from the one Jared is given. Yes, either one of us could become pregnant through no decision of our own. And you know what our cross is at that moment? To care for and protect the baby growing inside us. Jared will *never* have to carry this cross, and it's horribly unfair, but we don't decide the right thing based on what's fair."

Gina was quiet for a minute, and then, with a look of fierce resolve in her eyes, she said, "Okay."

Gina loved the Lord and desired to serve Him. Thinking that she might be put in an unfair situation scared her. But submitting to Christ? Remaining faithful no matter the situation? She had already made that decision a long time ago. So she looked that fear square in the eye and decided, "Nothing will change my resolve to follow the Lord—not even the fear of rape and pregnancy." Once she realized that the issue was ultimately about submission to God, it became a nonissue, and I could see a weight lifted from her shoulders. I felt privileged to stand there in that moment, witnessing a warrior for Christ preparing for the battle. That, my friends, is what infusing biblical courage looks like.

Christian encouragement means that we see this world for the broken mess that it is and remind each other that we were created for another world (John 15:18-19). Christian encouragement means that we acknowledge the pain, the strife, the difficulties of being a disciple of Jesus, but then remind each other *why* we are running the race (Hebrews 12). We remind each other that the glories that await us will far outweigh these momentary trials (2 Corinthians 4:17) and that we are storing up for ourselves treasures in heaven that moth and rust cannot destroy (Matthew 6:19-20). That is biblical encouragement.

Gina needed encouragement that God had already given her the strength and the ability to be faithful. Mama Bears, we all need someone who infuses courage in us from time to time. And part of our jobs as mamas is to infuse that courage into our kids.

The call to discipleship with Jesus is a heavy one, and we shouldn't pretend otherwise with our kids. In Luke 9:23-24, Jesus says to His disciples, "Whoever wants to be my disciple must deny themselves and take up their cross daily and follow me. For whoever wants to save their life will lose it, but whoever loses their life for me will save it." Here, Jesus is saying bluntly that the Christian walk will not be an easy one; we'll all have burdens to bear. Is this scary? Yup. Do we know what crosses we'll be called to carry in our own individual lives? Nope. Do we know what crosses our *children* will be called to carry? Also, no. So what can we know?

First, we can know God's will for our lives.

> It is God's will that you should be sanctified: that you should avoid sexual immorality; that each of you should learn to control your own body in a way that is holy and honorable, not in passionate lust like the pagans, who do not know God...For God did not call us to be impure, but to live a holy life. Therefore, anyone who rejects this instruction does not reject a human being

> but God, the very God who gives you his Holy Spirit (1 Thessalonians 4:3-5, 7-8).

Yes, friends, sexual holiness is itself a cross we will have to carry—each one of us. As Christopher Yuan puts it, "Holy sexuality—chastity in singleness and faithfulness in marriage—is God's good standard for *everyone*."[1] Our kids need us to infuse them with the courage it will take to follow this command.

Carrying Our Sexual Crosses

A popular argument surrounding LGBTQ+ issues is that same-sex attraction and transgenderism are burdens too heavy to carry. After all, none of us privileged cisgendered heterosexuals have to carry this cross. God made us for relationship. Who are we to tell people that they're doomed to a life without love?

It is good to acknowledge others' burdens, and it is also good to help each other carry our burdens (Galatians 6:2). But this assumption that people who identify as LGBTQ+ are the only ones with a sexual cross to bear is just not true. Everyone has a cross they are called to carry. If we want to live with our brothers and sisters in kindness and in compassion, it helps to see what crosses they may be carrying that we might not.

Cross 1: Being Young and Celibate

We older Mama Bears (and Papa Bears, and Grandma and Grandpa Bears) may have forgotten what it is like to be young and struggling with a strong sex drive. Biologically speaking, humans are created with a certain window of time during which our bodies are practically *begging* us to go out and make a baby. And our society is *not* structured according to our biology. A century ago, it was fairly normal to get married right out of high school. Even further back, societies were structured so that when young people hit puberty and sexual maturity, they didn't have to wait long before fulfilling their biological destiny.

Nowadays, that is not the case. And we who are older must recognize what a massive cross this is for our young people to carry. They are having to wait for sexual relationships ten, sometimes twenty years beyond the time when their bodies become ready. For those of you who are young and still maintaining sexual chastity, I commend you. You are loved by God and He sees your suffering. *How can we as the church help you carry this cross?*

Cross 2: Being Male (or Having a High Libido) and Celibate

In *general*, male and female sex drives are different. This has been common knowledge for eons, but it's now suddenly politically incorrect to say so. Are there ladies with a higher-than-average libido? Absolutely. So this is for you too. But ladies, the average girl we will *never* fully understand what our guys go through to remain sexually chaste. Yes, we want to be loved. Yes, we long for touch. Yes, it can feel like we have to chew on a piece of leather to prevent ourselves from going full sex-kitten on the guy we're dating. But no matter how hard it is for us to maintain self-control, *most of us will never fully understand what is going on in our guys' bodies* and the struggle they face to obey God in this area. (Testosterone is literally prescribed for low sex drive!)

So ladies, we need to be kind to our guys, especially the ones who are trying to maintain a faithful witness as disciples of Jesus. And for our guys out there who are trying to not only keep it in their pants but also fend off all the predatory girls who read *Teen Vogue*, I salute you. Your plight is not easy, especially not in a society where sex is so visible, so prevalent, so easily accessible, and where you are encouraged to "be a man" by disobeying God. You have a cross to carry that most of your sisters in Christ will never understand. And for my ladies with a high libido, the same goes for you. You are loved by God, and He sees your suffering. Obedience is a cross to carry. *How can we as the church help you carry this cross?*

Cross 3: Being Single and Celibate When Your Friends Are Married

Married people, remember the plight of your single friends. Human bodies were created for touch. Scientific studies have shown the importance of touch for normal childhood development[2]—and I suspect we will start seeing studies on the elderly population being deprived of touch during the pandemic lockdowns. Skin hunger is especially painful for people whose love language is touch.

Married people receive regular touch that their single friends do not—a quick kiss as you're running out the door, your husband's hand lingering on your back. It isn't easy for single people to watch, knowing that their sexual faithfulness means waiting for a spouse who may never appear. For those of you who are single while all your friends are married, taking up your sexual cross means that you suffer from not having touch. Sexual faithfulness means waiting for a guy or girl who may never appear. My eyes fill with tears as I remember the longing I had during my time as an older single. Friends, you are loved by God and He sees your suffering. *How can we as the church help you carry this cross?*

Cross 4: Living in a Loveless Marriage

Maybe your marriage hasn't gone the way you hoped. Perhaps you can't even remember why you got married. You know what the only thing lonelier than being single is? Feeling alone in a marriage. Not only are you isolated, but you're stuck in a lifelong commitment, and you can't imagine feeling in love again. At least a single person has the possibility of meeting Mister or Miss Right! For those of you carrying this cross, I commend you, friends. Taking up your cross means being sexually faithful to a person whom you may not even like. You are loved by God and He sees your suffering. *How can we as the church help you carry this cross?*

Cross 5: Inability to Have Sex in Marriage

This is one of those topics that few people ever discuss. Maybe you had a traumatic birth and carry scar tissue that makes sex almost impossible now. Maybe there's been illness, accident, or paralysis, and sex is no longer an option. Or maybe you have no clue what is going on with your body. All you know is that sex hurts…a lot. What do you do then? Who has it worse—the spouse in pain, or the other spouse who would cause pain by trying to be sexually intimate?

There are no winners in this situation. But there are disciples of Jesus, who, despite the hardships they have been handed, continue to be sexually faithful in whatever situation they have been placed. For those of you who have been given this hand, we mourn with you. You are loved by God and He sees your suffering. *How can we as the church help you carry this cross?*

Cross 6: Infertility

We have an epidemic of infertility in our world. Men and women who desire so badly to start a family suffer miscarriage after miscarriage. They grieve the death of child after child, hope after hope. Looking around, it seems everyone else has children. *The 16-year-old down the street just got pregnant. What's wrong with me? This is supposed to be a natural process!* For those of you in this situation, we grieve with you. Being a disciple of Jesus may mean not having children, or it may mean loving on your adopted children! The Lord can make beauty from ashes. You are loved by God and He sees your suffering. *How can we as the church help you carry this cross?*

Cross 7: Unwanted Pregnancy

Women were given the unique ability to grow the next generation in their bodies. For whatever reason, you have now unexpectedly found yourself with child. We stand with you as you choose life. Being a disciple of Jesus doesn't mean having to choose motherhood now; it just means providing this new life a place of safety until it can join the rest of us out in this world. Even if you can't raise this child to adulthood, another family will. Sacrificing the next nine months might be a greater sacrifice than anyone even knows. Or maybe it will be the most life-changing blessing you never saw coming. Either way, we acknowledge your fear. We grieve that this blessing did not happen at a time that you preferred. But you are loved by God and He sees your suffering. *How can we as the church help you carry this cross?*

Cross 8: Same-Sex Attraction

You grew up feeling different from the other kids of your gender. You watched them all get crushes, and then boyfriends and girlfriends. Maybe someone suspected your secret and ridiculed you. They made you feel like a freak, like you didn't belong, like you were broken. Maybe people told you that you were an abomination, hated by God. Carrying your cross could mean never kissing your lover goodnight. Never having a family. Never having that wedding, growing old with someone you love. Your parents might grieve the loss of potential grandchildren, and you could feel like you aren't just breaking your own heart, but theirs as well. Being a disciple of Jesus means willingly laying down a part of yourself and denying its power. It's lonelier than anyone ever knows. You are loved by God and He sees your suffering. *How can we as the church help you carry this cross?*

Cross 9: Not Fitting In with Other People of Your Gender

You're a girl and you feel like there is some mysterious girl-codebook that all the other girls got…and somehow you missed out. All the adults say to "be yourself," but when you are "yourself," the other girls withdraw. They don't want to play with you. Every time you've tried to be vulnerable, you got crushed. The Lord sees you.

Maybe you are a boy, and the other boys called you a sissy. You were picked on, harassed, bullied, and made to feel like you'd never be man enough, so why even try? All the things your mom praised you for, the other boys used to ridicule you for.

I know it feels easier to go where you fit in, to change yourself to match other people's expectations. For you, taking up your cross means that you might walk a lonely road and have a harder time making friends. *You will find them.* God created you as a man or woman with the exact qualities He wanted you to have as a man or a woman. You don't have to act like all the other men or women. For our guys, I celebrate the unique way God has created you as a man. For our girls, I celebrate the unique way God has created you as a woman. You can be your authentic self while still remaining in your God-given body. Taking up your cross means you accept the body He gave you while pursuing the gifts He also put inside of you—even if other people make fun of you for it. Do it anyway! You are a perfect fit in God's family. He loves you and He sees your suffering. *How can we as the church help you carry this cross?*

Cross 10: Sexual Abuse

Someone ripped a part of you away that you can never get back. You can't look at people the way you used to. You can't trust the way you used to. Maybe some people said it was your fault. You might have nightmares; you may have anger. You have an entire burden placed on you which clawed its way from your body to your brain, tainting the way you see everything and everyone around you.

Being a disciple of Jesus means that you place your anger in His hands so that it doesn't come out on other people, people who have nothing to do with what happened to you. It might mean that you protect future survivors by coming out and carrying your cross publicly. Or maybe that is just too much to bear, so you carry it silently.

The abuse was not your fault, and you are not forgotten. You are loved by God and He sees your suffering. *How can we as the church help you carry this cross?*

We Submit...Even When It's Unfair

You see, Church, we all have a cross to carry. If we could stop looking at our own, we might just see that we are truly all in this together. We all suffer. Maybe it shows up in our sexuality; maybe it shows up in other ways. There are those who struggle with finances, those who struggle with mental illness, those who struggle with relationships, learning disabilities, chaotic families of origin, betrayal, lust, addiction...should I go on? There are innumerable ways that sin can break this world. And yet, it is in this world that we are called to follow Christ.

Believers can submit to God no matter how unfair the circumstances. There are a lot of crosses to bear—a lot of sexual burdens we might be asked to carry. No matter how unfair they are, no matter how inborn the desire is, they do not negate Jesus's command to carry the cross of Christ. When we submit to Christ as Lord, we submit to Him in every area of our lives. Some areas are more difficult to surrender than others, but our submission isn't predicated on the ease of the task.

And here's the secret about sin: *We were all born that way*. We are all on equal footing—we're all flawed, guilty, and burdened with hardships. And we are all equally covered by the grace of Jesus Christ. When we realize how much we've been forgiven, we can turn and extend that same grace and compassion to others.

Sometimes the grief and trials feel too great to bear. But we can rejoice that "we do not have a high priest who is unable to empathize with our weaknesses" (Hebrews 4:15). Jesus doesn't look down from heaven thinking, "Gee, that looks hard." No, He suffered all that we suffer so He could look back at us and say, "Here's how you suffer. I'll do it first so you won't be afraid."

He is the imminent, the ever-present, the good God whom we serve. And He is infinitely worthy of us taking up our crosses—no matter what they may be—and following Him unto death. Nothing we lose here can compare to the life that we have gained. May the Lord grant us love and compassion and understanding as we all carry our crosses, together.

DISCUSSION QUESTIONS

1. **Icebreaker:** Give an example of encouragement that didn't fill you with courage. Share the situation with the group and have them reimagine the response as biblical encouragement. What words would have helped you to face the situation with strength?

2. **Main theme:** *We are all called to submit to God's will, no matter how unfair His will seems.* Describe a time you felt God's commands were too burdensome to take up. What was the cross God asked you to carry?

3. **Self-evaluation:** Have you shown judgment and lacked compassion toward those carrying sexual crosses? Bring this confession to God and receive His forgiveness.

4. **Brainstorm:** Discuss ways you can support those in your community who carry sexual crosses. Are there any tangible ways you can care for

those who are struggling with the burdens of same-sex attraction, singleness, or past abuse?

5. **Release the bear:** Talk with your kids this week about the crosses they carry as disciples of Christ.

Prayer of Lament

Choose to Trust

LAMENTATIONS 3:21-22, 55-57; JUDE 20-21, 24

This we recall and therefore have hope and expectation: Your mercy and kindness allow us not to be consumed by all this. Your tender compassion fails not. We called upon Your name, O Lord, out of the depths of the mire of the filth. You heard our voices: O hide not Your ear at our prayer for relief. You drew near on the day we called to You; You said, "Fear not." You are the One who can help us build up our children on our faith, rising higher and higher, praying in the Spirit. Guard and keep us in the love of God. You are able to keep us from stumbling or slipping or failing to present ourselves and our children blameless and faultless before the presence of Your glory.

You are worthy to be trusted, Lord, even when things don't look so good. You are the lamp to our feet and the light to our path. The Good Shepherd who can keep the enemy from slipping in the side door. You have already overcome the evil one. We can trust You to help us implement what we know for now. Just as we want our children to accept our discipline, we want to accept Yours as well. You are the Way when we lose ours, the Truth when we are surrounded by lies, and the Life when our world is trying to be the death of us, our sanity, and our kids' sexuality. Let us boldly live and proclaim the truth that despite what the world looks like, You have overcome the world. By Your power, You will bring us through it! Amen. So be it.

AFTERWORD

Things to Repeat to Your Kids Until They Want to Gag

The Lasting Effects of a Good Maxim

HILLARY

See if you can complete the following sentences:

If you don't have something nice to say...

Do unto others as you would have them...

Well, life isn't always...

Growing up in the South, we heard these statements constantly. If we didn't have anything nice to say, we didn't say anything at all. We did unto others what we would have them do unto us, and we learned not to complain about fairness because any adult within hearing distance would remind us that life wasn't fair. My favorite maxim came from my grandmother as I was learning to drive. She would scream in terror whenever I pulled away from a four-way stop sign in the presence of another car. I'd lovingly reassure her, "It's okay, Grandmommy. I have the right of way." And each time she'd snap back, "Well, there's a graveyard *full* of people who had the right of way."

Maxims are easy-to-remember, bite-sized pieces of a worldview that were repeated to us so many times we could recite them in our sleep. They tell us *general* truths about the world and how we should behave as humans. These little sayings not only teach us how to act but also reinforce what is *true* about our world, our identity, and our life's purpose. Through the sayings above, I learned my words shouldn't be used to tear people down, that life wasn't always fair, and that I could follow the rules and *still* get hurt because there was no guarantee that other people were following the rules.

Today, maxims about self-control and common courtesy are less common, and in their place are battle cries to "speak your truth," "follow your heart," or "you deserve the best." Those are the nuggets of wisdom that culture is passing on to your child, and they ain't *gold* nuggets, if you know what I mean.

As we said in chapter 6, human beings have a difficult time distinguishing that which is true from that which is familiar. The purpose of a maxim is to reinforce a particular worldview. And reinforcing biblical concepts for your kids through maxims might seem cheesy, but it's only weird if it doesn't work. (And yes, that's my life motto.)

Let's face it. An oft-touted maxim can be harder to shake than mono. My cousin's parting words to her daughter whenever she leaves the house are, "Have fun! Keep your clothes on!" I can all but guarantee that if her daughter even *thinks* about stripping down with a boy, she will immediately hear her mother's voice in her head—the last person you want in your thoughts when you are trying to get jiggy with Mr. Right Now.

Here, then, are some maxims you can try repeating to your kids. When they've heard it enough for it to really sink in, you'll know. Their eyes will roll back in their heads and there will be audible gagging sounds. At which point, you have permission to pat yourself on the back for a job well done.

1. What You Do with Your Body Matters

This one deals not just with sexuality, but with basically *every* aspect of human life, and there is no age too young to reinforce this truth. So, Mama Bears, when you ask your kids to take a bath or brush their teeth and they ask why, remind them that it's because *what they do with their body matters*.

The more you say it, the more this truth will be reinforced across different areas of life. But for the young kids, this statement will usually be followed by an even longer "But *whyyyyy*? Why does it matter what I do with my body?" Instead of saying "Because I said so," follow this maxim up with the next one.

2. God Gave You Your Body to Take Care of It

This one *also* applies to most anything you can think of. When they ask why they have to eat broccoli instead of candy, you can remind them that God gave them their body to take care of it, and too much candy can make their body sick.

Now, some parents try to get this point across by telling their child that their body is a gift from God, but I would discourage this language. First, gifts imply ownership, and that's not what our bodies are. First Corinthians 6:19-20 says, "Do you not know that your bodies are temples of the Holy Spirit, who is in you, whom you have received from God? You are not your own; you were bought at a price. Therefore honor God with your bodies."

A more practical second reason I don't recommend using the "gift" language is because your child has probably seen you throw away or regift a gift. And if you think they don't pick up on that kind of minutiae, to our chagrin, they do. So when they ask *why* we are to take care of our bodies, the statement above presents the concept of stewardship, a theme which is heavy throughout Scripture.

Adam and Eve were stewards of God's creation. We as humankind continue that stewardship. Not only does this reinforce how to be a good steward but also how to be a good *authority*. Part of authority is taking care of that which you rule. We are to rule over our bodies (and our urges) in a way that reflects *self-control*. This is an example of being a good steward *and* a good authority.

3. Sex Is the Bodily Renewal of Marital Vows

This would have changed my whole outlook on sex as a teen. When sex is properly defined, "sex outside of marriage" becomes nonsensical. How can you repeat vows you haven't taken?

4. Authority Isn't the Same Thing as Oppression

All the isms in this book operate on the assumption that authority = oppression. When the concept of authority is seen as inherently bad, our kids will not know what to do with the *authority* of the Bible or any other (legitimate) *authorities* in their lives (like you, their teachers, the police, etc.). Furthermore, the more they are taught to despise authority, the less likely they are to want to undertake those leadership roles. This is a problem since God's plan for us in Genesis 1:28 and Revelation 22:5 is to *rule over the earth and ultimately reign with God forever.*

Our kids need to recognize that a hierarchical structure itself is not bad. It's what you do with it. With the proper definition of authority, our kids can learn to recognize a person who is a good authority and one who is a bad authority. Some authorities you can get out from under and others you can't. It is important that we recognize and place ourselves under good authority—if we have the option.

5. You Can't Flourish in What You Weren't Created For

One of the buzzwords that we hear a lot is that people will "flourish" once they can finally live as their authentic selves. And yet, as we've cited throughout the book, there's also a ton of research touting how people who identify as LGBTQ+ are suffering from every ailment you can imagine, both emotionally and physically—generally more so than non-LGBTQ+ identified people. Secular science keeps trying to explain this away as a result of homophobia or "minority stress" (meaning that people are oppressed by the "stigma" their minority status carries). So why are countries like Sweden and Norway, who are supposedly the most accepting countries in the world for LGBTQ+ people, *still showing the same level of distress?* Can I maybe suggest that we have it backward: People are not experiencing distress because they aren't accepted; maybe they are experiencing distress because they are fighting against their design? Maybe because we cannot "flourish" in what we weren't created for.

6. You Can Say the Right Thing in the Wrong Way

We want our kids to speak truth, but we don't want them to become little crusaders for God by dropping a bunch of truth-grenades and letting the pieces fall where they may. As women have complained for millennia, "It's not *what* you said, it's the *way you said it*." They aren't wrong, y'all. Our delivery matters.

7. Just Because You Feel It Doesn't Make It True

This bit of wisdom goes against ev-ah-ree-thing the world is telling our kids. It cuts to the heart of emotional reasoning and helps remind our kids that we don't determine truth by our feelings. We can't prevent culture from following after the god of emotions; all we have control over is ourselves. Our kids need to remember that they will experience all sorts of feelings that are not grounded in truth. We don't ignore feelings. We dignify them for what they are. We also care about other people's feelings, but we don't judge *reality* based on feelings. You can press this maxim a little further from time to time by asking them, "Are your feelings lying to you right now?" This allows them to express the emotion while still understanding that it may not be pointing toward truth. (Fun fact: My husband frequently asks me this.)

8. Not All Change Is Progress

As humans we tend to think that any change is for the better. But anyone who saw my first-grade haircut knows that ain't the case. Some change is progress, and some is regressive. Some is neutral. It's best that we don't take a naive approach by assuming that anything different is automatically *better*.

9. What Do You Mean by That? How Did You Come to That Conclusion? What Actually Happened?

Remember from chapter 6 that there is a difference between categorical words and actual information. Linguistic theft is alive and well. When someone uses a categorical term (healthy, good, wrong, right, oppressive, injustice, harmful), we should never assume we're all on the same page unless they have defined the word and we know the circumstances surrounding the label.

When someone is trying to get your kids to agree with them without giving them details, teach them to ask, "What do you mean by that word?" and, "How did you come to that conclusion?" or even, "So what *actually* happened?" This reminds our kids that they are *not* to turn their brains off. We should all ask clarifying questions before committing ourselves to a position. Remember: If they can't accurately reenact the situation, then they don't really know what happened. They are believing the category without knowing the facts.

10. It's Okay to Be Normal, and It's Okay to Be Different

When I was a kid, all I wanted in life was to be like everyone else. All the other kids seemed to have a handle on their personality. They were shy, or boisterous, or funny. I was just *intense.* My brain was constantly seeking to understand every facet of the world I lived in, to find patterns, explain behaviors. I wanted everyone to be as keenly interested in life as I was. It's a great trait to have as a 40-year-old writer. It does *not* make you popular on the playground as a 10-year-old, though. I would always think, "Why can't I just be like everyone else?" I would have loved to know that it was okay to be different and that God had a plan for my special kind of weird.

Fast-forward to now, and suddenly the world belongs to the geeks, the nerds, and the weirdos (just like *Breakfast Club* prophesied!). Now the struggle kids face is "how can I be different?" Suddenly, being average, ordinary, dare I say *the norm* is what terrifies them. Being a minority used to mean sitting on the fringes. Now, it confers status to the point that all the kids in the majority-type are squeezing and reshaping their identities so that they, too, can be different and special...just like everybody else.

But let's look at this objectively: *Trying* to fit in and *trying* to be different both carry baggage because neither reflects being at peace with how God made you. We all have areas where we blend in and areas where we stand out. Do you have a little boy who doesn't fit the rough-and-tumble mold? What about a little girl who's more mud than Malibu Stacy? There are some molds that are just fine to break—so, honey, go right ahead.

11. It's Okay to Be on the Wrong Side of History If You're on the Right Side of Eternity

The phrase "being on the wrong side of history" pops up a lot, especially with the politicization of sex. And there's a legitimate point there. Humans do have a history of misquoting Scripture to justify the mistreatment of other people. Heroes like Abigail Adams and Rosa Parks improved our world by pushing back against the status quo—*when the status quo was wrong*. Kids today are being taught that every act of rebellion is just as noble. Uhhhh...no. Some rebellion is just good, old-fashioned rebellion and not to be admired. So if they are told that following Jesus means "being on the wrong side of history," then get used to being hated—because it's a *lot worse* to be on the wrong side of eternity.

12. Just Because It Feels Good Doesn't Make It Good for You

Now, there are some things that feel good that are actually good for you! Like a massage! But that's not the way it is for everything. This applies to food. It applies to pleasure. It applies to sex. It applies to most everything. Pleasure is not the same thing as moral or good, and just because it tastes good, looks good, or feels good doesn't mean it's good for you.

13. Personality, Interests, and Aptitudes Are on a Spectrum...Gender Is Not

I know I beat this horse dead in the gender identity chapter, but I really don't think our kids can hear this maxim enough. Every time I turn around, there's another story of parents who got their daughter a double mastectomy because she liked math and jujitsu. Another version of this statement is going back to our graphs and reminding our kids, "There is room for a boy/girl like you" and even "Your husband/wife is going to love having a man/woman with those traits!" (Even if they choose to be single, we want them to know that having gender-nonconforming interests does not mean they are automatically gay.)

14. Feelings Are Terrible Leaders but Great Followers

When it comes to obedience, discipline, and forming good habits, you can't wait till you *feel* like it or it'll never happen. So lead your feelings in the right direction till they catch up. Obedience becomes a lot simpler when we accept the fact that we can do the right thing even when we don't feel like doing it. The beautiful thing about how the mind works, though, is that when a person chooses to do stuff they don't want to do, it eventually helps them *want* to do those things. So give your feelings to God, and do the right thing anyway. With practice, it gets easier over time.

15. What Are You Training Your Brain to Crave?

We like to think that habits are things we can make or break at will. The reality is that every decision you make, every action you take, every thought on which you choose to dwell is changing your brain for better or worse. Each time you do something, your brain builds new connections that help you focus more on those things. It doesn't distinguish between good and bad; *it just responds to repetition.* (This is especially true when it comes to pornography.) When you notice your kids starting to have unhealthy fixations or habits, ask them: What are you training your brain to crave?

16. We Are Only Responsible for What We Have Been Given

Kids (okay, let's be honest...all of us) tend to play the game of comparisons. It's easy to judge ourselves by looking at the gifts and resources God has given someone else. But remember: You are not responsible for what the Lord has given me, and I am not responsible for what the Lord has given you. Each of us is only responsible for that which He has put on our plate. If your child has been blessed with intelligence, athletic ability, or popularity, remind them that to whom much is given much is expected (Luke 12:48). For the child who feels like they aren't as smart or talented as other people, remind them that they are responsible only for cultivating what God has given them. None of us will be judged in comparison to others. We stand alone before the throne of God, giving account for what we did with what we had. And remember, this also means that we can't judge others, because we don't know the load God has given them.

17. Everyone Is Suffering, Just in Different Ways

It's easy to imagine that everyone else's life is easier than our own. But everyone suffers in a unique and different way. Instead of letting our own pain steal all our attention, letting it isolate and divide us, we can remember how pain and suffering are global realities. These are ties that bind us together, in shared humanity. We can find company in our struggles, vulnerable connections through our pains, and shared community in overcoming adversity. Tracing each trail of tears, we can find lines of empathy and understanding. We are all human, and we are all in this thing together. Let's start living like it.

A Final Word

We are so grateful to have been able to journey alongside you as we tackled some of the biggest ideological challenges facing you and your children. Each one of these chapters could have been a book in itself, and naturally some points didn't get their due turn under the microscope. But here's the great news: There is a wealth of books, articles, and studies to explore next.

We challenge you not to let your studies stop with this book. The cultural conversation is always shifting. New arguments will be neatly packaged and offered as Turkish delight to your little ones. Let's do our best to arm our little Lucys and Susans and Peters while taking hope in the God who rescues every Edmund who calls out to Him!

You also have a whole community of Mama Bears standing beside you, ready to equip and encourage you on your journey as you disciple your children in their sexuality and gender identity. We take great joy in pouring into one another, so if you have a question or concern, please reach out to us through our website.

Finally, know that we are praying for you. The conversations we need to have as parents can be awkward at times, but God's design is worth it. Take up your cross, Mama Bears, and put on the armor of God, so that "you may be able to stand your ground, and after you have done everything, to stand" (Ephesians 6:13).

Recommended Resources

Books

Sam Allberry, *Why Does God Care Who I Sleep With?*

Ricky Chelette, DVDs, "*Why? Understanding Gender Development and Homo-sexuality in Males*" and "*Why? Understanding Female Gender Development*," livehope.org.

Vicki Courtney, *5 Conversations You Must Have with Your Son*

Kevin DeYoung, *What Does the Bible Really Teach About Homosexuality?*

Luke Gilkerson, *The Talk: 7 Lessons to Introduce Your Child to Biblical Sexuality*

Rachel Gilson, *Born Again This Way: Coming Out, Coming to Faith, and What Comes Next*

Miriam Grossman, *Lost in Trans Nation: A Child Psychologist's Guide Out of the Madness*

Miriam Grossman, *Unprotected: A Campus Psychiatrist Reveals How Political Correctness in Her Profession Endangers Every Student*

Maria Keffler, *Desist, Detrans & Detox: Getting Your Child Out of the Gender Cult*

Gabriele Kuby, *The Global Sexual Revolution: Destruction of Freedom in the Name of Freedom*

Logan Lancing with James Lindsey, *The Queering of the American Child: How a New School Religious Cult Poisons the Minds and Bodies of Normal Kids*

Sean McDowell, *Chasing Love: Sex, Love, and Relationships in a Confused Culture*

Joe S. McIlhaney Jr. and Freda McKissic Bush, *Hooked: The Brain Science on How Casual Sex Affects Human Development*

Nancy R. Pearcey, *Love Thy Body: Answering Hard Questions About Life and Sexuality*

Clifford and Joyce Penner, *The Gift of Sex: A Guide to Sexual Fulfillment*

Jackie Hill Perry, *Gay Girl, Good God: The Story of Who I Was, and Who God Has Always Been*

John Piper and Justin Taylor, editors, *Sex and the Supremacy of Christ*

Helen Pluckrose and James Lindsay, *Cynical Theories: How Activist Scholarship Made Everything About Race, Gender, and Identity—and Why This Harms Everybody*

Neil Shenvi and Pat Sawyer, *Critical Dilemma*

Abigail Shrier, *Irreversible Damage: The Transgender Craze Seducing Our Daughters*

Juli Slattery, *Rethinking Sexuality: God's Design and Why It Matters*

Juli Slattery, *Sex and the Single Girl*

John Stonestreet and Brett Kunkle, *A Practical Guide to Culture: Helping the Next Generation Navigate Today's World*

Christopher West, *Our Bodies Tell God's Story: Discovering the Divine Plan for Love, Sex, and Gender*

Christopher Yuan, *Holy Sexuality and the Gospel: Sex, Desire, and Relationships Shaped by God's Grand Story*

Curriculum

(For Elementary-Age Children)

Foundation Worldview, *God's Good Design* by Elizabeth Urbanowicz, https://foundationworldview.com/curriculum/gods-good-design

(For Teens)

Christopher Yuan, *The Holy Sexuality Project*, https://HolySexuality.com/

Podcast Episodes or YouTube Videos

Mama Bear Apologetics, "The Four Types of Love and Why Our Kids Need to Understand Them," episode 97

Take Back Our Schools, "Saving My Daughter from the Transgender Cult," February 25, 2023

Lisa Diamond, *"Lisa Diamond on Sexual Fluidity of Men and Women,"* Cornell University, December 6, 2013, https://www.youtube.com/watch?v=m2rTHDOuUBw

Notes

Introduction. My Kid's Cartoon Showed *What?*

1. Juli Slattery, *Rethinking Sexuality: God's Design and Why It Matters* (Multnomah, 2018), 31.
2. Jeff Diamant, "Half of U.S. Christians Say Casual Sex Between Consenting Adults Is Sometimes or Always Acceptable," Pew Research Center, August 31, 2020, www.pewresearch.org/fact-tank/2020/08/31/half-of-u-s-christians-say-casual-sex-between-consenting-adults-is-sometimes-or-always-acceptable/.
3. Erik Kain, "Study Finds Majority of Young Evangelicals Have Premarital Sex," *Forbes,* October 1, 2011, www.forbes.com/sites/erikkain/2011/10/01/study-finds-majority-of-young-evangelicals-have-premarital-sex/.
4. Slattery, *Rethinking Sexuality*, 24.
5. "Survey Says: Parent Power," Power to Decide, October 2016, https://powertodecide.org/what-we do/information/resource-library/parent-power-october-2016-survey-says.
6. Chris Savino, dir. "The Loud House," Season 2, episode 75, "L is for Love," June 15, 2017, on Nickelodeon.
7. *Pliny's Letters*, trans. Alfred Church and W.J. Brodribb (William Blackwood and Sons, 1872), 153–54. Emphasis mine.
8. Julia Marnin, "Neuroscience Professor Removed From APA Discussion After Saying There Are Only Two Sexes," *Newsweek,* May 14, 2021, https://www.newsweek.com/neuroscience-professor-removed-apa-discussion-after-saying-there-are-only-two-genders-1591697#:~:text=Neuroscience%20Professor%20Removed%20From%20APA,Are%20Only%20Two%20Sexes%20%2D%20Newsweek. See also Bea Swallow and PA Media, "Wiltshire teacher fired for not using preferred pronouns, tribunal told," *BBC News*, March 19, 2024, https://www.bbc.com/news/uk-england-wiltshire-68609392. See also House of Commons of Canada, Bill C-16: An Act to amend the Canadian Human Rights Act and the Criminal Code, May 17, 2016, https://www.parl.ca/DocumentViewer/en/42-1/bill/c-16/first-reading.

Part 1: Things I Probably Already Knew...But Kinda Forgot

1. Prayers of Lament based on the work of Mark Vroegop, *Dark Clouds, Deep Mercy: Discovering the Grace of Lament* (Crossway, 2019).

Chapter 1. Sexually Set Apart

1. Clay Jones, *Why Does God Allow Evil?* (Harvest House Publishers, 2017), 29.
2. Tim Keller, "The Gospel and Sex," The Gospel and Life Conferences, 2004 and 2005, https://gospelinlife.com/downloads/the-gospel-and-sex.
3. Clay Jones, "Killing the Canaanites: A Response to the New Atheism's 'Divine Genocide' Claims," Christian Research Institute, updated August 26, 2022, www.equip.org/article/killing-the-canaanites.
4. Clay Jones, "We Don't Hate Sin So We Don't Understand What Happened to the Canaanites,"

Philosophia Christi 11, no. 1 (2009), https://www.clayjones.net/wp-content/uploads/2011/06/We-Dont-Hate-Sin-PC-article.pdf.

5. See Ezekiel 16:36; Leviticus 18:21; 20:2-5; 2 Kings 23:10; Jeremiah 32:35.
6. The other two laws address meat sacrificed to idols (since idolatry was still a stronghold for them) and the meat and blood of strangled animals. That was it.
7. Greg Koukl, "Never Read a Bible Verse," Stand to Reason, February 4, 2013, https://www.str.org/w/never-read-a-bible-verse#.Vb4mGBNViko.
8. Tim Keller, "The Gospel and Sex," https://www.christ2rculture.com/resources/Ministry-Blog/The-Gospel-and-Sex-by-Tim-Keller.pdf.
9. Crow, Cameron, dir. *Vanilla Sky* (United States: Paramount Pictures, 2001), film.
10. The Beaver's Dam Building Behavior (Why, Where, and How Do Beavers Build Lodges and Dams?), AnimAnswers.com, July 15, 2022, https://animanswers.com/american-beaver-dams/.
11. This is currently being changed with the practice of "ethical nonmonogamy," polyamory, and open marriages. But I have not seen any of those working out well. Have you?
12. Christopher West, *Our Bodies Tell God's Story: Discovering the Divine Plan for Love, Sex, and Gender* (Brazos Press, 2020), 47.

Chapter 2. Sex Is Spelled W-O-R-L-D-V-I-E-W

1. John Piper, *Sex and the Supremacy of Christ* (Crossway, 2005), 26.
2. C.S. Lewis, *The Weight of Glory* (HarperCollins, 1980), 140.
3. George Barna, American Worldview Inventory 2024, April 23, 2024, https://www.arizonachristian.edu/wp-content/uploads/2024/04/CRC-Release-AWVI-2-April-23-2024.pdf.
4. College Fix Staff, "UCSF Professor: Trans Kids Who ID as 'Minotaurs' Merely Part of 'Gender Revolution,'" *The College Fix*, August 19, 2023, https://www.thecollegefix.com/ucsf-professor-trans-kids-who-id-as-minotaurs-merely-part-of-gender-revolution/. See orignal video, Diane Ehrensaft, "Diane Ehrensaft 'Reading in a Gender Creative World' at the San Francisco Public Library," April 13, 2018, YouTube, https://www.youtube.com/watch?v=1Q8D52SlAnA.
5. Crystal Cheatham, "Part 1: Deconstruction" in *The Deconstructionist Playbook: An Anthology*, Crystal Cheatham and Theresa Ta, eds. (Bemba Press, 2021), 1.
6. Most of the cartoons for teaching kids comprehensive sex education repeat the phrase "oral, anal, and vaginal" whenever they talk about sex, as if these are all equally healthy versions of sex. But that's not true, and our kids will need us to explain why. Anal sex has all sorts of complications like tearing (which leads to infection), rectal prolapse (where the rectum actually falls outside of the anus), and fecal incontinence where people are so stretched out that they begin pooping their pants regularly. The vagina is the only orifice God *designed* for penetration.
7. It may refer to 1) the way we co-exercise dominion over the earth, 2) how the marital relationship mirrors God's internal relationship within the Trinity, 3) our eternal souls, or 4) our creative faculties and cognitive abilities which allow us to partake in the creative process to a degree unparalleled within the animal kingdom. Regardless of how *imago dei* is defined, the point is that we reflect God's image to the world in a unique way, and that's both a privilege and a responsibility.
8. For a good picture of what this looks like, read C.S. Lewis's book *Perelandra*. The "green lady" is a depiction of what it would look like to only want that which God wanted and to be totally content in it. The diatribe between the green lady and Weston is a long, drawn-out, and chillingly accurate portrayal of what happened in the super-condensed conversation between the snake and Eve in Genesis 3:1-5.

9. Hillary Morgan Ferrer, "Why Did God Create the Tree in the First Place?" Mama Bear Apologetics, https://mamabearapologetics.com/god-create-tree-first-place/.

10. Robbie Meredith, "Gay men given electric shocks 'to cure homosexuality' at QUB," *BBC News*, September 30, 2019, https://www.bbc.com/news/uk-northern-ireland-49838964.

11. Granted, he probably wanted to make sure that LGBTQ+ identifying people know their fallenness isn't worse than others, but this should still have been a really simple "yes."

Chapter 3. A Pretty Great Design, When Followed

1. For excellent examples of this type of biography, see Jackie Hill Perry, *Gay Girl, Good God: The Story of Who I Was, and Who God Has Always Been* (B&H, 2018) and Rachel Gilson, *Born Again This Way: Coming Out, Coming to Faith, and What Comes Next* (The Good Book Company, 2020).

2. The metaphor of cultivating a garden as a symbol of *good* authority appears frequently in Scripture. It begins with Genesis 1 and Adam and Eve's role in the Garden of Eden. We see it in in Isaiah 5 and Isaiah 58:11 where Israel is likened to a vineyard. Paul also uses this imagery in 1 Corinthians 3:9, where he compares workers in the Lord to gardeners, tending to those under their care.

3. Rachel Gilson, *Born Again This Way: Coming Out, Coming to Faith, and What Comes Next* (The Good Book Company, 2020), 39–40.

4. Christopher West, *Our Bodies Tell God's Story: Discovering the Divine Plan for Love, Sex, and Gender* (Baker, 2020), 82.

Chapter 4. Demolishing Arguments, Not People

1. The Shema is considered the most important Jewish prayer—the first to be memorized by children—and is often spoken or sung at important moments, like Shabbat.

2. Jen Hatmaker, *Fierce, Free, and Full of Fire: The Guide to Being Glorious You* (Thomas Nelson, 2020), 91.

Chapter 5. Are You Sex-Smarter than a Fifth Grader?

1. National Sex Education Standards: Core Content and Skills, K-12, second edition, 2020, https://advocatesforyouth.org/wp-content/uploads/2020/03/NSES-2020-web.pdf.

2. Miriam Grossman, "A Brief History of Sex Ed: How We Reached Today's Madness," *Public Discourse: The Journal of the Witherspoon Institute*, July 16, 2013, https://www.thepublicdiscourse.com/2013/07/10408.

3. National Sex Education Standards, 7.

4. John S. Santelli et al., "Abstinence-Only-Until-Marriage: An Updated Review of U.S. Policies and Programs and Their Impact," *Journal of Adolescent Health* 61, no. 3 (2017): 273–80, doi: 10.1016/j.jadohealth.2017.05.031.

5. For example, many curricula liberally instruct kids on using lubrication for anal sex to reduce friction, implicitly acknowledging the dangers, but teaching kids how to make a damaging practice less damaging.

6. See Amaze.org's playlists here: https://www.youtube.com/@amazeorg.

7. Planned Parenthood, "How Do You Know if Someone Wants to Have Sex with You?" YouTube, September 21, 2015, www.youtube.com/watch?v=qNN3nAevQKY.

8. Nadia Bolz-Weber, *Shameless: A Case for Not Feeling Bad About Feeling Good (About Sex)* (Random House, 2020), 17.

9. In one video titled "Am I Ready to Have Sex?" one of the "important questions" kids should ask themselves is: "Do I actually know anyone I'd like to have sex with?" See around the 40-second mark here: https://www.youtube.com/watch?v=rj3wBPZjy-8.

10. The Gender Unicorn has also become very popular. Similar teaching, different animal. See Trans Student Educational Resources, Gender Unicorn, https://transstudent.org/gender/.

11. Deven Clarke, "Gender-Based Assignment at Texas High School, 'Genderbread Person,' Sparks Controversy," Click 2 Houston, March 27, 2024, https://www.click2houston.com/news/2024/03/27/gender-based-assignment-at-texas-high-school-genderbread-person-sparks-controversy/.

12. William H. Jeynes, "A Meta-Analysis on the Factors That Best Reduce the Achievement Gap," *Education and Urban Society* 47, no. 5 (2015): doi: 10.1177/0013124514529155.

13. William H. Jeynes, "The Effects of Black and Hispanic 12th Graders Living in Intact Families and Being Religious on Their Academic Achievement," *Urban Education* 38, no. 1 (2003): doi: 10.1177/0042085902238685. Conclusions: "The results indicate that Black and Hispanic children who lived in an intact family and showed a high level of religiosity scored as well as White students on most measures of academic achievement, even when controlling for socioeconomic status and gender. These same Black and Hispanic students also performed better than their Black and Hispanic counterparts who were not from intact families and/or were not high in religiosity. These results suggest that parental family structure and religiosity may play a larger role in explaining the academic gap between Black and Hispanic students, on one hand, and Whites, on the other hand, than was previously believed."

14. National Sex Education Standards, 11.

15. Shaziya Allarakha, "What Are the 72 Other Genders?," MedicineNet, February 9, 2024. https://www.medicinenet.com/what_are_the_72_other_genders/article.htm.

16. Russell Goldman, "Here's a List of 58 Gender Options for Facebook Users," ABC News, February 13, 2014, https://abcnews.go.com/blogs/headlines/2014/02/heres-a-list-of-58-gender-options-for-facebook-users.

17. Michel Foucault, *The History of Sexuality*, vol. 1 (Pantheon Books, 1979), 100.

18. Michel Foucault, *The History of Sexuality*, 25.

19. Erin R. Markman, "Gender Identity Disorder, the Gender Binary, and Transgender Oppression: Implications for Ethical Social Work," *Smith College Studies in Social Work* 81, no. 4 (2011): 314–27, doi: 10.1080/00377317.2011.616839.

20. Judith Butler argues against the reductive categories of normal in her book *Gender Trouble: Feminism and the Subversion of Identity* (Routledge, 1990).

21. Read Saul Alinsky's *Rules for Radicals* to see a how-to manual for this.

22. C.S. Lewis, *God in the Dock: Essays on Theology and Ethics*, ed. Walter Hooper (Eerdmans, 1970), 292.

23. Maurianne Adams, Lee Anne Bell, and Pat Griffin, eds, *Teaching for Diversity and Social Justice,* 2nd ed. (Routledge, 2007), appendix C.

24. Jeffrey M. Jones, "LGBTQ+ Identification in U.S. Now at 7.6%," Gallup, March 13, 2024, https://news.gallup.com/poll/611864/lgbtq-identification.aspx.

25. Abigail Shrier, *Irreversible Damage: The Transgender Craze Seducing Our Dauthers* (Regnery Publishing, 2020), xxi.

26. There are a few Christian organizations that teach that if you do everything "God's way" you're guaranteed to have kids not walk away. This, Mama Bears, is a lie. Both of God's first children rebelled. Take responsibility for what you can, and leave the results to God.

Chapter 6. The Enemy's New Playbook

1. For a broader discussion of these tactics, see Gabriele Kuby, *The Global Sexual Revolution: Destruction of Freedom in the Name of Freedom* (LifeSite, 2015).
2. Saul D. Alinsky, *Rules for Radicals: A Practical Primer for Realistic Radicals* (Random House, 1971), 36, 44.
3. Daniel Kahneman, *Thinking, Fast and Slow* (Farrar, Straus and Giroux, 2011), 62. Emphasis mine.
4. These are two main themes in Greg Koukl's book *Tactics: A Game Plan for Discussing Your Christian Convictions* (Zondervan, 2019).
5. Bolz-Weber, *Shameless*, 82. Emphasis mine.
6. The Council on Biblical Manhood and Womanhood, *Nashville Statement* (August 2017), https://cbmw.org/nashville-statement.
7. Cima, Maaike, Franca Tonnaer, and Marc D Hauser. "Psychopaths Know Right from Wrong but Don't Care." Social cognitive and affective neuroscience, March 2010. https://pmc.ncbi.nlm.nih.gov/articles/PMC2840845/.
8. Ed Komenda, "Transgender Minors Protected from Estranged Parents under Washington Law," *Associated Press*, May 9, 2023, https://www.pbs.org/newshour/politics/transgender-minors-protected-from-estranged-parents-under-washington-law.

Chapter 7. The Genderbread Person

1. "Genderbread Person & LGBTQ Umbrella," The Safe Zone Project, http://thesafezoneproject.com/wp-content/uploads/2015/08/GenderbreadPersonLGBTQUmbrella.pdf.
2. *Merriam-Webster Dictionary*, "identity," accessed December 8, 2020, www.merriam-webster.com/dictionary/identity.
3. "Genderbread Person & LGBTQ Umbrella."
4. "Genderbread Person & LGBTQ Umbrella."
5. "Genderbread Person & LGBTQ Umbrella."
6. Sue Bohlin, "Raising Gender Healthy Kids," Probe for Answers, July 30, 2015, https://probe.org/raising-gender-healthy-kids.
7. Ivan Reitman, dir. *Kindergarten Cop* (United States: Imagine Entertainment, 1990), film.
8. Lianne Laurence, "Court Orders Christian to Pay $55,000 to Trans Politician for Calling Him 'Biological Male,'" LifeSite, March 28, 2019, www.lifesitenews.com/news/court-orders-christian-to-pay-55000-to-trans-politician-for-calling-him-biological-male.
9. "Genderbread Person & LGBTQ Umbrella."
10. "Does ISNA Think Children with Intersex Should Be Raised Without a Gender, Or in a Third Gender?" Intersex Society of North America, accessed December 8, 2020, https://isna.org/faq/third-gender.
11. Paula Johnson, "His and Hers…Health Care," TED: Ideas Change Everything, December 2013, https://www.ted.com/talks/paula_johnson_his_and_hers_health_care.
12. "Genderbread Person & LGBTQ Umbrella."
13. Cara Lee Arndorfer and Elizabeth A. Stormshak, "Same-Sex Versus Other-Sex Best Friendship in Early Adolescence: Longitudinal Predictors of Antisocial Behavior Throughout Adolescence," *Journal of Youth and Adolescence* 37, no. 9 (October 2008): 1059–70, doi: 10.1007/s10964-008-9311-x.

14. "Genderbread Person & LGBTQ Umbrella."
15. "Genderbread Person & LGBTQ Umbrella."
16. Evan L. Ardiel and Catharine H. Rankin, "The Importance of Touch in Development," *Paediatrics & Child Health* 15, no. 3 (March 1, 2010): 153–56, doi: 10.1093/pch/15.3.153.
17. "Genderbread Person & LGBTQ Umbrella."

Chapter 8. Sex-Positivity

1. Reich is not the only one who encouraged this movement. Alfred Kinsey, Margaret Sanger, Robert Rimmer, and others led the charge for sexual liberation. Nancy Pearcey gives an excellent account of each of these people in her book *Love Thy Body,* which we encourage you to read ASAP!
2. Nancy Pearcey, *Love Thy Body: Answering Hard Questions About Life and Sexuality* (Baker Books, 2018), 133.
3. Quoted in Gail Mitchell, "The Real Story Behind 'WAP': Cardi B's Business Parnter Brooklyn Johnny Tells All," Billboard, August 28, 2020, https://www.billboard.com/music/music-news/wap-cardi-b-business-partner-brooklyn-johnny-story-9441667/.
4. Pearcey, *Love Thy Body*, 135.
5. Chantelle Ivanski and Taylor Kohut, "Exploring Definitions of Sex Positivity Through Thematic Analysis," *The Canadian Journal of Human Sexuality* 26, no. 3 (2017): 216-25, doi: 10.3138/cjhs.2017-0017.
6. Jess O'Reilly, "What Sex Positivity Means to Me," Sex with Dr. Jess, March 6, 2019, www.sexwithdrjess.com/2019/03/what-sex-positivity-means-to-me.
7. Erica Smith, quoted in "What Does It Actually Mean to Be 'Sex Positive'?" by Gabrielle Kassel, Healthline, September 3, 2020, www.healthline.com/health/healthy-sex/sex-positive-meaning.
8. The K-2 standard requires children to define the different kinds of "family" including same-sex parents and non-married cohabitating parents (Standard CHR.2.CC.4). Grades 3–5 begin defining sexual orientation (Standard SO.5.CC.CC.2). Students in grades 6 through 8 have to explain the difference between people who are heterosexual, bisexual, lesbian, gay, queer, two-spirit, asexual, and pansexual (Standard SO.8.CC.2). See National Sex Education Standards: Core Content and Skills, K–12, Second Edition, 2020, https://advocatesforyouth.org/wp-content/uploads/2020/03/NSES-2020-web.pdf.
9. NSES Standard SH.8.CC.1
10. West, *Our Bodies Tell God's Story*, 8.
11. Sarah L. Brown et al., "Suicide Risk Among BDSM Practitioners: The Role of Acquired Capability for Suicide," *Journal of Clinical Psychology* 73, no. 12 (December 2017): 1642–54, doi: 10.1002/jclp.22461.
12. CHR.12.INF.2 – "Analyze cultural and social factors (e.g., sexism, homophobia, transphobia, racism, ableism, classism) that can influence decisions regarding sexual behaviors." See National Sex Education Standards: Core Content and Skills, K–12, Second Edition, 2020, https://advocatesforyouth.org/wp-content/uploads/2020/03/NSES-2020-web.pdf.
13. By the end of eighth grade, your child should "develop a plan for the school to promote dignity and respect for all people of all sexual orientations in the school community." While we are all in favor of promoting dignity for all people *period*, the only reason to specify sexual orientation is to get kids to be promoting the orientation under the guise of promoting the person. Just another example of sneaking in the ideological bomb attached to a hurting person in need of love.
14. Myriam Grossman, *Unprotected: A Campus Psychiatrist Reveals How Political Correctness in Her Profession Endangers Every Student* (Penguin Group, 2007), 23.

15. Meg Meeker, *Epidemic: How Teen Sex Is Killing Our Kids* (Regnery, 2002), 12.

16. Grossman, *Unprotected*, 27.

17. Planned Parenthood, "Let's Talk About Sex—Sexual Health Advice from Dr. Vanessa Cullins," YouTube, October 20, 2009, www.youtube.com/watch?v=wvlCx3w_tss.

18. Grossman, *Unprotected*, 16.

19. A phrase Grossman borrows from the literature from the Medical Institute for Sexual Health.

20. Kirk Johnson, "Sexually Active Teenagers Are More Likely to Be Depressed and to Attempt Suicide," The Heritage Foundation, June 3, 2003, www.heritage.org/education/report/sexually-active-teenagers-are-more-likely-be-depressed-and-attempt-suicide.

21. Kara Joyner and J. Richard Udry, "You Don't Bring Me Anything but Down: Adolescent Romance and Depression," *Journal of Health and Social Behavior* 41, no. 4 (December 2000): 369, doi: 10.2307/2676292.

22. See the app "Our Bible App" at www.ourbibleapp.com.

23. C.S. Lewis, *The Screwtape Letters* (Touchstone, 1961), 44.

24. Dr. Nick Pitts, "Former Secretary of Defense Gen. Jim Mattis Speaks at DBU," Dallas Baptist University, September 20, 2019, https://www.dbu.edu/ige/resources/2019/09/general-jim-mattis-speaks-at-dbu.html.

Chapter 9. Queer Theory

1. Grace Abels, *Transgender Day of Visibility Always Falls on March 31. This Year, So Did Easter*, Politifact, The Poynter Institute, April 1, 2024, https://www.politifact.com/article/2024/apr/01/did-biden-declare-easter-sunday-as-trans-day-of-vi/.

2. Karl Marx says, "Abolition of the family!…On what foundation is the present family, the bourgeois family, based? On capital, on private gain." Karl Marx, *The Communist Manifesto: A Norton Critical Edition*, 2nd ed., Frederic L. Bender, ed. (W. W. Norton & Company, 2012), 78.

3. Karl Marx, *The Communist Manifesto*, 72 and 81. For clarity, I used "oppressor" for the bourgeoisie and "oppressed" for proletariat.

4. Logan Lancing and James Lindsay, *The Queering of the American Child: How a New School Religious Cult Poisons the Minds and Bodies of Normal Kids* (New Discourses, 2024), 17.

5. Hailey Nicole Otis, "Tess Holliday's Queering of Body-Positive Activism: Disrupting Fatphobic Logics of Health and Resignifying Fat as Fit," *Women's Studies in Communication* 43, no. 2 (March 25, 2020): 157–80, doi: 10.1080/07491409.2020.1737287.

6. Andre ChenFeng, Dani Wadlington, and Sonia Michelle Cintron, "A Pathway to Equitable Math Instruction: Dismantling Racism in Mathematics Instruction," www.equitablemath.org, May 2021, https://equitablemath.org/wp-content/uploads/sites/2/2020/11/1_STRIDE1.pdf, 66.

7. Although, blue hair has become almost like waving a flag that that you are either queer or queer friendly.

8. Furry: FURScience, *What's a Furry?* updated February 9, 2021, accessed November 23, 2024, https://furscience.com/whats-a-furry/. Therian: Therian-Guide.com, *An Updated Alter-Human Term List*, https://forums.therian-guide.com/Thread-An-updated-Alter-Human-Term-List.

9. Amber Roberts, *Otherkin Are People Too; They Just Identify as Nonhuman*, Vice, July 16, 2015, https://www.vice.com/en/article/mvxgwa/from-dragons-to-foxes-the-otherkin-community-believes-you-can-be-whatever-you-want-to-be.

10. While queer theorists don't actively say "our worldview is true because of evolution," they will usually punt to evolution if you ask them how humans were created. If someone is a Christian and identifying with queer theory, they just have an inconsistent worldview. You cannot believe in queer theory *and* truly believe that God designed humans for a purpose only He can define.
11. In fact, this is currently being changed from a "disorder" (lycanthropy) and into another "dysphoria" called *species dysphoria*. And trying to help a person identify as a human will soon be seen as another type of abusive conversion therapy as seen in the movie *Wolf.* See also Natalia Winkelman, "'Wolf Review: Animal Behavior,'" *New York Times*, December 2, 2021, https://www.nytimes.com/2021/12/02/movies/wolf-review-animal-behavior.html.
12. Postmedia News, "Trans Teacher Shows up at New Hamilton School Without Massive Prosthetic Breasts," *Toronto Sun*, September 1, 2023, https://torontosun.com/news/local-news/trans-teacher-shows-up-at-new-hamilton-school-without-massive-prosthetic-breasts#comments-area.
13. Yuka Obuno, "What Happened to the Japanese Man Who 'Married' Virtual Character Hatsune Miku?" *The Mainichi*, January 11, 2022, https://mainichi.jp/english/articles/20220111/p2a/00m/0li/028000c.
14. Lyrick Raccoon, "What Are ABDL Conventions & Should I Attend?" PretendAgain, August 17, 2024, https://www.pretendagain.com/blogs/news-tips-community-information/what-are-abdl-conventions-should-i-attend.
15. Madeleine Van der Bruggen, "Why It's Our Shared Responsibility to Protect Kids," TEDxTalks, YouTube, April 13, 2018, https://www.youtube.com/watch?v=egiBgmvv8wA. See also Allyson Walker, "Understanding Resilience Strategies Among Minor-Attracted Individuals," PhD diss., City University of New York, https://academicworks.cuny.edu/. See also Corinne Murdock, "'Minor-Attracted Person': Inside the Growing Effort to Destigmatize Pedophilia," *The Daily Wire*, November 30, 2021, https://www.dailywire.com/news/minor-attracted-person-inside-the-growing-effort-to-destigmatize-pedophilia.
16. Ian Oxnevad, "Professor's Redefinition of Pedophilia Could Help Offenders Demand Rights," *New York Post*, January 1, 2022, https://nypost.com/2022/01/01/professors-redefinition-of-pedophilia-could-help-offenders-demand-rights/.
17. Amelia Walters, "Bestiality References Allegedly Made During Presentation at Renmark High School," ABC News Australia, April 4, 2024, https://www.abc.net.au/news/2024-04-04/alleged-bestiality-references-renmark-high-school-presentation/103653438.
18. Fr. Dwight Longenecker (@dlongenecker1), "First we overlook evil. Then we permit evil. Then we legalize evil. Then we promote evil. Then we celebrate evil. Then we persecute those who still call it evil," Twitter (now X), October 31, 2019, https://x.com/dlongenecker1/status/1190075527840833536.
19. You can find hundreds of options of pronoun pins on Esty, https://www.etsy.com/market/pronoun_pin.
20. For more information on these clubs see LGBT+ Groups in Schools, The Proud Trust: Home for LGBT+ Youth, https://www.theproudtrust.org/schools-and-training/lgbt-groups-in-schools/.
21. George P. Bush, "Doss Elementary Pride Parade," Facebook, April 8, 2022, https://www.facebook.com/watch/?v=255205400159785.
22. Joshua Rhet Miller, "Disney Exec Vows More Gay Characters Amid Huge Inclusivity Push," *New York Post*, March 30, 2022, https://nypost.com/2022/03/30/disney-executive-wants-more-lgbtqia-minority-character/.
23. Catherine Giddings, "15 LGBTQ Books for Kids and Teens Recommended by Queer Librarians, Educators and Independent Booksellers," *New York Times*, updated June 27, 2024, https://www.nytimes.com/wirecutter/reviews/15-lgbtq-books-for-kids-and-teens/.

24. Elizabeth Keohan, "Misgendering: Exploring the Harmful Impact of It," Talkspace, September 8, 2023, https://www.talkspace.com/blog/misgendering-impact/. A new Colorado bill considers deadnaming a type of discrimination that could affect custody, First Regular Session, Seventy-fifth General Assembly State of Colorado, "House Bill 25-1312," https://leg.colorado.gov/sites/default/files/documents/2025A/bills/2025a_1312_ren.pdf.
25. Jesse O'Neil, "Father Arrested for Discussing Child's Gender Transition in Defiance of Court Order," New York Post, March 18, 2021, https://nypost.com/2021/03/18/man-arrested-for-discussing-childs-gender-in-court-order-violation/.
26. Jules Gleeson, "Judith Butler: The Early Years," JSTOR, June 19, 2019, https://daily.jstor.org/judith-butler-the-early-years/.
27. Madison Vanderberg, "Photographer Captures Boys Dressed as Their Favorite Princesses in Empowering Series," Scary Mommy, updated January 28, 2021, https://www.scarymommy.com/boys-can-be-princesses-too.
28. See Katy Faust's book *Them Before Us: Why We Need a Global Children's Rights Movement* (Post Hill Press, 2021).
29. When it comes to sexuality, practices like anal sex, sado-masochism, pedophelia, and incest have carried stigmas because they result in preventable diseases, reflect warped desires, or cause emotional damage to kids.

Chapter 10. Purity Culture

1. Leah MarieAnn Klett, "Liberal Lutheran Pastor Melts Purity Rings into Vagina Sculpture, Presents It to Gloria Steinem," *Christian Post*, February 15, 2019, www.christianpost.com/news/liberal-lutheran-pastor-melts-purity-rings-into-vagina-sculpture-presents-it-to-gloria-steinem.html.
2. Tina Schermer Sellers, "How the Purity Movement Causes Symptoms of Sexual Abuse," TinaSchermerSellers.com, updated September 1, 2020, www.tinaschermersellers.com/post/how-the-purity-movement-causes-symptoms-of-sexual-abuse.
3. Sharayah Colter, "True Love Waits Returns to Where It Began 20 Years Ago," *Baptist Press*, February 14, 2013, https://www.brnow.org/news/True-Love-Waits-returns-to-where-it-began-20-years/.
4. *True Love Waits: Crossing Bridges with Purity* (Lifeway Press, 1998), 10–12.
5. Joshua Harris, *I Kissed Dating Goodbye: A New Attitude Toward Romance and Relationships* (Multnomah, 1997).
6. Hannah Lee Powers, quoted in "My Life Inside the Purity Movement," YouTube, October 10, 2018, www.youtube.com/watch?v=c0vTn177UVg.
7. Linda Kay Klein, *Pure: Inside the Evangelical Movement that Shamed a Generation of Young Women and How I Broke Free* (Touchstone, 2018). This happened in Klein's small-town church, and she implied that all evangelical churches were the same.
8. Jessica Valenti, *The Purity Myth: How America's Obsession with Virginity Is Hurting Young Women* (Seal Press, 2010), 24.
9. Elise Forte, quoted in Amanda Robb's "The Innocence Project," *O: The Oprah Magazine* (March 2007), www.oprah.com/relationships/father-daughter-purity-balls-to-promote-abstinence-chastity-pledges/6.
10. Klein, *Pure,* 3.
11. In case you haven't read Margaret Atwood's book *The Handmaid's Tale* or seen the show or the feminist

protesters, this was the dress code of the enslaved fertile women forced to bear children for the wealthy couples of the Republic of Gilead.

12. As quoted in the documentary *Give Me Sex, Jesus* at www.youtube.com/watch?v=wp5HkXw9Rag.
13. Nicholas H. Wolfinger, "Does Sexual History Affect Marital Happiness?" Institute for Family Studies, October 22, 2018, https://ifstudies.org/blog/does-sexual-history-affect-marital-happiness.
14. Taylor Alesia, "How Modesty Changed My Life," November 15, 2024, YouTube, https://www.youtube.com/watch?v=i9vSKDfxePo.

Chapter 11. Pornography

1. Pornhub Team, "The 2019 Year in Review," Pornhub, December 11, 2019, www.pornhub.com/insights/2019-year-in-review#2019.
2. Josh McDowell, "The Porn Epidemic: Facts Stats & Solutions," https://www.josh.org/wp-content/uploads/sites/607/2024/02/Porn-Epidemic-Executive-Synopsis-9.25.2018.pdf.
3. Nicholas Kristof, "The Children of Pornhub: Why Does Canada Allow This Company to Profit off Videos of Exploitation and Assault?" *New York Times*, December 4, 2020, https://www.nytimes.com/2020/12/04/opinion/sunday/pornhub-rape-trafficking.html.
4. Ron DeHaas "What Are the Most Up-to-Date Stats on Porn?" Covenant Eyes, January 19, 2016, www.covenanteyes.com/2016/01/19/what-are-the-most-up-to-date-stats-on-pornography.
5. "Pornography Statistics," Covenant Eyes, accessed March 25, 2021, www.covenanteyes.com/pornstats.
6. Dale Kunkel et al., "Sex on TV: A Biennial Report for the Kaiser Family Foundation," accessed March 25, 2021, www.kff.org/wp-content/uploads/2013/01/sex-on-tv-a-biennial-report-to-the-kaiser-family-foundation-1999-executive-summary.pdf. Unfortunately, an equally exhaustive survey of the presence of sexualized content has yet to be repeated on today's content. Something tells me the numbers would not be pretty, especially in music videos.
7. Elizabeth McDade-Montez, "New Media, Old Themes: Sexualization in Children's TV Shows," ETR.org, March 28, 2017, www.etr.org/blog/research-childrens-media/. Sexualization and objectification ranged from seductive clothing to unwanted touching and suggestive behavior.
8. Karen E. Dill and Kathryn P. Thill, "Video Game Characters and the Socialization of Gender Roles: Young People's Perceptions Mirror Sexist Media Depictions," *Sex Roles* 57, 851–64 (2007), doi: 10.1007/s11199-007-9278-1.
9. "Consider This," The Novus Project, accessed March 25, 2021, http://thenovusproject.org/resource-hub/parents. We can't even go to the store anymore without having a game plan in place to distract their attention from the eye-level backside hanging out of the bottom of a pair of "fashionable" cut-offs waiting to check out in front of them.
10. "Pornography Statistics," Covenant Eyes, accessed March 25, 2021, www.covenanteyes.com/pornstats.
11. For a Christian perspective on this see John Piper, "Pornography: The New Narcotic," Desiring God, October 9, 2013, https://www.desiringgod.org/articles/pornography-the-new-narcotic and for a secular perspective see Ryan Singel, "Internet Porn: Worse than Crack?" *Wired*, November 19, 2004, www.wired.com/2004/11/internet-porn-worse-than-crack.
12. Joe S. McIlhaney Jr. and Freda McKissic Bush, *Hooked: The Brain Science on How Casual Sex Affects Human Development* (Northfield Publishing, 2019), 32.
13. Frances E. Jensen, *The Teenage Brain: A Neuroscientist's Survival Guide to Raising Adolescents and Young Adults* (Harper Collins, 2015), 107.
14. Brian J. Willoughby, Dean M. Busby, and Bonnie Young-Petersen, "Understanding Associations

Between Personal Definitions of Pornography, Using Pornography, and Depression," *Sexuality Research and Social Policy* 16 (2019): 342–56, doi: 10.1007/s13178-018-0345-x.

15. Catharine A. MacKinnon, "X-Underrated: Living in a World the Pornographers Have Made," in *Big Porn, Inc.: Exposing the Harms of the Global Pornography Industry*, Melinda Tankard Reist and Abigail Bray, eds. (Spinifex Press, 2012), 12.
16. Gert Martin Hald, Neil M. Malamuth, and Carlin Yuen, "Pornography and Attitudes Supporting Violence Against Women: Revisiting the Relationship in Nonexperimental Studies," *Aggressive Behavior* 36, no. 1 (2010): 14–20, doi: 10.1002/ab.20328.
17. Melinda Tankard Reist, "Growing Up in Pornland: Australian Girls Have Had It with Porn-Conditioned Boys," Feminist Current, March 13, 2016, www.feministcurrent.com/2016/03/13/growing-up-pornland-australian-girls.
18. Jean Mackenzie, "Vagina Surgery 'Sought by Girls as Young as Nine,'" BBC, July 3, 2017, www.bbc.com/news/health-40410459.
19. "Landmark Report: U.S. Teens Use an Average of Nine Hours of Media Per Day, Tweens Use Six Hours," Common Sense Media, November 3, 2015, www.commonsensemedia.org/about-us/news/press-releases/landmark-report-us-teens-use-an-average-of-nine-hours-of-media-per-day.
20. Robert Jensen, "Stories of a Rape Culture: Pornography as Propaganda," in *Big Porn, Inc.: Exposing the Harms of the Global Pornography Industry*, Melinda Tankard Reist and Abigail Bray, eds. (Spinifex Press, 2012), 30.
21. Sandra Laville, "Most Boys Think Online Pornography Is Realistic, Finds Study," *The Guardian*, June 14, 2016, www.theguardian.com/culture/2016/jun/15/majority-boys-online-pornography-realistic-middlesex-university-study.
22. Colin Hesse and Kory Floyd, "Affection Substitution: The Effect of Pornography Consumption on Close Relationships," *Journal of Social and Personal Relationships* 36, no. 11-12 (2019): 3887–3907, doi: 10.1177/0265407519841719.
23. Shrier, *Irreversible Damage*, 47.
24. See Gary Wilson, *Your Brain on Porn: Internet Pornography and the Emerging Science of Addiction* (Commonwealth Publishing, 2018). You can view the associated website at www.yourbrainonporn.com. It has both anecdotal evidence and a lot of scientific studies.
25. Linda Cusick, "Youth Prostitution: A Literature Review," *Child Abuse Review* 11, no. 4 (July August 2002), 230–251, doi: 10.1002/car.743.
26. To learn more about Fight the New Drug, you can visit their site at www.fightthenewdrug.org.
27. To learn more about VidAngel, go to https://www.vidangel.com/.

Chapter 12. Same-Sex Attraction

1. There are still churches fighting to remain orthodox regarding this issue, but the culture is not on their side. And another side note, for those feisty enough to look at the endnotes, the next big ones are polyamory and then pedophilia. Gird your loins, Mama Bears. It's a'coming.
2. We also need to realize that there is a difference between *struggling* with same-sex attraction and *not struggling*—meaning the person has accepted homosexuality as part of their identity and believes it to be compatible with Christianity.
3. Katy Faust calls this your "no flinch face." Caroline Woods, "Viewpoint: Raising conservative kids in a 'woke' world," The Dakota Scout, December 9, 2023, https://www.thedakotascout.com/p/viewpoint-raising-conservative-kids.

4. Lisa Diamond, "Lisa Diamond on Sexual Fluidity of Men and Women," YouTube, December 6, 2013, www.youtube.com/watch?feature=player_embedded&v=m2rTHDOuUBw.

5. Lisa Diamond, "Sexual Fluidity in Males and Females," *Current Sexual Health Reports* 8 (December 2016): 249–56, doi: 10.1007/s11930-016-0092-z.

6. Order Ricky's talk on males here: www.livehope.org/product/why-understanding-male-gender-development-on-demand. For a scientifit study, see Mehmet Eskin, Hadiye Kaynak-Demir, and Sinem Demir, "Same-Sex Sexual Orientation, Childhood Sexual Abuse, and Suicidal Behavior in University Students in Turkey," *Archives of Sexual Behavior* 34, no. 2 (April 2005): 185–95, doi: 10.1007/s10508-005-1796-8.

7. Marie E. Tomeo et al. "Comparative Data of Childhood and Adolescence Molestation in Heterosexual and Homosexual Persons," *Archives of Sexual Behavior* 30 (2001): 535–541, doi: 10.1023/A:1010243318426.

8. Lawrence S. Mayer and Paul R. McHugh, "Sexuality and Gender: Findings from the Biological, Psychological, and Social Sciences," *The New Atlantis,* Fall 2016, www.thenewatlantis.com/publications/executive-summary-sexuality-and-gender.

9. Matthew Vines, *God and the Gay Christian: The Biblical Case in Support of Same-Sex Relationships* (Convergent Books, 2015), 31.

10. Vines, *God and the Gay Christian*, chapter 4.

11. Vines, 99.

12. Vines, 29.

13. Peter Enns and Jared Byas, hosts, *The Bible for Normal People*, podcast, season 2, episode 34, "Jen Hatmaker—Changing Your Mind About the Bible: A Survivor's Guide," January 29, 2018, https://thebiblefornormalpeople.podbean.com/e/episode-34-jen-hatmaker/.

14. DeYoung, *What Does the Bible Really Teach About Homosexuality?* (Crossway, 2015).

15. Hobbes, Michael. "Together Alone: The Epidemic of Gay Loneliness" The Huffington Post, March 2, 2017. https://highline.huffingtonpost.com/articles/en/gay-loneliness/.

16. Hillary Morgan Ferrer and Amy Davison, *The Mama Bear Apologetics Podcast*, podcast, episode 97, "The Four Types of Love and Why Our Kids Need to Understand Them," February 6, 2024, https://mamabearapologetics.com/97-the-four-types-of-love/.

17. Mama Bear Apologetics, "The Overhauling of Straight America," https://mamabearapologetics.com/wp-content/uploads/2024/12/overhauling-straight-america.pdf.

Chapter 13. I Identify as a [Fill in the Blank]

1. I believe this is largely due to what we saw in public school special education programs when kids were not taught how to *overcome* their difficulties, but rather had the work made easier to accommodate them. Removing half of the answers in a multiple choice test does *nothing* to help kids with learning disabilities. And kids aren't stupid. Once they realized that having a "diagnosis" meant that they would get special treatment, they all started clamoring for their own diagnosis. In the realm of LGBTQ+, review page 244. Kids are clamoring for any kind of minority "identity" so that they can 1) get out of the oppressor catgory and 2) get special protection from bullying. In terms of the mental health diagnoses, many kids are gaining social media fame by "educating the public" on their unique brand of suffering. British researcher Tara Murphy noted that conditions like Tourrettes suddenly become in vogue (especially among teen girls), but it essentially involved inserting the word *beans* into every other sentence, as seen here: Lauren Milici, "Teen Girls Developing Sudden Severe Tics and Blurting

out the Word 'Beans'—And It Could Be Linked to TikTok," indy500, October 19, 2021, https://www.indy100.com/news/doctors-theorize-tiktok-as-reason-for-teen-girls-developing-tics-b1941305.

2. True intersex conditions that leave the gender of an individual ambiguous account for only about 0.018 percent of the population. Leonard Sax, "How Common Is Intersex? A Response to Anne Fausto-Sterling," *The Journal of Sex Research*, no. 39 (2002), 174–178, doi: 10.1080/00224490209552139.

3. Side note, there is *some* truth in this when you compare the percentage of male and females who fall into the thinker vs. feeler categories for the Myers Briggs. And I'm not just slightly more "thinker." I'm on the extreme spectrum, even for guys. For more on the statistics, see Rachel Suppok, "Not So Rare: Feeler Men and Thinker Women," TrueYou Journal, October 5, 2015, https://www.truity.com/blog/feeler-men-and-thinker-women.

4. For more about John Money, see: https://kinseyinstitute.org/collections/archival/john-money.php.

5. Simon Baron-Cohen, "The Essential Difference: The Truth About the Male and Female Brain," https://www.researchgate.net/profile/Simon-Baron-Cohen/publication/232430614_The_Essential_Difference_The_Truth_About_The_Male_And_Female_Brain/links/547cdb7a0cf2cfe203c1fde2/The-Essential-Difference-The-Truth-About-The-Male-And-Female-Brain.pdf.

6. Charles Murray, *Human Diversity: The Biology of Gender, Race, and Class* (Hachette Book Group, 2020), 12.

7. Simone de Beauvoir, *The Second Sex*, Constance Borde and Sheila Malovany-Chevallier, trans. (Vintage Books, 2011), 267. Originally published in 1949.

8. Gayle Rubin, "The Traffic in Women: Notes on the 'Political Economy' of Sex," in *Toward an Anthropology of Women*, ed. Rayna R. Reiter (Monthly Review Press, 1975), 157.

9. Judith Butler, *Gender Trouble: Feminism and the Subversion of Identity* (Routledge, 2007), 191.

10. It's one, the other, or (as in some intersex conditions) neither. And even though some intersex people used to be referred to as hermaphrodites due to ambiguous genitalia, there is no actual human hermaphroditism because no human has ever produced fully functioning egg and sperm to where they could theoretically fertilize their own egg. That is why we don't use the word *hermaphrodite* for intersex individuals anymore. There is no such thing as a true hermaphroditic human.

11. "Genderbread Person & LGBTQ Umbrella," The Safe Zone Project, http://thesafezoneproject.com/wp-content/uploads/2015/08/GenderbreadPersonLGBTQUmbrella.pdf. See also on Mama Bear Apologetics blog, https://mamabearapologetics.com/wp-content/uploads/2024/12/GenderbreadPersonLGBTQUmbrella.pdf.

12. I really recommend the organization at www.whatmakesaman.org. I think they've got a great start at defining biblical manhood, and I hope a similar website for women comes along too!

13. Have you seen the man online who knits sweaters for penguins? Find his story here: That Good News Girl (@thatgoodnewsgirl), "It's never too late to find a new purpose," March 6, 2025, https://www.instagram.com/reel/DG3mBvIPn7i/?utm_source=ig_web_copy_link&igsh=MzRlODBiNWFlZA==.

14. Scottie Andrew, "A Guide to Neopronouns: From AE to ZE," CNN, August 12, 2023, https://www.cnn.com/us/neopronouns-explained-xe-xyr-wellness-cec/index.html.

15. The Lost Boys, "Demon Pronouns Explained," YouTube, October 29, 2021, https://www.youtube.com/watch?v=shYtruajkw0.

16. Abigail Shrier, *Irreversible Damage: The Transgender Craze Seducing our Daughters* (Regnery, 2020), 7.

17. Alia E. Dastagir, "Marsha Blackburn Asked Ketanji Brown Jackson to Define 'Woman.' Science Says There's No Simple Answer," *USA Today*, updated March 27, 2022, https://www

.usatoday.com/story/life/health-wellness/2022/03/24/marsha-blackburn-asked-ketanji-jackson-define-woman-science/7152439001/.

Chapter 14. *Trans*cending the Gender Cult

1. Chloe Cole, "'My Childhood was RUINED:' Detransitioner Chole Cole Talks About Trans Procedures," The Daily Signal, July 27, 2023, YouTube, https://www.youtube.com/watch?v=DSGgR3W_jjg.
2. Statista Research Department, "LGBT Identification in the U.S. 2012-2023," Statista, July 5, 2024, https://www.statista.com/statistics/719685/american-adults-who-identify-as-homosexual-bisexual-transgender-by-generation/.
3. *Encyclopedia Britannica*, "cult," accessed March 6, 2025, https://www.britannica.com/search?query=cult.
4. The Free Dictionary, "cult," accessed March 6, 2025, https://www.thefreedictionary.com/cult. Emphasis added.
5. Stephen A. Hassan, "Understanding Cults: The Basics," *Psychology Today*, June 5, 2021, https://www.psychologytoday.com/us/blog/freedom-mind/202106/understanding-cults-the-basics.
6. "Lisa," "The Cult of Transgenderism: My Brother's Crisis of Identity in an America Gone Mad," Family Research Council, https://www.frc.org/blog/2019/11/cult-transgenderism-my-brothers-crisis-identity-america-gone-mad/#gsc.tab=0.
7. Kathleen Hayes, "Gender Ideology's True Believers," Quillette, May 19, 2022, https://quillette.com/2022/05/19/gender-ideologys-true-believers/.
8. Will Hall, "UK's Foremost Expert: Gender Ideology Is 'A Cult Belief,'" *The Baptist Message*, May 30, 2023, https://www.baptistmessage.com/uks-foremost-expert-gender-ideology-is-made-up/.
9. Stephen A. Hassan, "Understanding Cults."
10. Abigail Shrier, "How Activist Teachers Recruit Kids," The Truth Fairy, November 18, 2021. https://www.thetruthfairy.info/p/how-activist-teachers-recruit-kids.
11. Logan Lancing and James Lindsay, *The Queering of the American Child: How a New School Religious Cult Poisons the Minds and Bodies of Normal Kids* (New Discourses, 2024), xiii–xiv.
12. Maria Keffler, *Desist, Detrans & Detox: Getting Your Child out of the Gender Cult* (Partners for Ethical Care, 2021), 17.
13. A leaked document from the California Teachers Association Celebrate Pride State Council of Education Program June 1-2, 1019 states, "Current interpretation of California state law does not allow trans students to begin gender identity confirming hormonal therapy with the consent of a both legal guardians; however it does allow for cis minors to receive hormonal (e.g. birth control) *without the barrier of parental permission.*" Emphasis mine. See the document on the Mama Bear Apologetics blog, https://mamabearapologetics.com/20241219_114335/.
14. Here's an example, but I've personally seen this sign in a lot of places, including on T-shirts. Carly Mayberry, "Sign Telling Identity-Confused Kids 'I'm Your Mom Now' Sparks Controversy," *Newsweek*, March 8, 2022, https://www.newsweek.com/sign-telling-identity-confused-kids-im-your-mom-now-sparks-controversy-1685713.
15. Vicky Holt, Elin Skagerberg, and Michael Dunsford, "Young People with Features of Gender Dysphoria: Demographics and Associated Difficulties," *Clinical Child Psychology and Psychiatry* 21, no. 1 (November 26, 2014): 108–18, doi: 10.1177/1359104514558431.
16. Aimilia Kallitsounaki and David M. Williams, "Autism Spectrum Disorder and Gender Dysphoria/Incongruence. A Systematic Literature Review and Meta-Analysis," *Journal of Autism and Developmental Disorders* 53 (May 20, 2022): 3103–17, https://link.springer.com/article/10.1007/

s10803-022-05517-y. Emily Thrower et al., "Prevalence of Autism Spectrum Disorder and Attention-Deficit Hyperactivity Disorder amongst Individuals with Gender Dysphoria: A Systematic Review," *Journal of Autism and Developmental Disorders* 50, no. 3 (November 15, 2019): 695–706, https://doi.org/10.1007/s10803-019-04298-1.

17. Elizabeth Hisle-Gorman et al., "Gender Dysphoria in Children with Autism Spectrum Disorder," *LGBT Health* 6, no. 3 (April 2, 2019): 95–100, doi: 10.1089/lgbt.2018.0252.
18. Temple Grandin, "Calming Effects of Deep Touch Pressure in Patients with Autistic Disorder, College Students, and Animals," *Journal of Child and Adolescent Psychopharmacology* 2, no. 1 (January 1992): 63–72, doi: 10.1089/cap.1992.2.63.
19. Emily Thrower et al., "Prevalence of Autism Spectrum Disorder."
20. Jenna McHenry, Nicole Carrier, Elaine Hull, and Mohamed Kabbaj, "Sex Differences in Anxiety and Depression: Role of Testosterone," *Frontiers in Neuroendocrinology* 35, no. 1 (January 2014): 42–57, doi: 10.1016/j.yfrne.2013.09.001.
21. Brian C. Thoma et al., "Disparities in Childhood Abuse between Transgender and Cisgender Adolescents," *Pediatrics* 148, no. 2 (August 1, 2021), doi: 10.1542/peds.2020-016907. This article points out the correlation, but draws the conclusion that the LGBTQ identity can be made "healthy" instead of it being the distortion that came from the abuse. Annie M.Q. Wang et al., "Outcomes Following Gender Affirming Phalloplasty: A Systematic Review and Meta-Analysis." *Sexual Medicine Reviews* 10, no. 4 (August 26, 2022): 499–512, doi: 10.1016/j.sxmr.2022.03.002.
22. Niki Fritz, Vinny Malic, Bryant Paul, and Yanyan Zhou, "A Descriptive Analysis of the Types, Targets, and Relative Frequency of Aggression in Mainstream Pornography–Archives of Sexual Behavior," *Archives of Sexual Behavior* 49 (July 13, 2020): 3041-3053, doi: 10.1007/s10508-020-01773-0.
23. Karin Nadrowski, "A New Flight from Womanhood? The Importance of Working through Experiences Related to Exposure to Pornographic Content in Girls Affected by Gender Dysphoria," *Journal of Sex & Marital Therapy* 50, no. 3 (November 25, 2023): 293–302, doi: 10.1080/0092623X.2023.2276149.
24. Mary Margaret Olohan, *Detrans: True Stories of Escaping the Gender Ideology Cult* (Regnery, 2024), 21.
25. *Britannica*, "6 Cultures That Recognize More than Two Genders," last updated January 12, 2023, https://www.britannica.com/list/6-cultures-that-recognize-more-than-two-genders.
26. Patti Wigington, "Inanna, Goddess War, Sex, and Justice," Learn Religions, updated February 27, 2020, https://www.learnreligions.com/inanna-goddess-4796590.
27. J.A. Black et al., *The Electronic Text Corpus of Sumerian Literature* (Oxford 1998,) 115–131, http://www-etcsl.orient.ox.ac.uk/.
28. Morg Daniels, "Ancient Mesopotamian Transgender and Non-Binary Identities," Academus Education, June 30, 2021, https://www.academuseducation.co.uk/post/ancient-mesopotamian-transgender-and-non-binary-identities.
29. American Psychiatric Association (1980), *Diagnostic and Statistical Manual of Mental Disorders* (3rd ed.). Washington, DC: American Psychiatric Association, 261.
30. "Gender Dysphoria Diagnosis," American Psychiatric Association, https://www.psychiatry.org/psychiatrists/diversity/education/transgender-and-gender-nonconforming-patients/gender-dysphoria-diagnosis.
31. Sara Dahlen et al., "International Clinical Practice Guidelines for Gender Minority/Trans People: Systematic Review and Quality Assessment," BMJ Open 11, no. 4 (April 2021), doi: 10.1136/bmjopen-2021-048943.
32. Shrier, *Irreversible Damage*, xxi.

33. Deborah Soh, *The End of Gender: Debunking the Myths About Sex and Identity in Our Society* (Simon & Schuster, 2020), 141. This section references and cites all 11 studies.
34. *Britannica*, "6 Cultures That Recognize More than Two Genders," last updated January 12, 2023, https://www.britannica.com/list/6-cultures-that-recognize-more-than-two-genders.
35. Lisa Littman, "Parent Reports of Adolescents and Young Adults Perceived to Show Signs of a Rapid Onset of Gender Dysphoria," *Yearbook of Paediatric Endocrinology* 13, no. 8 (September 12, 2019), doi: 10.1530/ey.16.6.13.
36. Shrier, *Irreversible Damage*, 26.
37. For more information on this, see Shrier's book *Irreversible Damage*.
38. A quick Google search will bring up numerous lists and definitions of gender identities. And as you'll see, they all seem to be defining various shades masculine or feminine leanings.
39. There are about 30 known intersex conditions. For more information, see The Intersex Society of North America at www.isna.org.
40. Leonard, Sax, "How Common Is Intersex? A Response to Anne Fausto-Sterling," *Journal of Sex Research* 39, no. 3 (2002): 174–8, doi:10.1080/00224490209552139.
41. Arthur P. Arnold and S. Marc Breedlove, "Organizational and Activational Effects of Sex Steroids on Brain and Behavior: A Reanalysis," *Hormones and Behavior* 19, no. 4 (December 1985): 469–98, doi: 10.1016/0018-506X(85)90042-X.
42. Melissa Hines, "Prenatal Testosterone and Gender-Related Behaviour," *European Journal of Endocrinology* 155, supplement no. 1 (November 2006): S115-S121, doi: 10.1530/eje.1.02236.
43. See Jonathan Wells's Transgenderism Series on Evolution News at https://evolutionnews.org/tag/transgenderism-series. You can also see the executive summary of all the literature summarized by Lawrence S. Mayer and Paul R. McHugh at www.thenewatlantis.com/publications/executive-summary-sexuality-and-gender.
44. Sara Dahlen, "International Clinical Practice Guidelines."
45. Wylie C. Hembree et al., "Endocrine Treatment of Gender-Dysphoric/Gender-Incongruent Persons: An Endocrine Society Clinical Practice Guideline," *Endocrine Practice* 23, no. 12 (December 2017): 3869–3903, doi: 10.4158/1934-2403-23.12.1437.
46. Jo Taylor et al., "Interventions to Suppress Puberty in Adolescents Experiencing Gender Dysphoria or Incongruence: A Systematic Review," *Archives of Disease in Childhood*, April 9, 2024, doi: 10.1136/archdischild-2023-326669.
47. Food and Drug Administration, "Risk of Pseudotumor Cerebri Added to Labeling for Gonadotropin-Releasing Hormone Agonists," July 1, 2022, https://www.fda.gov/media/159663/download.
48. Genevieve Gluck (@WomenReadWomen), "'Every single child who was truly blocked at Tanner stage 2 (9–11 years old) has never experienced orgasm,'—Marci Bowers, trans-identified male, President of WPATH. This is medical experimentation on children. It is chemical castration and genital mutiliation." Twitter (now X), May 3, 2022, https://x.com/WomenReadWomen/status/1521692875242688512.
49. "Puberty Blockers Are Chemical Castration. Marci Bowers (WPATH) Casually Reveals Extent of Damage," September 16, 2022, RubbleOfEmpires, YouTube, https://www.youtube.com/watch?v=kuwOx9YdHXY.
50. Paulette Cutruzzula Dreher et al., "Complications of the Neovagina in Male-to-Female Transgender Surgery: A Systematic Review and Meta-Analysis with Discussion of Management," *Clinical Anatomy* 31, no. 2 (November 10, 2017): 191–99, doi: 10.1002/ca.23001.
51. Mauro E. Kerckhof et al., "Prevalence of Sexual Dysfunctions in Transgender Persons: Results from

the ENIGI Follow-Up Study," *The Journal of Sexual Medicine* 16, no.12 (2019): 2018–29, doi:10.1016/j.jsxm.2019.09.003.

52. Gabriela Gonzalez and Jennifer T. Anger, "Voiding Dysfunction in Transgender Patients: What We Know and What We Do Not Know," *Current Urology Reports* 26, no. 16 (November 5, 2024), doi: 10.1007/s11934-024-01234-4.

53. Annette Kuhn, Alessandro Santi, and Martin Birkhäuser, "Vaginal Prolapse, Pelvic Floor Function, and Related Symptoms 16 Years after Sex Reassignment Surgery in Transsexuals," *Fertility and Sterility* 95, no. 7 (2011): 2379–82, doi:10.1016/j.fertnstert.2011.03.029.

54. Annie M.Q. Wang, et al., "Outcomes Following Gender Affirming Phalloplasty: A Systematic Review and Meta-Analysis," *Sexual Medicine Reviews* 10, no. 4 (August 26, 2022): 499–512, doi: 10.1016/j.sxmr.2022.03.002.

55. Isabel S. Robinson, et al., "Surgical Outcomes Following Gender Affirming Penile Reconstruction: Patient-Reported Outcomes from a Multi-Center, International Survey of 129 Transmasculine Patients," *The Journal of Sexual Medicine* 18, no. 4 (2021): 800–811, doi:10.1016/j.jsxm.2021.01.183.

56. See *detrans*, https://www.reddit.com/r/detrans/.

57. Lisa Littman, "Individuals Treated for Gender Dysphoria with Medical and/or Surgical Transition Who Subsequently Detransitioned: A Survey of 100 Detransitioners," *Archives of Sexual Behavior* 50, no. 8 (October 19, 2021): 3353–69, doi: 10.1007/s10508-021-02163-w.

58. Elie Vandenbussche, "Detransition-Related Needs and Support: A Cross-Sectional Online Survey," *Journal of Homosexuality* 69, no. 9 (April 30, 2021): 1602–20, doi: 10.1080/00918369.2021.1919479.

59. Jo Taylor et al., "Interventions to Suppress Puberty in Adolescents Experiencing Gender Dysphoria or Incongruence: A Systematic Review," *Archives of Disease in Childhood*, April 9, 2024, doi: 10.1136/archdischild-2023-326669.

60. For instance, see Yolanda Smith et al., "Sex Reassignment: Outcomes and Predictors of Treatment for Adolescent and Adult Transsexuals," *Psychological Medicine* 35, no. 1 (2005): 89–99, doi: 10.1017/s0033291704002776.

61. C. M. Wiepjes, "Trends in Suicide Death Risk in Transgender People: Results from the Amsterdam Cohort of Gender Dysphoria Study (1972–2017)," *Acta Psychiatrica Scandinavica* 141, no. 6 (March 12, 2020): 486–91, doi: 10.1111/acps.13164.

62. Cecilia Dhejne et al., "Long-Term Follow-up of Transsexual Persons Undergoing Sex Reassignment Surgery: Cohort Study in Sweden," *PLoS ONE* 6, no. 2 (February 22, 2011), doi: 10.1371/journal.pone.0016885.

63. Lisa Littman, "Parent Reports of Adolescents and Young Adults."

64. Charlie Jacobs, "What I've Learned Rescuing My Daughter from Her Transgender Fantasy," The Daily Signal, December 13, 2021, https://www.dailysignal.com/2021/12/13/what-ive-learned-rescuing-my-daughter-from-her-transgender-fantasy/.

65. Mama Bear Apologetics, "Ministry to Detransitioners," https://mamabearapologetics.com/ministry-to-detransitioners/.

66. Hilary Cass, "Final Report," Cass Review, April, 2024, https://cass.independent-review.uk/home/publications/final-report/.

67. Dorey Scheimer, Meghna Chakrabarti, and Tim Skoog, "'Cass Review' Author: More 'Caution' Advised for Gender-Affirming Care for Youth," WBUR, May 8, 2024, https://www.wbur.org/onpoint/2024/05/08/hilary-cass-review-caution-nhs-gender-affirming-care-youth.

68. Scheimer, Chakrabarti, and Skoog, "'Cass Review' Author."

69. Sara Dahlen, "International Clinical Practice Guidelines."
70. "What Deadnaming Is and Why It's Harmful," Cleveland Clinic, September 13, 2024. https://health.clevelandclinic.org/deadnaming.

Chapter 15. Taking Up Your Sexual Cross

1. Christopher Yuan, *Holy Sexuality and the Gospel: Sex, Desire, and Relationships Shaped by God's Grand Story* (Multnomah, 2018), 52.
2. Evan L. Ardiel and Catharine H. Rankin, "The Importance of Touch in Development," *Paediatrics & Child Health* 15, no. 3 (March 2010): 153–56, doi: 10.1093/pch/15.3.153.

Acknowledgments

HILLARY

This book is the epitome of what it means for me to conquer fear. Thank you, Harvest House, for pushing me to write it even when I kept saying no.

Thank you, Amy and Lindsey, my partners in ministry, who were willing to listen to every insecurity and fear, and especially for Amy for agreeing to conquer this cultural behemoth with me.

Thank you to my husband, who loves me like Christ loved the church.

For my editor and agent, Kathleen, who endured about five FaceTimes per day to discuss anything and everything. You have been my defender and you are officially part of my "writing process." And Audrey, who gave me the space to keep working till this book was right.

For all my Mama Bears, who kept our ministry running while Amy and I worked on this book. Thanks to Emily Pelley, who helped in a million different ways.

Thank you to those who read early versions and lent support or just served as a sounding board—Teasi Cannon, Hillary Short, Bethany Woodward, Beth Barber, Ricky Chelette, Katy Faust, Joe Graybill, Anja Westerhaus, Alycia Wood, Kelly Schenkoske, DeeAnna Ownby, Bruno Borges, Christopher Yuan, Chris and Alice Morgan (the best publicists and parents anyone could ask for), the Hocksbergens (for a million reasons, least of which is our awesome cover!), Julie Loos (and her amazing prayers), and countless others who were willing to lend feedback.

As with everything that is Mama Bear Apologetics, this is a group project. Mama Bear is all of us. We truly are all in this together. And as in all things, to my God and Savior who is the Artist of artists. May we all have eyes to see and ears to hear how He reveals Himself through our bodies, our sexuality, our gender, our marriages, and our families.

AMY

This book would never have been possible without the support of so many. Thank you to R.K.L., T.D., P.G., and R.I., who first sparked the love of apologetics in me and gave me my first chance to speak. To my classmates Kyle, Travis, and the countless ladies who shared their stories, advice, and wisdom. To my folks, who knew I wanted to be a writer but probably didn't think it would be on this topic. To my boys Jake, Josh, and Drew. You ate cereal for dinner more than once and never complained. I'm so proud of the godly men you are becoming! To little Maddie, may God make you bold in the faith. To my gorgeous! Thank you for all the sacrifices you made, the dinners you cooked, for telling me I was pretty even though I wore the same sweatpants for days on end. You are my dearest blessing. Most importantly, to God, whose beauty and wisdom guided this whole process. May the many mamas and papas who read this feel Your love, grace, and truth.

About the Authors

HILLARY MORGAN FERRER is the founder and president of Mama Bear Apologetics. She feels a burden for providing accessible apologetics resources for busy moms. She is the chief author and editor of the best-selling books *Mama Bear Apologetics: Empowering Your Kids to Challenge Cultural Lies* and *Honest Prayers for Mama Bears.* Hillary has her master's degree in biology and loves helping moms to discern truths and lies in culture from both a biblical and scientific perspective. She is passionate about understanding the root causes of doubt and helping people identify the sources of their barriers to faith. Hillary and her husband, John, have been married since 2007 and minister together as an apologetics team.

AMY DAVISON is a former Air Force veteran turned podcast cohost, writer, and speaker for Mama Bear Apologetics. She received her MA in Christian apologetics from Southwestern Baptist Theological Seminary and her work has been published by the Evangelical Philosophical Society and The Stream. She and her husband are raising their four children in Texas.

JULIE LOOS is the contributor of the "Prayers of Lament" and the "PAWS for Prayer" sections, wrote the prayers in the first Mama Bear book and coauthored *Honest Prayers for Mama Bears.* She has been involved in various leadership roles with Moms in Prayer International for over two decades. Julie uses her certificate in apologetics from Biola University to be an ambassador for apologetics in her church. She is enjoying starting a prayer legacy for her grandchildren.

To learn more about Harvest House books and to read sample chapters, visit our website:

www.HarvestHousePublishers.com